Configurations of Rape in the Hebrew Bible

Studies in Biblical Literature

Hemchand Gossai
General Editor

Vol. 109

PETER LANG
New York • Washington, D.C./Baltimore • Bern
Frankfurt am Main • Berlin • Brussels • Vienna • Oxford

Frank M. Yamada

Configurations of Rape
in the Hebrew Bible

A Literary Analysis
of Three Rape Narratives

To Jacq,
Thank you for your
careful eye, your guidance, and
your support.
            Best wishes,
            Frank Yamada

PETER LANG
New York • Washington, D.C./Baltimore • Bern
Frankfurt am Main • Berlin • Brussels • Vienna • Oxford

Library of Congress Cataloging-in-Publication Data

Yamada, Frank M.
Configurations of rape in the Hebrew Bible:
a literary analysis of three rape narratives / Frank M. Yamada.
p. cm. — (Studies in biblical literature; v. 109)
Includes bibliographical references and index.
1. Rape in the Bible. 2. Bible. O.T. Genesis XXXIV—Criticism, interpretation, etc.
3. Bible. O.T. Samuel, 2nd, XIII, 1–13—Criticism, interpretation, etc.
4. Bible. O.T . Judges XIX—Criticism, interpretation, etc. I. Title.
BS1199.R27Y36   221.8'3641532—dc22   2007013529
ISBN 978-1-4331-0167-0
ISSN 1089-0645

Bibliographic information published by **Die Deutsche Bibliothek**.
Die Deutsche Bibliothek lists this publication in the "Deutsche
Nationalbibliografie"; detailed bibliographic data is available
on the Internet at http://dnb.ddb.de/.

The paper in this book meets the guidelines for permanence and durability
of the Committee on Production Guidelines for Book Longevity
of the Council of Library Resources.

Printed in Germany

TABLE OF CONTENTS

EDITOR'S PREFACE

More than ever the horizons in biblical literature are being expanded beyond that which is immediately imagined; important new methodological, theological, and hermeneutical directions are being explored, often resulting in significant contributions to the world of biblical scholarship. It is an exciting time for the academy as engagement in biblical studies continues to be heightened.

This series seeks to make available to scholars and institutions, scholarship of high order, and which will make a significant contribution to the ongoing biblical discourse. This series includes established and innovative directions, covering general and particular areas in biblical study. For every volume considered for this series, we explore the question as to whether the study will push the horizons of biblical scholarship. The answer must be yes for inclusion.

In this volume, Frank Yamada examines three rape narratives in the Hebrew Bible: Genesis 34, Judges 19, and 2 Samuel 13. While extensive studies have been conducted on these texts and indeed on the theme of "rape" in the Bible, Frank Yamada's approach takes the conversation in a very helpful and new direction. He not only develops an argument that demonstrates a movement from rape to excessive male violence to social fragmentation, but argues persuasively for a pattern and relationship between these three texts. Scholars who have been looking for a systematic and expansive study on the relationship between these three texts will find in this volume much that will extend the scholarly discourse.

The horizon has been expanded.

Hemchand Gossai
Series Editor

ACKNOWLEDGMENTS

This project, which is a revision of my doctoral dissertation (2005), was completed with the help of many people. The folks at Peter Lang Publishing have been great partners in the making of this book. I would like to thank the General Editor of the *Studies in Biblical Literature* series, Hemchand Gossai, for his engagement and acceptance of my work. Heidi Burns, the Senior Editor, has provided excellent communication and leadership throughout this process. Thank you, you have been great.

During my doctoral work, Choon Leong Seow was the one who initially encouraged me to pursue this topic. I would especially like to thank my dissertation advisor, Jacqueline Lapsley, whose patience, wisdom, and insight helped me bring this project to a conclusion. I had two very careful and meticulous readers on my committee in F. W. (Chip) Dobbs-Allsopp and Dennis Olson. Their perspectives and input helped me to envision and expand my work in helpful and crucial ways. Katharine Doob Sakenfeld and Brian Blount also gave me valuable guidance at the early stages of my process.

I would also like to thank my colleagues and students at Seabury-Western Theological Seminary, who provided me with the encouragement, support, and space needed to finish this project. Newland Smith, Ruth Meyers, James Lemler, and Gary Hall allowed me to have a reduced course load as I was finishing my Ph.D. and provided moral and administrative support. I extend a special word of thanks to my colleagues A. K. M. Adam and John Dreibelbis, who offered perspective and friendship throughout this process. I also would like to acknowledge my hard working research assistants, Richard Easterling, John Hickey, and Siobhán Patterson. They saved me many hours. Heidi Haverkamp provided me an invaluable service by working on my indices. Michelle Warriner Bolt put me in touch with valuable editing resources. It makes a huge difference to work in a community that supports me and my scholarship in so many ways.

I am very appreciative of Paul Myhre and the people at the Wabash Center for Teaching and Learning in Theology and Religion. Their 2007 Summer Fellowship provided me with the funding and time necessary to bring this project to its completion. The fellowship helped me to secure the services of Michael Koplow at the University of Chicago Press, who put in many after-work hours to edit early drafts of this book. I would also like to thank the leadership and participants in the Asian and Asian North American Pre-Tenure workshop, who gave me sound advice and wisdom.

I have many friends and colleagues to thank, who read drafts of chapters, provided timely insights, and gave me moral support: Anne Joh, Cheryl Anderson, Gale Yee, Henry Rietz, Horace Griffin, Benny Liew, Jeffrey Kuan, Mary Foskett, Julie Duncan, Caroline Chen, Matthew Stith, Elisabeth Johnson, and I cannot forget the Shomer League, OTFL, and the guys from the Saturday softball pick-up game.

My parents, Karen Furuichi and Frank Yamada, Sr. sustained me financially and emotionally throughout my graduate and doctoral work, even when they were unsure of what a Ph.D. in biblical studies would do for me. Most of all I would like to thank my spouse, Michelle, for her unwavering support and love. Thank you for the many nights and weekends that you gave to me so that I could finish this project. Your understanding gives me the motivation to do what I do. Finally, to my two children, Stephen and Adam, who inspire me to finish things that would otherwise be left undone.

ABBREVIATIONS

AAA	American Anthropological Association
ABD	*Anchor Bible Dictionary.* Edited by D. N. Freedman. 6 vols. New York, 1992
AEL	*Ancient Egyptian Literature.* M. Lichtheim. 3 vols. Berkeley, 1971–1980
AnBib	Analecta biblica
ANETS	Ancient Near Eastern Texts and Studies
BHK	*Biblia Hebraica.* Edited by R. Kittel. 3rd ed. Stuttgart, 1937.
BHS	*Biblia Hebraica Stuttgartensia.* Edited by K. Elliger and W. Rudolf. Stuttgart, 1983
BibInt	*Biblical Interpretation*
BibOr	Biblica et orientalia
BR	*Biblical Research*
BTB	*Biblical Theology Bulletin*
BWANT	Beiträge zur Wissenschaft vom Alten und Neuen Testament
BZAW	Beihefte zur Zeitschrift für die alttestamentliche Wissenschaft
CBC	Cambridge Bible Commentary
CBQ	*Catholic Biblical Quarterly*
DBAT	*Dielheimer Blätter zum Alten Testament und seiner Rezeption in der Alten Kirche*
HL	Hittite Laws
HS	*Hebrew Studies*
IBC	Interpretation: A Bible Commentary for Teaching and Preaching
IDB	*The Interpreter's Dictionary of the Bible.* Edited by G. A. Buttrick. 4 vols. Nashville, 1962
Int	*Interpretation*
ISBE	*International Standard Bible Encyclopedia.* Edited by G. W. Bromiley. 4 vols. Grand Rapids. 1979–1988
JANES	*Journal of the Ancient Near Eastern Society of Columbia University*, New York
JBL	*Journal of Biblical Literature*
JBQ	*Jewish Bible Quarterly*
JSOT	*Journal for the Study of the Old Testament*
JSOTSup	Journal for the Study of the Old Testament: Supplement Series
MAL	Middle Assyrian Laws

NIB	*The New Interpreter's Bible.* Edited by L. E. Keck. 12 vols. Nashville, 1994–2002
OTL	Old Testament Library
RB	*Revue biblique*
SBLDS	Society of Biblical Literature Dissertation Series
SBLSymS	Society of Biblical Literature Symposium Series
SBT	Studies in Biblical Theology
TDOT	*Theological Dictionary of the Old Testament.* Edited by G. J. Botterweck and H. Ringgren. Translated by J. T. Willis, G. W. Bromiley, and D. E. Green. 14 vols. Grand Rapids, 1974–1998
ThWAT	*Theologisches Wörterbuch zum Alten Testament.* Edited by G. J. Botterweck and H. Ringgren. 10 vols. Stuttgart, 1970–1998
UF	*Ugarit-Forschungen*
VT	*Vetus Testamentum*
VTSup	Vetus Testamentum Supplements
WBC	Word Biblical Commentary
WTJ	*Westminster Theological Journal*

CHAPTER ONE

Introduction: The Problem of Rape in the Biblical Texts and Culture

Introduction

Rape is a pervasive problem that has captured the attention of writers and scholars both modern and ancient. Sociologists and anthropologists have shown that rape is prevalent in most cultures of the world, though other cultures do not always understand the act in the same categories as in the West.[1] Similarly, literary critics have shown that authors, modern and ancient, have dealt with the topic of rape throughout the history of literature.[2] The biblical authors were not an exception.

---

[1] Representative studies on rape and culture include: Susan Brownmiller, *Against Our Will: Men, Women and Rape* (New York: Bantam, 1975); Lynn A. Higgins and Brenda R. Silver, eds., *Rape and Representations* (New York: Columbia University Press, 1991); Patricia Searles and Ronald J. Berger, eds., *Rape and Society: Readings on the Problem of Sexual Assault* (Boulder: Westview, 1995); Emilie Buchwald, Pamela R. Fletcher, and Martha Roth, eds., *Transforming a Rape Culture* (Minneapolis: Milkweed, 1993); Patricia D. Rozeé, "Forbidden or Forgiven? Rape in Cross-Cultural Perspective," *Psychology of Women Quarterly* 17 (1993): 499–514; and Peggy Reeves Sanday, "The Socio-Cultural Context of Rape: A Cross-Cultural Study," *Journal of Social Issues* 37, no. 4 (1981): 5–27. Susanne Scholz surveys the scholarly literature on rape in her published dissertation (*Rape Plots: A Feminist Cultural Study of Genesis 34* [Studies in Biblical Literature 13; New York: Peter Lang, 2000], 19–44). Harold Washington also provides an intriguing synthesis of rape research in his analysis of biblical texts. See Harold C. Washington, "Violence and the Construction of Gender in the Hebrew Bible: A New Historicist Approach," *BibInt* 5 (1997): 324–63.

[2] Laura E. Tanner, *Intimate Violence: Reading Rape and Torture in Twentieth-Century Fiction* (Bloomington: Indiana University Press, 1994); Kathryn Gravdal, *Ravishing Maidens: Writing Rape in*

There are three narrative incidents of rape in the Hebrew Bible: Gen 34; Judg 19; and 2 Sam 13. In each of these texts there is a progression that moves from rape to male responses that are excessively violent to some kind of social fragmentation. In Gen 34, Shechem the Hivite rapes (ענה in the Piel) Dinah, the daughter of Jacob. Simeon and Levi slaughter all the males in the village as an act of revenge. This retaliation severs Jacob's previous relationship with the people of Shechem and raises the possibility of future reprisals from the peoples of the land (Gen 34:30). The scene ends with the family divided as father and sons are at odds with each other in the aftermath of the bloody slaughter of Shechem.

In Judg 19, an unruly mob in the town of Gibeah of Benjamin tortures and rapes (עלל in the Hithpael) the concubine of a Levitical priest. The priest reports to the tribal leaders that the lords of Gibeah had raped (ענה in the Piel) and killed his concubine. A bloody civil war follows that nearly destroys the entire tribe of Benjamin. The intertribal battle, which is narrated as a holy war of Israel with itself, is symptomatic of the larger social and moral decline at the end of the period of Judges—a period that the narrator characterizes as a time without a king, where "every man did the right in his own eyes" (Judg 17:6 and 21:25).

In 2 Sam 13, Amnon, son of David, rapes (ענה in the Piel) Tamar, his half-sister. After hearing about the rape, Absalom plots secretly against Amnon and has him killed. The rape itself and the post-rape responses of David and Absalom fuel dynamics that lead eventually to the son's rebellion against his father. The events of 2 Sam 13 ff. point to the fulfillment of Nathan's oracle against David, in which violence and strife will mark the king's house (2 Sam 12:10–12).

Each of these texts embodies the progression of rape → excessive male violence → social fragmentation in ways that are unique to the themes and contexts of its story. Complicated forces and themes within each text determine the different male responses that result from the rape. Similarly, the different types of social fragmentation within each story take on configurations that are particular to that story's characters and context. However, the similar

Medieval French Literature and Law (Philadelphia: University of Pennsylvania Press, 1991); and Froma Zeitlin, "Configurations of Rape in Greek Myth," in *Rape* (ed. Sylvana Tomaselli and Roy Porter; Oxford: Basil Blackwell, 1986), 122–51.

progression and outcome of these three different texts about rape is striking, suggesting that an extensive study on the relationship between them is overdue.

The similarities among these texts become more intriguing when one considers the fact that the Hebrew Bible contains a less violent option for dealing with rape in Deut 22:28–29.[3] In this law, if a man encounters a virgin who is not engaged, seizes her (תְּפָשָׂהּ) and lies with her (שָׁכַב עִמָּהּ), he is to pay her father fifty shekels, and the man is forbidden to divorce the woman. The similar issues between Deut 22:28–29 and Gen 34 are significant. In fact, many scholars, when addressing the dynamics in either of these passages, will often provide discussion of the other text as support for their interpretation.[4] It is not the purpose of this study to provide a detailed analysis of these legal texts or to propose how their understandings of sexual violence determine the meaning of rape within the different narratives. Instead, I argue that the rapes in Gen 34, Judg 19, and 2 Sam 13 have different configurations of meaning that are specific to the contexts and themes within each of these stories. The legal material on rape, however, suggests that within Israel's culture and worldview, there existed less violent options for dealing with rape. Hence, beyond the similar progression described above, the three rape texts share the feature of being excessively violent. In each of these texts, the male responses that follow the rape move beyond the accepted social norms of the text—norms that find

---

[3] For discussion of this law and other laws that relate to the issue of rape in the Hebrew Bible, see below. The difficulty of navigating a definition of rape in these laws is similar to the debate among scholars concerning Dinah in Gen 34. Most scholars recognize that the events within Judg 19 and 2 Sam 13 constitute rape. The case of Dinah is debated because the issue of consent is ambiguous in Gen 34. As I will argue below, Shechem's crime is best understood as rape within the context of the narrative. Dinah's silence has a particular function within the story in that it draws the reader's attention to the conflicted and problematic male responses that result from the rape.

[4] Lyn M. Bechtel, "What If Dinah Is Not Raped?" *JSOT* 62 (1994): 19–36; Tikva Frymer-Kensky, "Virginity in the Bible," in *Gender and Law in the Hebrew Bible and the Ancient Near East* (ed. Victor H. Matthews, Bernard M. Levinson, and Tikva Frymer-Kensky; JSOTSup 262; Sheffield: Sheffield Academic Press, 1998), 86–91; Washington, "Violence and the Construction of Gender," 324–63; and Cheryl B. Anderson, *Women, Ideology, and Violence: Critical Theory and the Construction of Gender in the Book of the Covenant and the Deuteronomic Law* (JSOTSup 394; London: T & T Clark, 2004), 86–89.

their expression within the legal materials.[5] The reasons for these excessively violent responses are different in each text. The fact, however, that each of these narratives progresses toward excessive male violence is significant.

While there have been numerous treatments of these individual texts, and a few works that point to connections between Gen 34 and 2 Sam 13, no significant study to date has thoroughly examined the potential relationship of these three rape narratives.[6] In addition, when biblical scholars examine the topic of rape, their discussions typically polarize into two positions—one that assumes modern definitions of rape, which emphasize the will of the victim, and another that subsumes all representations of rape into ideas of culture (e.g., honor and shame). In both positions, understandings of rape and culture tend to force the narrative(s) into patterns and definitions that are external to the texts themselves.

In order to address these deficiencies, the present study examines the relationship between Gen 34, Judg 19, and 2 Sam 13, through a narrative analysis of all three texts. The governing question for the present analysis is: Given the fact that a less violent alternative for addressing rape exists within the

---

[5] Westbrook makes this point about Gen 34 and 2 Sam 13 in his brief discussion of rape within the context of biblical and ANE legal texts. See Raymond Westbrook, "Punishments and Crimes," *ABD* 5:552.

[6] The following works recognize significant connection between Gen 34 and 2 Sam 13: Esther Fuchs, *Sexual Politics in the Biblical Narrative: Reading the Hebrew Bible as a* Woman (JSOTSup 310; Sheffield: Sheffield Academic Press, 2000), 200–224; David Noel Freedman, "Dinah and Shechem, Tamar and Amnon," *Austin Seminary Bulletin: Faculty Edition* 105 (1990): 51–63; Pamela Tamarkin Reis, "Cupidity and Stupidity: Woman's Agency and the 'Rape' of Tamar," *JANES* 25 (1997): 43–60; Naomi Graetz, "Dinah the Daughter," in *A Feminist Companion to Genesis* (ed. Athalya Brenner; The Feminist Companion to the Bible 2; Sheffield: Sheffield Academic Press, 1993), 306–17; and Mary Anna Bader, *Sexual Violation in the Hebrew Bible: A Multi-Methodological Study of Genesis 34 and 2 Samuel 13* (Studies in Biblical Literature 87; New York: Peter Lang, 2006). Of these scholars, Fuchs, Freedman, and Bader are among the few who develop significantly the literary connections between these two texts. Mishael Maswari Caspi recognizes three rape narratives, but focuses exclusively on Gen 34 in his article, "The Story of the Rape of Dinah: The Narrator and the Reader," *Hebrew Studies* 26, no. 1 (1985): 25–45. Alice Keefe examines all three rape narratives collectively (see "Rapes of Women/Wars of Men," *Semeia* 61 [1993]: 79–97). The next section looks at problems with Keefe's methodology, which uses women's experience metaphorically to understand the larger social chaos. For a critique of Keefe, see Mieke Bal, "Metaphors He Lives By," *Semeia* (1994): 185–207, esp. 196; and Francis Landy, "On Metaphor, Play and Nonsense," *Semeia* (1994): 219–37, esp. 232–33.

Hebrew Bible through the legal material, why do all three narrative examples of rape move toward excessive male violence? I will argue that these texts bear a family resemblance to one another in that they move through the progression of rape to excessively violent male responses to social fragmentation.[7] This resemblance, while displaying characteristics of similar movement and outcome, still allows for the particular expression of each of these texts. That is, within each text, different thematic and context-related forces contribute to the significance and meaning of the rape. Thus, the excessive male violence and social fragmentation that result from the initial sexual violation find different expression within Gen 34, Judg 19, and 2 Sam 13.

---

[7] The notion of "family resemblance" is both well established and contested in literary theory. The idea of family resemblance derives originally from Ludwig Wittgenstein (*Philosophical Investigations* [trans. G. E. M. Anscombe; Oxford: Basil Blackwell, 1958], 31–32) but has been applied in many different fields of study, including genre studies. For an introduction and discussion, see Alastair Fowler, *Kinds of Literature: An Introduction to the Theory of Genres and Modes* (Cambridge: Harvard University Press, 1982), 37–53, esp. 40–44; and, David Fishelov, *Metaphors of Genre: The Role of Analogies in Genre Theory* (University Park: Pennsylvania State University Press, 1993), 53–83, esp. 55–68. See, however, Jacques Derrida and Vincent Leitch, who argue for the contradictory and destabilizing aspects of genre (Jacques Derrida, "The Law of Genre," *Glyph* 7 [1980]: 202–29; and, Vincent B. Leitch, *Cultural Criticism, Literary Theory, Poststructuralism* [New York: Columbia University Press, 1992], 62–82). See also, Stanley Fish, who argues for the socially constructed nature of literary classifications within interpretative communities (Stanley Fish, "How To Recognize a Poem When You See One," in *Is There a Text in This Class? The Authority of Interpretative Communities* [Cambridge: Harvard University Press, 1980], 322–37). For a good survey and application of family resemblance as it relates to the genre of the city-lament in biblical and ANE texts, see F. W. Dobbs-Allsopp, *Weep, O Daughter of Zion: A Study of the City-Lament Genre in the Hebrew Bible* (BibOr 44; Rome: Editrice Pontificio Istituto Biblico, 1993), 15–27. It is not the purpose of this chapter to survey or resolve the debates around the topic of family resemblance or genre. My use of this designation is strictly functional and rhetorical. That is, the notion of family resemblance is suggestive of both issues of similarity and particularity within literature. Thus, formalists and post-structuralists alike have used the term to argue for the usefulness and problematic nature of genre classifications (see Fishelov, *Metaphors of Genre*, 55–68). I use "family resemblance" as an interpretive metaphor for understanding the congruent elements among the rape narratives, even when the particularity of these three texts calls into question any similarities that could be assimilated under the rubric of genre. What unites these stories into a family of texts is their movement from rape → excessive male violence → some form of social fragmentation. Thus, their similarity results more from dynamics associated with rape and sexual violence than with a particular literary form.

The degree and extent of the violence within the different texts varies, from Absalom's premeditated killing of Amnon in 2 Samuel to the slaughtering of the entire city of Shechem in Genesis to the massive killing and near extinction of an entire tribe in Judges. Similarly, the type and degree of social fragmentation find expression in disputes between father and sons (Jacob and Simeon/Levi), strife and division within David's house, and the complete social and moral collapse of Israel in the period of the Judges. Hence, the three rape texts bear their family resemblance through the progression of rape → excessive violence → social fragmentation. However, the reasons that each of these texts moves toward excessive violence is different, and the expressions of social fragmentation that results are unique to the themes and context of each story.

Scope of the Study

The present work is a narrative analysis of Gen 34, Judg 19, and 2 Sam 13. While other biblical texts (e.g., Gen 19 and Deut 22) inform the present reading of the rape stories, the primary focus of the study will be on these three narratives. I will show that the rape stories betray similar elements, development, and outcome, even though they embody this progression in ways that are particular to the themes and contexts of each individual narrative. Any one of these congruities, by itself, is not unusual. In fact, one would expect to find similar expressions and word use in texts that address a similar subject matter. The combination of all of these congruities, however, points to a more significant relationship between these texts. Before reviewing the research on the rape narratives, some justification is needed for analyzing these texts collectively.

Reading the Rape Texts Collectively

A cursory examination of these texts reveals some striking similarities. As shown above, all three rapes are followed by violent social and political struggles among men, and all three end in some kind of social fragmentation. These texts also have common vocabulary. In addition to the verb, ענה in the Piel, which is commonly translated as "rape," these texts share an evaluative term, נְבָלָה, "senselessness, disgraceful folly."[8] This second term represents a moral judgment on the rape by certain characters in the narrative. In all three texts, נְבָלָה occurs within the idiom, "to do (עשה) a disgraceful thing (נְבָלָה) in Israel (בְּיִשְׂרָאֵל)." In Gen 34:7, Jacob's sons are outraged at Shechem's actions: כִּי־נְבָלָה עָשָׂה בְיִשְׂרָאֵל לִשְׁכַּב אֶת־בַּת־יַעֲקֹב, "for he has done a disgraceful thing in Israel by lying with the daughter of Jacob." In Judg 19:22, a mob has gathered outside of the house where the Levitical priest and his concubine are staying. They ask the owner of the house to release the man to them so that they might know him (וְנֵדָעֶנּוּ), i.e., have sexual relations with him. The old man, who took the couple in, implores the mob outside, אַל תַּעֲשׂוּ אֶת־הַנְּבָלָה הַזֹּאת, "do not do this disgraceful thing" (19:23). After offering both his daughter and the Levite's concubine to the crowd, he once again begs them, לֹא תַעֲשׂוּ דְּבַר הַנְּבָלָה הַזֹּאת "do not do this disgraceful thing" (19:24). Thus, the old man considers the evil intentions that the mob has for the Levite as נְבָלָה, "a disgraceful thing." Later, after the mob rapes the unnamed woman, the Levite describes his outrage at Gibeah to the gathered tribes, עָשׂוּ...נְבָלָה בְּיִשְׂרָאֵל, "they have done…a disgraceful thing in Israel" (Judg 20:6). Even though the "disgraceful thing" earlier in Judg 19 refers to the mob's request to sexually humiliate the Levite, the Levite's comment makes it clear that he includes the violent act of the mob against the woman as part of the "disgraceful" act. In 2 Sam 13, Tamar pleads with Amnon not to sexually violate her: כִּי לֹא־יֵעָשֶׂה כֵן בְּיִשְׂרָאֵל אַל־תַּעֲשֵׂה אֶת־הַנְּבָלָה הַזֹּאת, "for such a thing is not done in Israel; do not do this disgraceful thing" (13:12).

The idiom "to do (a form of the verb, עשה) a disgraceful thing (נְבָלָה) in Israel (בְּיִשְׂרָאֵל)" appears in all three texts.[9] As stated above, this phrase

---

[8] ענה in the Piel means "humble" or "afflict." In the context of sexual violence, the humiliation refers to the subduing of a woman sexually. Lyn Bechtel has challenged the interpretation of "rape" for the Piel of ענה in Gen 34. She argues that the term is more appropriately translated "humiliate," i.e., Shechem has humiliated or shamed Dinah in that she is no longer of marriageable status (see "What If Dinah Is Not Raped?" 19–36). She acknowledges, however, that ענה can mean rape when words of force are used. For a more detailed discussion of this root and its meaning, see Chapter 2 below. For more discussion on the semantic range of the root ענה, see Ellen van Wolde, "Does 'INNÁ Denote Rape? A Semantic Analysis of a Controversial Word," *VT* 52, no. 4 (2002): 528–44.

[9] Claudia Camp, recognizing that the three rape narratives under discussion all use this phrase, proposes that the idiom points specifically to illicit sexual relations (see Claudia V. Camp,

represents a significant value judgment by particular characters within the narratives about the rape. Of the thirteen occurrences of the abstract noun, נְבָלָה, nine are found in the expression described above—"to do a disgraceful thing." Within this formula, נְבָלָה represents a violation of social norms,[10] including legal and/or covenantal transgressions,[11] which result in communal disorder. Thus, Alice Keefe, following Wolfgang Roth and Anthony Phillips, suggests that the term, נְבָלָה connotes a serious breach of social relations. In this way, the term reflects a cultural understanding of rape that has significant social ramifications.[12] In the eyes of these characters and/or in the perception of the narrator, such a disgraceful thing is not done in Israel.

Despite the similarities mentioned above—the pattern of initial rape that leads to further violence and resulting social fragmentation, and the overlapping vocabulary—there is a noticeable lack of research that examines the rape texts together.[13] This lack calls for a study that examines the similarities between the rape narratives, paying attention to the particular ways that rape in these texts develops toward excessive male violence and social fragmentation.

Wise, Strange and Holy: The Strange Woman and the Making of the Bible (JSOTSup 320; Gender, Culture, Theory 9; Sheffield: Sheffield Academic Press, 2000), 302–4.

[10] Gen 34:7, Judg 19:23, 24; 20:6, 10; and 2 Sam 13:12.

[11] Deut 22:21, Josh 7:15, and Jer 29:23.

[12] See Wolfgang M. W. Roth, "*NBL*," *VT* 10 (1960): 394–409, and Anthony Phillips, "*NEBALAH*," *VT* 25 (1975): 237–41, cited in Keefe, "Rapes of Women," 82. For a complete discussion on the root, see Johannes Marbök, "נָבָל *nābāl*," *TDOT* 9:157–71.

[13] Freedman points out many other striking similarities between Gen 34 and 2 Sam 13 (see discussion below). He goes so far as to suggest that the same author wrote these two stories and belong to the same work, what Richard Elliot Friedman has called "Super-J" (essentially, Genesis–2 Samuel). See Freedman, "Dinah and Shechem," 51–63. While Freedman's conclusion is awkward, his article does point to significant points of similarity between Gen 34 and 2 Sam 13. Fuchs also provides insightful analyses of Gen 34 and 2 Sam 13, emphasizing the androcentric assumptions in stories that subsume the rape of a sister to the revenge of her brother(s) (see Fuchs, *Sexual Politics in Biblical Narrative*, 200–224). Bader, in a recently published dissertation, also examines narrative and literary congruencies between Gen 34 and 2 Sam 13. She provides a brief excursus on Judg 19 ff., but she does not include this text in her overall narrative analysis in spite of the literary similarities among these rape stories. She minimizes the Judges material because the primary focus of her work is on the interactions between daughters, fathers, and brothers (Bader, *Sexual Violation in the Hebrew Bible*).

Survey of Research on the Rape Narratives

As stated above, most scholarly treatments of the rape narratives have focused on individual texts. In Chapters 2 through 4, I consider interpretations and critical issues that are specific to Gen 34, Judg 19, and 2 Sam 13. The purpose of this section is to survey the secondary literature that intentionally focuses on the issue of rape in these three texts. This review will highlight trends in the recent debate on the rape narratives and the confusion surrounding the definition of rape in the biblical text. I will also look at those scholars who see connections between these texts and suggest that their analyses have not been nearly as exhaustive in seeking to understand the texts' interrelatedness. Finally, at the end of this chapter, I will summarize briefly some of the issues related to the legal texts on rape, since this material provides the basis from which one can understand the responses in the rape texts as excessively violent.

Traditionally, scholars have examined the individual rape texts using the methodologies of historical, form, and tradition-historical criticism. In recent decades, however, there has been a noticeable shift in the examination of biblical narrative more generally. Literary critical and narrative critical readings of the Bible have added much to biblical scholarship during this period. Such readings have refocused the scholarly discussion on the "final form" of the text and the text's artistic and literary qualities.[14] In this vein, scholars have

---

[14] The expression "final form of the text" can be misleading. The MT, especially in books like 2 Sam, is notoriously corrupt. As modern critical translations show, readers of the Hebrew Bible, at times, must reconstruct the text using the versions and sound text critical reasoning to make better sense of the material. Hence, the notion of a "final form" of the Hebrew Bible is bound to provoke controversy. Canonical critics like Brevard Childs use the term "final form" to speak of a text's authoritative reception within certain religious communities (see *Introduction to the Old Testament as Scripture* [Philadelphia: Fortress, 1979], 75–77). Literary and narrative critics have used the terminology to suggest a particular kind of reading practice. Such a method presumes that meaningful interpretation can emerge when the reader assumes a certain literary unity of the text. Thus, the tools of modern literary criticism are used to produce interpretations using some received text, usually MT. This type of literary criticism has produced compelling interpretations of biblical narrative. In the present study, "final form" is meant within the context of these literary readings of the Hebrew Bible. The present work is not text critical in nature. Where possible, I will try to make sense of the received tradition as expressed in the MT. For a useful discussion on the topic of literary criticism and the Bible, including issues related to the "final form" of the text, see Kenneth R. R. Gros Louis, "Some Methodological Considerations," in *Literary Interpretations of Biblical Narrative II* (ed. Kenneth R. R. Gros Louis and James S. Ackerman;

concentrated less on issues such as source critical analysis and historical reconstruction and have emphasized topics of inquiry such as characterization, narration, and plot.[15] This trajectory in scholarship is also evident in the recent literature concerning the biblical rape narratives.[16] Despite the proliferation of literary and narrative critical readings on the rape texts, no significant study has looked at all three rape stories collectively despite the texts' thematic similarities.

Feminist Interpretations of the Rape Texts

Phyllis Trible's *Texts of Terror: Literary-Feminist Readings of the Biblical Narrative*, was the first substantial literary-critical treatment of two of the rape texts, Judg 19 and 2 Sam 13. Her study focuses on the lives of four women characters—Hagar

---

Nashville: Abingdon, 1982), 13–24. For methodological issues between literary critical and historical critical biblical scholarship from the perspective of literary critics, see Robert Alter, *The Art of Biblical Narrative* (New York: Basic Books, 1981), 3–22, esp. 19–20; idem, "Introduction," in *The Literary Guide to the Bible* (ed. Robert Alter and Frank Kermode; Cambridge: Belknap, 1987), 11–35; Meir Sternberg, *The Poetics of Biblical Narrative: Ideological Literature and the Drama of Reading* (Bloomington: Indiana University Press, 1987), 7–23; and David M. Gunn, "What Does the Bible Say? A Question of Text and Canon," in *Reading Bibles, Writing Bodies: Identity and the Book* (ed. Timothy K. Beal and David M. Gunn; New York: Routledge, 1997), 242–61. For a new historicist perspective on the interrelation between literary and historical criticism see F. W. Dobbs-Allsopp, "Rethinking Historical Criticism," *BibInt* 7 (1999): 235–71.

[15] For examples of this trend, see Alter, *Art of Biblical Narrative*; Shimeon Bar-Efrat, *Narrative Art in the Bible* (JSOTSup 70; Sheffield: Almond Press, 1989); David M. Gunn and Danna Nolan Fewell, *Narrative in the Hebrew Bible* (New York: Oxford University Press, 1993); Paul R. House, ed., *Beyond Form Criticism: Essays in Old Testament Literary Criticism* (Winona Lake: Eisenbrauns, 1992); Sternberg, *Poetics of Biblical Narrative*; and Mieke Bal, *Death and Dissymmetry: The Politics of Coherence in the Book of Judges* (Chicago: University of Chicago Press, 1988).

[16] Recent examples of literary or narrative analyses of the individual rape texts are extensive: Caspi, "Rape of Dinah"; Danna Nolan Fewell and David M. Gunn, "Tipping the Balance: Sternberg's Reader and the Rape of Dinah," *JBL* 110 (1991): 193–211; Sternberg, *Poetics of Biblical Narrative*, 441–81; Mieke Bal, "A Body of Writing: Judg. 19," in *A Feminist Companion to Judges* (ed. Athalya Brenner; Feminist Companion to the Bible 4; Sheffield: Sheffield Academic Press, 1993), 208–30; idem, "The Rape of Narrative and Narrative of Rape," in *Literature and the Body: Essays on Populations and Persons* (ed. Elaine Scarry; Baltimore: Johns Hopkins University Press, 1984), 1–32; Phyllis Trible, *Texts of Terror* (Philadelphia: Fortress, 1984), 37–63 and 65–91; J. Cheryl Exum, "Raped by the Pen," in *Fragmented Women: Feminist (Sub)versions of Biblical Narratives* (Valley Forge: Trinity, 1993), 170–201; Bar-Efrat, "The Narrative of Amnon and Tamar," in *Narrative Art*, 239–82; and, Gunn and Fewell, *Narrative in the Hebrew Bible*, 148–51.

(Gen 16:1–16; 21:9–21), Tamar (2 Sam 13), an unnamed woman (Judg 19), and Jephthah's daughter (Judg 11:29–40). She offers feminist interpretations of the biblical passages, examining the ways in which these texts create a world that is inhospitable and terrifying for women. She interprets each of the four stories independently, though they all share the common theme of terror.[17] Thus, while Trible's study examines two of the three rape narratives, she interprets these texts individually, without exploring explicit thematic or functional connections between them.[18] She combines a form of literary criticism that emphasizes the final form of the text with a feminist hermeneutic.[19] This last aspect of her method serves to critique the misogynistic and patriarchal tendencies of culture, both past and present.[20] She suggests three different ways that feminist

---

[17] Trible, *Texts of Terror*, 3–5.

[18] Trible does recognize certain themes between the four texts, but these themes, as she acknowledges, are informed by an intention that is extrinsic to the texts (ibid., 4). One of the goals of the present book is to suggest ways that one can interpret the common themes and assumptions that are intrinsic to the texts themselves.

[19] For a comprehensive treatment of Trible's methodology, see Phyllis Trible, *Rhetorical Criticism: Context, Method, and the Book of Jonah* (Minneapolis: Fortress, 1994).

[20] Feminist biblical scholars and theologians do not agree on how feminist interpretation should/can negotiate the patriarchal nature of the biblical text. In addition, Carol Meyers has raised a substantial criticism against feminist uses of the term "patriarchy," since it fails to recognize the complex configuration of male and female relationships in other cultures, including the culture of ancient Israel. In *Discovering Eve*, Meyers uses anthropological theory and data to clarify the distinction between authority and power. Following Michelle Rosaldo, Meyers defines authority as "the culturally legitimated right to make decisions and command obedience." Power, by contrast, is "the ability to effect control despite or independent of official authority" (*Discovering Eve: Ancient Israelite Women in Context* [New York: Oxford University Press, 1988], 41). She argues that women exercised significant informal power within Israelite society though they possessed little if any formal authority, as is evident in the biblical material (for full discussion, see Meyers, *Discovering Eve*, 24–46). Meyers' corrective is helpful in that it suggests that configurations of male and female relations cannot be subsumed into a monolithic notion of patriarchy that assumes male dominance cross-culturally. Each form of male/female power and authority will have culturally particular expressions. Her analysis, however, tends to minimize the ways in which ideology both masks and reinforces social realities. Meyers' analysis rightly points out the ways in which "the myth of male dominance" does not reflect social realities (45). Her work, however, does not always take seriously how such a male-centered ideology affects the lived reality of women on the ground. For a critique of Meyers' position, see Phyllis A. Bird, *Missing Persons and Mistaken Identities: Women and Gender in Ancient Israel* (Minneapolis: Fortress, 1997), 257–58. Also, for different ways that feminist scholars have incorporated social scientific materials in their

interpreters have approached the Bible. The first exposes the patriarchal bias of the biblical texts. The second seeks liberating themes within the text or reinterprets familiar texts to critique a culture of patriarchy. The third, and Trible's own emphasis in *Texts of Terror*, assumes the first two approaches but seeks to memorialize those abused women within the biblical texts.[21] Thus, the intention of Trible's approach is to recover a "neglected history" of women within the Bible, so that the violence of the texts is not forgotten. The present work, while not falling neatly into one of Trible's categories, hopes to contribute to the growing area of scholarship that explores narrative depictions of violence against women within the biblical texts. By exploring the rape texts' family resemblance and by showing how these texts move toward excessive violence and social fragmentation, this study will provide a more complete understanding of how rape is portrayed in the narratives of the Hebrew Bible.

Trible's scholarship, and the work of other feminist biblical interpreters, helpfully emphasizes women characters and women's issues in the Bible. Thus, feminist interpreters have tended to focus on the experience of women within these texts, raising issues that revolve around the lives of women. It is not surprising, therefore, that feminist literature on the individual rape narratives has increased in proportion to feminist studies done on rape within the last twenty years.[22] Modern understandings of rape emphasize that it is an act of power and sexual violence done against the will of another. Such an understanding has affected the ways in which biblical scholars, especially feminist biblical scholars, have understood rape in the Bible.

Alice A. Keefe is one of the few scholars who attempts to address the complex dynamic of rape using all three rape narratives. She argues that the violated body of the raped woman is "a metonym for the social body as it is

---

analysis of patriarchy and gender in the Hebrew Bible and the ancient Near East, see Peggy L. Day, ed., *Gender and Difference in Ancient Israel* (Minneapolis: Fortress, 1989); Tikva Frymer-Kensky, *In the Wake of the Goddesses: Women, Culture, and the Biblical Transformation of Pagan Myth* (New York: Free Press, 1992); and Gale A. Yee, *Poor Banished Children of Eve: Woman as Evil in the Hebrew Bible* (Minneapolis: Fortress, 2003).

[21] Trible, *Texts of Terror*, 3. For a good summary of feminist approaches to the biblical texts, see Katharine Doob Sakenfeld, "Feminist Uses of Biblical Materials," in *Feminist Interpretation of the Bible* (ed. Letty M. Russell; Philadelphia: Fortress, 1985), 55–64.

[22] For a survey of feminist rape research, see Linda Brookover Bourque, *Defining Rape* (Durham: Duke University Press, 1989), 14–58, and Scholz, *Rape Plots*, 19–44.

disrupted by war."[23] Keefe focuses her analysis on the women characters' experience of rape in the text. She argues for a correspondence between the degree of intimacy allowed into the woman's experience and the degree of intimacy between the warring parties. For example, the narrator of 2 Samuel allows the reader into Tamar's experience of rape through her response to the violation, i.e., her verbal reaction and her subsequent mourning. This high degree of intimacy into the woman's experience corresponds to the close familial intimacy between the two warring parties—the half-brothers, Absalom and Amnon—in this narrative.

While Keefe's article is intriguing, it falls short in at least two ways. First, her focus on the woman's experience of rape is misplaced given the biblical evidence. In fact, the only time that the reader is allowed access to the woman's experience is in the example above, 2 Sam 13. In both Gen 34 and Judg 19, the women are noticeably silent. Second, her analysis does not adequately address the respective responses to rape by the men in the narrative. These responses are crucial in that they represent a significant similarity among these texts, that is, war between men results from the initial rape of a woman. As stated above, this dynamic of rape followed by violent conflict reflects a significant connection among the rape texts. By focusing primarily on the women's experiences, Keefe has produced a reading that has difficulty accounting for the complex social interactions and male responses to rape within the narratives.

Susanne Scholz, in her published dissertation, argues that the history of interpretation on Gen 34 betrays a trivialization of what she recognizes as the central event of the text—the rape of Dinah.[24] Scholz's study is informed consciously by research done in the last twenty years on rape. This research emphasizes the ways in which social forces participate in a complicated way to reinforce a culture of rape, contributing to what feminist scholars have called a rape script. Within this script, certain masculine and feminine behaviors are assumed and reinforced. Presupposing such a framework, scholars understand rape as a complex cultural construct rather than a strictly physical or emotional phenomenon. Scholz argues that contemporary and historical interpretations of Gen 34 contribute to this culture of rape. She proceeds by examining and comparing nineteenth-century German commentaries on Gen 34 and forensic

---

[23] Keefe, "Rapes of Women," 79.

[24] Scholz, *Rape Plots.*

medical textbooks from the same period in Germany. After surveying recent biblical scholarship of this passage, Scholz provides her own feminist interpretation of Gen 34 using a rhetorical/literary model that is informed by Trible's methodology. Scholz's interpretation stresses rape as the primary event in the passage and emphasizes that Gen 34 is a story about Dinah.

Scholz's observations about the complex relationship between text and the culture of readers are helpful, and her point about the ways in which biblical interpretation reflects the cultural assumptions of the interpreter is a needful corrective. Her interpretation of Gen 34, however, is noticeably forced. She admits that focusing on Dinah's experience is difficult because Dinah does not speak.[25] Scholz justifies her claim that Dinah is the main character of the story by pointing out that even after Dinah has left the narrative scene, the characters continue to talk about her. In other words, all actions and speech that occur later in the chapter stem directly from the initial rape.[26] While the rape is, without a doubt, the precipitating event in the story, it pushes the interpretative limits of the text for one to propose that Dinah is the central character. Dinah acts only once in Gen 34, when she "goes out" to visit the women of the land, after which she is acted upon by men. Dinah does not speak in the story; she is spoken to (34:3) and spoken about. By such criteria, Dinah is not a central character, though Shechem's rape of Dinah is the pivotal event that drives the narrative forward.

Cultural Interpretations of the Rape Texts:
Explorations in Honor and Shame

Some scholars have focused on the cultural assumptions implicit in the individual rape narratives.[27] Such interpretations use sociology or cultural anthropology, especially ethnographic studies done on Mediterranean societies, to reconstruct a social world reflected in the biblical texts. These scholars use

---

[25] Ibid., 168.

[26] Ibid., 133–34.

[27] For examples of cultural readings of the individual rape narratives from the perspective honor and shame, see Bechtel, "What if Dinah is Not Raped?"; Camp, *Wise, Strange and Holy*, 279–322; and Victor H. Matthews and Don C. Benjamin, "Amnon and Tamar: A Matter of Honor (2 Samuel 13:1–38)" in *Crossing Boundaries and Linking Horizons: Studies in Honor of Michael C. Astour on His 80th Birthday* (ed. Gordon D. Young, Mark W. Chavalas, and Richard E. Averbeck; Bethseda: CDL, 1997), 339–66.

the framework of honor and shame to understand the culture of the Bible, though they must use the research analogically. That is, the ethnographic studies of the Mediterranean were carried out among agricultural groups, mostly nomadic in nature, that still exist. The culture of honor and shame, therefore, must be applied to the biblical texts through analogy. In spite of this limitation, biblical scholars have found honor and shame culture to be a useful heuristic lens through which to evaluate the biblical material. Moreover, certain cultural ideas and themes within the biblical text suggest that honor and shame issues were meaningful within Israelite society. Honor and shame studies have had a significant following within scholarship in both the New Testament and the Hebrew Bible.[28] These proposals, however, do not acknowledge the similar

---

[28] Honor and shame studies focus on anthropological data from the Mediterranean region. Anthropologists have characterized these cultures as agonistic, male centric, and driven by codes of honor and shame. Within such cultures, people are "other" centered or dyadic, engage in competitive struggles for honor through challenge and riposte, and are marked by sharp differentiations between gender roles. For representative discussions, see Julian Pitt-Rivers, *The Fate of Shechem or the Politics of Sex: Essays in the Anthropology of the Mediterranean* (Cambridge: Cambridge University Press, 1977); Jean G. Peristiany, ed., *Honour and Shame: The Values of Mediterranean Society* (London: Weidenfeld and Nicolson, 1965); David G. Gilmore, ed., *Honour and Shame and the Unity of the Mediterranean*, American Anthropological Association Special Publication 22 (Washington, D.C.: American Anthropological Association, 1987); and J. G. Peristiany and Julian Pitt-Rivers, eds., *Honor and Grace in Anthropology* (Cambridge: Cambridge University Press, 1992). More recently, other anthropological scholars have challenged the assumptions and applications of this earlier work. See Lila Abu-Lughod, *Veiled Sentiments: Honor and Poetry in a Bedouin Society* (Berkeley: University of California Press, 1986); Michael Herzfeld, "Honour and Shame: Problems in the Comparative Analysis of Moral Systems," *Man* 15, no. 2 (1980): 339–51; Unni Wikan, "Shame and Honour: A Contestable Pair," *Man* 19, no. 4 (1984): 635–52; Alison Lever, "Honour as a Red Herring," *Critique of Anthropology* 6, no. 3 (1986): 83–106; Gideon M. Kressel, "Shame and Gender," *Anthropological Quarterly* 65, no. 1 (1992): 34–46; and Rosemary J. Coombe, "Barren Ground: Re-conceiving Honour and Shame in the Field of Mediterranean Ethnography," *Anthropologica* 32 (1990): 221–38. In biblical scholarship, see Victor H. Matthews and Don C. Benjamin, eds., "Honor and Shame in the World of the Bible," *Semeia* 68 (1994): 7–161. See also the responses in this volume from John K Chance, "The Anthropology of Honor and Shame: Culture, Values, and Practice," *Semeia* 68 (1994): 139–51; and Gideon M. Kressel, "An Anthropologist's Response to the Use of Social Scientific Models in Biblical Studies," *Semeia* 68 (1994): 153–61. New Testament studies include: Steven Richard Bechtler, *Following in His Steps: Suffering, Community, and Christology in 1 Peter* (SBLDS 162; Atlanta: Scholars Press, 1998); David Arthur deSilva, *Honor, Patronage, Kinship and Purity: Unlocking New Testament Culture* (Downers Grove: Intervarsity Press, 2000); idem, *Despising Shame: Honor Discourse and Community Maintenance*

narrative configuration or function of the rape texts. Such approaches also have tended to assume that the dynamics within the biblical narratives are related to cultural forces external to the text. In most cases, the interpreter's understanding of culture dominates their interpretation of different texts, subsuming diverse materials within the constructed cultural framework.

Ken Stone, in his work, *Sex, Honor, and Power in the Deuteronomistic History*, looks at biblical narratives that contain references to sexual activity.[29] Stone uses both anthropological studies on honor and shame and the narratological analysis of Mieke Bal to uncover patterns of sexuality within biblical culture. His

---

in the Epistle to the Hebrews (SBLDS 152; Atlanta: Scholars Press, 1995); John H. Elliot, "Disgraced Yet Graced: The Gospel According to 1 Peter in the Key of Honor and Shame," *BTB* 25 (Winter 1995): 166–78; and David M. May, "Mark 3:20–35 from the Perspective of Shame/Honor," *BTB* 17 (1987): 83–87. The individual and collective works of Malina and Neyrey have been influential in the use of honor/shame material in New Testament studies. For representative works see Bruce J. Malina, *The New Testament World: Insights from Cultural Anthropology* (rev. ed.; Louisville: Westminster/ John Knox, 1993); Jerome H. Neyrey, *The Social World of Luke-Acts: Models for Interpretation* (Peabody: Hendrickson, 1991). For studies of honor and shame and the Hebrew Bible, see Lyn M. Bechtel (Huber), "The Biblical Experience of Shame/Shaming: The Social Experience of Shame/Shaming in Biblical Israel in Relation to Its Use as Religious Metaphor" (Ph.D. diss., Drew University, 1983); idem, "The Perception of Shame Within the Divine-Human Relationship in Biblical Israel," in *Uncovering Ancient Stones: Essays In Memory of H. Neil Richardson* (ed. Lewis M. Hopfe; Winona Lake: Eisenbrauns, 1993), 79–92; idem, "Shame as a Sanction of Social Control in Biblical Israel: Judicial, Political, and Social Shaming," *JSOT* 49 (1991): 47–76; Dianne Bergant, "'My Beloved Is Mine and I Am His' (Song 2:16): The Song of Songs and Honor and Shame," *Semeia* 68 (1994): 23–40; Lillian R. Klein, "Honor and Shame in Esther," in *A Feminist Companion to Esther, Judith and Susanna* (ed. Athalya Brenner; The Feminist Companion to the Bible 7; Sheffield: Sheffield Academic Press, 1995): 149–75; Jacqueline E. Lapsley, *Can These Bones Live? The Problem of the Moral Self in the Book of Ezekiel* (BZAW 301; Berlin: de Gruyter, 2000), esp. 130–57; idem, "Shame and Self-Knowledge: The Positive Role of Shame in Ezekiel's View of the Moral Self," in *The Book of Ezekiel: Theological and Anthropological Perspectives* (ed. Margaret S. Odell and John T. Strong; SBLSymS 9; Atlanta: Society of Biblical Literature, 2000), 143–73; Margaret S. Odell, "An Exploratory Study of Shame and Dependence in the Bible and Selected Near Eastern Parallels," in *The Biblical Canon in Comparative Perspective: Scripture in Context IV* (ed. K. Lawson Younger, Jr., William W. Hallo, and Bernard F. Batto; ANETS 11; Lewiston: Edwin Mellon, 1991), 217–33; Timothy S. Laniak, *Shame and Honor in the Book of Esther* (SBLDS 165; Atlanta: Scholars Press, 1997); Ronald A. Simkins, "'Return to Yahweh': Honor and Shame in Joel," *Semeia* 68 (1994): 41–54; Gary Stansell, "Honor and Shame in the David Narratives," *Semeia* 68 (1994): 55–79; and Ken Stone, *Sex, Honor, and Power in the Deuteronomistic History* (JSOTSup 234; Sheffield: Sheffield Academic Press, 1996).

[29] Stone, *Sex, Honor, and Power*.

goal is to examine the ways in which biblical narrative reflects a certain cultural configuration of sexual behavior. Stone's analysis looks at both Judg 19 and 2 Sam 13. He does not examine, of course, Gen 34 since he is looking at texts in the Deuteronomistic History (DtrH). In addition, he focuses on the broader category of sexuality and is not interested in issues specific to the rape narratives. Stone concludes that these texts about sexuality within the DtrH reflect male struggles for honor and power. The Deuteronomistic writers were not concerned primarily with sexuality, but with the ways in which sexuality impacted the political and social environment of Israel. Thus, within the DtrH, issues of male power and prestige are directly related to sexual activity with women. Stone's conclusion is consistent with studies that examine honor and shame dynamics in Mediterranean cultures.

Stone provides a number of interesting interpretations of various texts within the Deuteronomistic History. By combining anthropological research and narratological analysis, he is able to provide a cultural analysis of the Deuteronomistic texts, specifically those narratives that contain references to sexuality. Stone's work provides a way to examine the cultural assumptions of the texts, using a method that is appropriate to such analysis. Stone's methodology, however, tends to subsume the meaning of texts, including their sometimes various understandings of sex and sexual contact, into categories of honor and shame. The honor and shame script of male prestige and competition becomes a filter through which the texts should be read. Thus, the particular expressions of each text tend to get lost within the larger cultural framework.

Lyn Bechtel, in her article, "What If Dinah Is Not Raped?" argues that Dinah is not sexually assaulted by Shechem.[30] She suggests that recent interpreters of Gen 34 misunderstand the biblical narrative in that they project modern understandings of rape onto the biblical text. Contemporary definitions of rape focus on the violation of an individual's will. Bechtel suggests other cultural dynamics are at work within Gen 34 since the biblical texts assume a culture that is group-oriented. She proposes that the Piel stem of ענה does not mean "to rape," in the modern sense of the word, but "to humiliate," or "to

---

[30] Bechtel, "What If Dinah Is Not Raped?" 19–36, followed by Mark Brett (Mark G. Brett, *Genesis: Procreation and the Politics of Identity* [Old Testament Readings; London and New York: Routledge, 2000], 101–3).

shame."[31] Bechtel develops her analysis of עִנָּה in the Piel by examining the word's use in Deuteronomy 22 and 2 Sam 13. She suggests that within group-oriented societies, shame functions as a way to control behaviors of those within the group. A group shames an individual whose behavior or situation is unacceptable to the group's standards. Shaming results in a loss of status for the person or persons involved.

According to Bechtel, in the culture of the biblical text, intercourse becomes shameful for women in two ways: 1) when the sexual act violates social obligations such as marriage or family ties; or 2) when sex does not lead to the prospect of marriage or familial bonding. Thus, the issue in Gen 34 is not that Dinah is raped, but that she is humiliated through Shechem's sexual act. Bechtel admits that עִנָּה in the Piel can mean "rape" when words of force are used in conjunction with the verb, e.g., 2 Sam 13.

Bechtel concludes that Gen 34 is not primarily about the rape of Dinah; in fact, Dinah is not raped at all. The central conflict in the text focuses on a disagreement between two parties—Dinah and Jacob, who look favorably on interaction with outsiders, and Simeon and Levi, who perceive that such interaction pollutes the family group.[32] The last two desire to maintain the purity of the group and are threatened by interactions with the people of the land.

Bechtel's analysis is helpful in that she properly takes issue with the ways in which modern scholars have assumed contemporary understandings of rape in their interpretations of Gen 34. Her reading of the Dinah story, which assumes group-orientation, also points to complex social dynamics at work within the biblical text. Her understanding of rape, however, requires modification. Bechtel argues that Dinah is not raped, but is sexually humiliated. Her understanding and definition of rape is a modern one: "a man's forcible, aggressive sexual intercourse with a woman who at the time does not consent and shows obvious resistance or vigorous struggle."[33] She suggests that since

---

[31] For a more complete discussion of this verb and the meaning of rape, see Chapter 2 below.

[32] See also Bernd Jörg Diebner, "Gen 34 und Dinas Rolle bei der Definition 'Israels,'" *DBAT* 19 (1984): 59–75.

[33] Bechtel, "What If Dinah Is Not Raped?" 20.

there is no indication of sexual violence or force in Gen 34, Shechem's act with Dinah cannot be considered rape.

There are at least two problems with her reasoning. First, Bechtel criticizes other biblical interpreters for reading modern understandings of rape into Gen 34, but she, herself, uses a contemporary definition of rape to determine that Dinah is not raped. For Bechtel, Dinah cannot be raped because Gen 34 does not conform to her contemporary understanding of rape. Second, while the verbs לקח and שכב do not always suggest the use of force, the words certainly can have such connotations, especially in certain contexts. The succession of לקח and שכב within the context of female abduction push the interpretation of ענה in the Piel toward the violent potential within the root.

Reading Connections between the Rape Texts

A number of scholars have recognized thematic connections between at least two of the three rape narratives, though no significant study to date has identified a relationship among all three. Indeed Keefe, whom I discussed above, is one of the only scholars to attempt a reading of all the rape narratives collectively.[34] Her focus on women's perception, however, provides an inadequate lens through which to analyze these texts. A more appropriate analysis would account for the ways in which the initial rape of a woman leads to further violence between men.

Esther Fuchs, in her monograph, *Sexual Politics in the Biblical Narrative: Reading the Hebrew Bible as Woman*, also focuses on women's issues in biblical

---

[34] Keefe, "Rapes of Women." In a recent volume, Joy Schroeder does a historical survey of Christian interpretation on texts involving sexual violence. She covers interpreters from 150 to 1600 C.E. She does examine all three rape narratives in question in the present study. However, her rationale for including these texts is held together loosely. She suggests that commentators would have considered these texts to be rapes according to their own historically contextual standards. See Joy A. Schroeder, *Dinah's Lament: The Biblical Legacy of Sexual Violence in Christian Interpretation* (Minneapolis: Fortress, 2007), 2–3. While her work does appeal to some studies in biblical scholarship, her primary focus is on specific historical periods of biblical interpretation. For a useful historical survey of the rape texts, see Chapter One, "Fallen Virgin, Violated Daughter: The Rape of Dinah (Genesis 34);" Chapter Three, "Dismembering the Adulteress: The Levite's Concubine (Judges 19);" and Chapter Four, "Violated Sister: The Tears of Tamar (2 Samuel 13)."

literature.[35] She does a better job, however, in articulating the function of female absence and male prominence in the rape stories. Using feminist literary analysis, Fuchs persuasively exposes the sexual politics in both Gen 34 and 2 Sam 13. She argues that there is a fundamental problem in these stories, namely that the rape of a sister gives way to a plot development that emphasizes a brother's revenge:

> Although she is clearly the direct victim of the villain's abuse, the sister in both stories is not *aided* by her brother in her attempt to punish the aggressor, but rather *replaced* by him. She is not even consulted by her brother, who determines himself how to punish the rapist. Having fulfilled her role as a rape victim, the sister clears the way for her brother-hero to step in and restore 'moral' order (emphasis hers).[36]

Thus, Fuchs' insightful interpretation of these two rape narratives moves the discussion forward in that she accounts for both the diminished role of women in these stories, while explaining why the plot moves increasingly toward male responses.

Fuchs' analysis emphasizes similarities and differences between Gen 34 and 2 Sam 13, while mentioning only briefly Judg 19 in her discussion of these rape narratives.[37] The Judges material is important to her discussion of the father's house, but she fails to notice the similar narrative trajectory in Judg 19–21, in which the rape of a woman moves quickly to issues of male vengeance and the wars of men. This oversight is likely due to limitations in the comparative categories. That is, by focusing primarily, though not exclusively, on the relationship between sisters and brothers, Fuchs' emphasizes texts that have the proper characters—sisters and brothers—but misses the significant plot trajectory of rape that leads to male revenge.

Finally, in his brief article, "Dinah and Shechem, Tamar and Amnon," David Noel Freedman recognizes striking literary and linguistic parallels between Gen 34 and 2 Sam 13.[38] He argues that a single author wrote the two

---

[35] Fuchs discusses two of the rape texts in question, Gen 34 and 2 Sam 13, in her chapter entitled, "The Biblical Sister: Redeemed by Her Brother?" (Chapter 7). While she does mention Judg 19, her primary point of comparison and contrast is between Dinah and Tamar (*Sexual Politics in the Biblical Narrative*, 200–224).

[36] Ibid., 202.

[37] Ibid., 209–11.

[38] Freedman, "Dinah and Shechem," 51–63.

texts, and that they represent "book-ends" within a larger narrative complex, what Richard Elliot Friedman has termed "Super-J" (Genesis–Samuel).[39] Freedman suggests that the similarities between the narratives create an "echo-effect" near the beginning and end of Super-J. The two stories contain enough similarities to create this effect; however, they also have enough variation to invite comparison. Thus, Super-J uses these two similar narratives about the violation of two virgins in Israel to elicit a comparison between the houses of David and Jacob.

Freedman has illuminated convincingly the similarities between Gen 34 and 2 Sam 13. He also has alluded to the parallel themes and narrative function operative in both of these texts. His reading and reconstruction, however, are dubious, relying on Richard Friedman's speculative proposal for J.[40] The present study also will suggest that Freedman's work misses the significance of the congruencies between Gen 34 and 2 Sam 13. As proposed above, Judg 19 also displays similar vocabulary, thematic elements, and progression. Freedman also fails to identify the particularity of these two rape narratives, since his intent is to argue that Gen 34 and 2 Sam 13 are the work of one author. Thus, his work focuses only on those congruent factors within the texts that one can explain under the rubric of authorial intention. I show in the following chapters that the similarities between the rape texts are best understood in light of their family resemblance, i.e., their similar progression of rape that leads to excessive violence, resulting in social fragmentation.

Legal Material on Rape

Before concluding, a word about the legal material on rape is needed. This book is not a comprehensive examination of the meaning of rape in the Hebrew Bible or in ancient Israel. The purpose of the study is to examine the interrelated and distinct representations of rape within biblical narrative. However, one is better equipped to interpret the rape narratives when one takes

---

[39] Friedman suggests that J's narrative extends from Genesis through the Deuteronomistic History. See Richard Elliot Friedman, *The Hidden Book in the Bible* (San Francisco: HarperSanFrancisco, 1998).

[40] For discussion and critique of Friedman's proposal, see Hershel Shanks, P. Kyle McCarter, Ronald S. Hendel, and Richard D. Nelson, "Has Richard Friedman Really Discovered A Long-Hidden Book in the Bible," *BR* 15 (April 1999): 30–39, 44–46.

into consideration the laws that deal with rape in the Hebrew Bible. For the present work, the legal material functions to provide an alternative to the violent post-rape responses that are found in Gen 34, Judg 19, and 2 Sam 13. I am not arguing that the biblical authors or editors had the laws in mind when the rape texts were written or edited into their present contexts. Nor is a complete examination of the legal material on rape and other sexual offenses within the scope of this study. The simple point that I am making about the law is that it represents a nonviolent response to rape within the Hebrew Bible, and therefore, provides a contrast with the excessively violent male responses in the rape texts. Hence, before I turn to the narrative material, it is necessary to address briefly the issues involved in the interpretation of the legal material on rape.

The primary texts under consideration are found in Deut 22:22–30. Scholars have long recognized that these laws deal with issues related to illicit sexual relations between men and women, including adultery and/or rape.[41] Two texts, 22:25–27 and 22:28–29, are often considered to be rape laws.[42] Scholars have identified three issues in these laws: 1) the marital status of the woman involved; 2) the question of the woman's consent or lack of consent; and 3) the issue of who is the injured party.[43] Moreover, the male's use of force in the rape laws is stated explicitly in both cases.[44]

---

[41] For further discussion on these texts, see Moshe Weinfeld, *Deuteronomy and the Deuteronomic School* (Oxford: Clarendon, 1972), 284–86; Carolyn Pressler, *The View of Women Found in the Deuteronomic Family Laws* (BZAW 216; Berlin: de Gruyter, 1993), 31–43; idem, "Sexual Violence and the Deuteronomic Law," in *A Feminist Companion to Exodus to Deuteronomy* (ed. Athalya Brenner; The Feminist Companion to the Bible 6; Sheffield: Sheffield Academic Press, 1994), 102–12; Frymer-Kensky, "Virginity in the Bible," 91–93; Harold C. Washington, "'Lest He Die in Battle and Another Man Take Her': Violence and the Construction of Gender in the Laws of Deuteronomy 20–22," in *Gender and Law in the Hebrew Bible and the Ancient Near East* (ed. Victor H. Matthews, Bernard M. Levinson, and Tikva Frymer-Kensky; JSOTSup 262; Sheffield: Sheffield Academic Press, 1998), 208–12; and Cheryl B. Anderson, *Women, Ideology, and Violence*, 40–42 and 86–91.

[42] Westbrook, "Punishments and Crimes," 552; and Tikva Frymer-Kensky, "Sex and Sexuality," *ABD* 5:1145. See, however, Pressler, who argues that the purpose of these laws was not to address sexual violence, but the loss of property of certain males (Pressler, "Sexual Violence," 102–12).

[43] Pressler, "Sexual Violence," 106. Pressler mentions the first two issues explicitly, though she is arguing that the laws are framed as violations of other men and do not address the bodily

In the laws of Deut 22:22–30, the woman's status is clearly defined with respect to marriage.[45] She is described as married, inchoately married, or not engaged. When the woman is married or engaged, the crime is treated as adultery, and is punishable by death.[46] In such cases, the woman's culpability is based on her consent. In biblical law, the woman's consent is tied to the context within which the act occurred. Thus, if the man had sex with the woman in the city (vv. 23–24), consent is assumed. Presumably, if the sexual act occurred in the town, and the woman cried out, someone would have heard her cry. If, however, the sexual intercourse happens in the open country (vv. 25–27), the act is considered to be non-consensual. The woman could have cried out without anyone hearing. In the last law (vv. 28–29), the rape of an unattached virgin, the woman's consent is not mentioned explicitly, though the male's use of force suggests that the sexual encounter was non-consensual.[47]

---

violation of women. For other studies that examine the ways in which Deuteronomic family laws protect the rights of men, see Pressler, *Family Laws*, 95–114; Washington, "Violence and the Construction of Gender," 324–63; and Cheryl B. Anderson, *Women, Ideology, and Violence*, 86–91.

[44] In the first case, the use of חזק in v. 25 is a clear reference to force. Some have questioned the use of force in 22:28–29, suggesting that תפש does not necessarily imply force, but can mean simply, "to hold" (Weinfeld, *Deuteronomy and the Deuteronomic School*, 286). As Pressler rightly argues, תפש, when its object is inanimate, can mean "to hold" or "to handle skillfully" an object or city. When the object is a human being, however, the verb "has to do with involuntary seizure" (Pressler, *Family Laws*, 37–38, and n. 49).

[45] Pressler identifies the status of women for the six laws in this section. In the first two cases, the woman is newly married. In the third law, the woman is "under the authority of a master/husband" (בְּעֻלַת־בַּעַל). The next two cases deal with a woman who has been engaged or is "inchoately married" (the two are treated here as synonyms), i.e., the bride price has been paid, but the marriage has not been consummated. The final law deals with an unbetrothed virgin ("Sexual Violence," 106).

[46] Cuneiform sources provide similar cases that suggest that sex with an engaged woman was considered to be adultery (Code of Ur-Nammu § 6, Code of Eshnunna § 26, and Code of Hammurabi § 130). See discussion in Westbrook, "Punishments and Crimes," 552.

[47] For a parallel in Middle Assyrian Law, see MAL § A 55. In this law, a man forcibly seizes a virgin girl who is not engaged. The man's use of force is a factor irrespective to the context within which the rape takes place (e.g., the city or in the open country). As with the laws in Deuteronomy, cuneiform sources suggest that the woman's consent was a key issue and usually was tied to the context of the crime (cf. MAL § A 12 and a Hittite law, HL § 197). Though Pressler argues that consent is not a primary legal concern in Deut 22:28–29, she acknowledges

On the third aspect of these laws, the issue of the injured party, scholars have recognized that these laws were designed to protect the rights and property of certain men. This is not to say, however, that the laws ignore the woman's situation. Carolyn Pressler clarifies this issue well:

> The laws are not oblivious to the woman's welfare. They do offer her certain protections. A married or betrothed woman who resists sexual intercourse with someone other than her husband is considered innocent of adultery and is protected from execution. An unbetrothed woman who is sexually violated is provided with the protection of marriage—a protection vital for her social status, economic security and honor. The laws do not show concern for her sexual integrity, however. They do not treat sexual violation of a woman as sexual assault against her.[48]

Thus, the laws against rape in Deuteronomy frame the issue predominantly as it relates to the economic and social losses of men. This fact helps to explain why restitution for the rape of a virgin involves the payment of the bride price.[49] The crime itself is seen as a financial loss of the father, since the sexual violation has made his daughter unmarriageable. The no-divorce clause of this law, however, does suggest security for the woman's future status.

The preceding discussion has at least two implications for the study of the rape narratives. First, since the legal material frames the act of rape as a crime against other men, one should not be surprised to find similar dynamics within the stories about rape. The progression from rape to excessive male violence suggests that the characters experience the rape as a crime against men. The difference between narrative and law, however, is that the narrator can tell the story in such a way that emphasizes the female victim's situation or plight. Such depictions can align the reader with the raped woman, distancing the reader from the male characters who perceive the event as a crime against themselves.

Second, the Deuteronomic laws, even if they do not address the crime of rape as sexual violence against a woman as such, do provide a less violent alternative for addressing the situation. Hence, when one reads the rape texts, the question must be asked: If a less violent option for dealing with rape is

---

that the use of force in this law suggests a non-consensual context (see Pressler, *Family Laws*, 38, n. 49).

[48] Pressler, "Sexual Violence," 109.

[49] See, however, Weinfeld, who argues that the fifty shekels of silver is a fine for violating the young woman, not the customary *mōhar* (*Deuteronomy and the Deuteronomic School*, 285).

available, why do these texts move toward excessive male violence? A related question also emerges concerning the interpretation of rape within the legal material. If the legal issue in rape is not sexual violence against women, but the economic or social losses of men, why are the male responses to rape so excessively violent in the rape narratives? For example, in Gen 34, the story involves elements that are very similar to those found in Deut 22:28–29. Dinah, presumably a virgin who is not engaged, is seized and raped by Shechem. Shechem and Hamor offer to pay the bride price; in fact, Shechem allows the sons of Jacob to set the price as high as they want (34:12). If the issue of rape is simply a matter of male economic loss, as scholars have suggested concerning the laws of Deuteronomy, then one would assume that Jacob and his sons would readily accept the offer. The fact that Simeon and Levi deceive and slaughter the inhabitants of the city in retaliation for the Shechem's crime suggests that much more is at stake than financial injury. The interpretations that follow will explore the different ways that each of these rape texts makes this movement to excessive violence.

Summary

The preceding discussion has highlighted at least three trends within scholarship on the rape narratives. First, despite the compelling literary and linguistic congruencies among the rape texts, there is no comprehensive study that examines the nature of these texts' relationship to one another in a satisfactory way. Second, biblical scholars often presuppose a modern definition of rape in their interpretations of Gen 34, Judg 19, and 2 Sam 13. This contemporary understanding of the sexual violence in the texts has led to interpretative confusion. Similarly, feminist interpreters have usually focused on women's experience within the text, even when the texts display little interest in such matters. Finally, scholars who focus on the cultural assumptions (e.g., honor and shame) within the biblical material tend to subsume their understandings of the texts into cultural frameworks that are admittedly external to the text. Scholarship on the rape texts has not considered a way to explore the connection of these three texts while maintaining the particular expressions of each of these rape stories.

The present work argues that Gen 34, Judg 19, and 2 Sam 13 bear a family resemblance to one another, displaying similar thematic elements, progression and outcome. The texts all display a similar movement from the original rape of one woman to further retributive violence between men to some form of social fragmentation. While these congruencies justify each story's place within this family of texts, the individual expressions of the progression—the various manifestations of rape, male violence, and social fragmentation—will vary according to the particular thematic and contextual elements of the different texts.

CHAPTER TWO

Genesis 34: The Rape of Dinah, the Disputes of Men and the Division of a Family

Introduction

Gen 34 describes the rape of Dinah and the consequent retaliation of her brothers on the city of Shechem. In this chapter, I will argue that the narrative follows the progression described earlier, namely, that the story moves from the initial rape to male responses that are excessively violent to social fragmentation. This rape text is set within the complicated issues of group identity, specifically, how the Israelite family negotiates its relationship to outsiders. In what follows, particular attention is given to the fracturing of Jacob's family, which is seen in the conflict between Jacob and his sons. The initial rape of Dinah sets in motion different male responses to the deed. Dinah's reaction to her violation is not narrated, which tends to focus the reader's attention all the more on the propriety or impropriety of the males' varied responses. As the narrative progresses, the rape of Dinah deteriorates into the negotiations and conflicts of men. The issue over how Israel is to relate to those outside of its group's boundaries is an important theme that complicates the males' disputes. The story ends with the family of Jacob in conflict over how the brothers dealt with the rape. In addition, Israel's relationship to other peoples of the land is made more problematic because of the excessive violence of the brothers' retaliation.

Sternberg, followed by Paul Noble, has suggested that this story is a complex narrative that deals with issues of crime and punishment. The present chapter will argue that such a designation only partially accounts for what is going on in this story, something that both scholars acknowledge. The narrative wrestles just as much with issues of how this Israelite family will negotiate with the inhabitants of Shechem, and how different opinions can divide a family. Both Sternberg and Noble understand that there is a significant connection between the relational dynamics in this story and the theme of crime and punishment.[1] However, while both address the former issues, their interpretations emphasize the latter theme. Thus, their interpretations tend to side with certain characters over others based on how they respond to the crime. As Noble acknowledges, and as I will show, the narrative portrayal of the conflicts between the characters is much more complicated. The plot never resolves around the theme of crime and punishment. In fact, one of the more compelling elements of this story is that the punishment does not fit the crime—the retaliation of the brothers is excessively violent. Indeed, in the end, the punishment does not address the crime satisfactorily. The final result is that the relationship between insiders and outsiders has become increasingly problematic with the potential for further retributive violence (Gen 34:30). In addition, the story closes with the family of Jacob divided over how the situation was handled. The family resemblance of this story, which is characterized by the progression of how rape leads to excessive violence and thence to social fragmentation, better explains the movement and dynamics of this story while allowing the story's complexities to come forward.

The Context of Rape

The rape of Dinah is set within a larger narrative context that addresses the issue of how Jacob and his family will deal with outsiders, specifically, with the inhabitants of the Canaanite city of Shechem.[2] This theme within Gen 34 is introduced in 33:18–20. In v. 18, the narrator sets the context by describing that

---

[1] Meir Sternberg, *The Poetics of Biblical Narrative*, 445–81; Paul Noble, "A 'Balanced' Reading of the Rape of Dinah: Some Exegetical and Methodological Observations," *BibInt* 4, no. 2 (1996): 173–204.

[2] Tikva Frymer-Kensky, *Reading the Women of the Bible* (New York: Schocken, 2002), 196–97; Bechtel, "What If Dinah Is Not Raped?" 31–36; Walter Brueggemann, *Genesis* (IBC; Atlanta: John Knox, 1982), 274–75; Terence E. Fretheim, "The Book of Genesis: Introduction, Commentary, and Reflections," *NIB* 1:577.

Jacob traveled "safely" (שָׁלֵם) within the region of Shechem. In a geographical sense, 33:18–20 serves as a narrative bridge between 33:1–17 and 34:1 ff., describing Jacob's journey from Succoth to the city of Shechem. Verse 18, however, also provides the reader with information that will be key to understanding the events and dynamics that follow in Gen 34. There has been much discussion about the translation of 33:18. The disagreement revolves around whether שָׁלֵם is a place name, "Salem," or is best translated with an adverbial sense, "safely."[3] The Hebrew is ambiguous, though Westermann argues on grammatical grounds for the place name.[4] In either translation, the city's name is not as important as its identification with the person of Shechem (עִיר שְׁכֶם), who figures prominently in the chapter that follows, and the place's description as being in the land of Canaan (בְּאֶרֶץ כְּנַעַן). The introduction to Shechem provides the reader with a first glimpse of the character who will eventually rape Dinah and subsequently fall in love with her. His actions will set in motion a chain of interactions between the inhabitants of this Canaanite city and the family of Jacob. The description of the city as being "in the land of Canaan" sets Gen 34 within the context of Israel among outsiders.[5] As I will show below, this context will prove to be important for understanding the post-rape responses of Jacob and his sons. שָׁלֵם foreshadows the perception that Hamor and Shechem will have of the Israelites later in 34:21, that they are "peaceful" (שְׁלֵמִים).

This perception is indicative of one of the relational possibilities between Jacob's family and the inhabitants of Shechem. In this understanding, the two groups interact peacefully with each other in negotiations. 33:18–20 introduces the reader to this relational trajectory in that Jacob and the sons of Hamor have a successful transaction. Jacob purchases land upon which he pitches his tent (v. 19) and builds an altar (v. 20). These initially peaceful dealings are consistent

---

[3] K.-J. Illman, "šālem," *ThWAT* 8:93–101.

[4] Claus Westermann, *Genesis 12–36* (trans. John J. Scullion; Continental; Minneapolis: Fortress, 1995), 528.

[5] While it is clear from archeological evidence that there is significant cultural continuity between Israel and Canaan, the biblical texts portray the Canaanites as foreigners or outsiders. Within the narrative context of Gen 34, the Hivites are characterized as a distinct ethnic group, related to groups of people living in the land of Canaan (33:18). For a discussion of Israelite ethnicity as it relates to the archaeological evidence, see William G. Dever, *Who Were the Early Israelites and Where Did They Come From?* (Grand Rapids: Eerdmans, 2003), 191–241.

with Hamor and Shechem's post-rape negotiations and Jacob's apparent acquiescence to their proposal in Chapter 34. The social interactions in 33:18–20 also will stand in stark contrast to Simeon and Levi's violent post-negotiation response later in 34:25–26, and the subsequent plundering of the city in 34:27–29. As will be seen below, the brothers' response is dictated by their perception of how to interact with outsiders.

Hence, the setting of this rape story in Gen 34 begins within the context of relational possibilities between insiders and outsiders, between Israel and these inhabitants of Canaan. This theme is a key element throughout the story: different attitudes toward dealing with outsiders inform the differences in how Dinah's brothers respond. The rape will make it necessary for the Israelites and Hivites to interact, leading to offers and counteroffers between the men around the topic of intermarriage. In what follows, I will show how the dynamic, set up between competing perspectives of how to deal with outsiders, contributes to the progression of rape → excessively violent male response → social fragmentation. The rape itself provides the impetus for the two groups to negotiate. As the story progresses, the sons' hostility toward Shechem propels the narrative forward toward its violent conclusion. The sons' violence makes the Israelite family's relationship to the inhabitants of the land problematic, providing one kind of social fragmentation. In addition, the actions of Jacob's sons and the inaction of Jacob lead to increasing family tensions within the Israelite family.

The Rape Text Progression

In this section, I will trace the progression of rape → male responses characterized by excessive violence → social fragmentation. My analysis will focus on the ways in which one element leads to the next, and how the initial rape creates the impetus for the male responses that follow. The social fragmentation that results is a direct consequence of the excessive retributive violence carried out by the offended males.

The Rape of Dinah

The rape of Dinah is the precipitating event of Gen 34. Shechem's rape of Dinah, including his subsequent proposal of marriage, creates a situation in which Jacob and his family must confront the issue of how to interact with outsiders. After a brief introduction to the characters of Dinah and Shechem, the rape itself is narrated quickly in v. 2. Throughout Gen 34, the narrator is clearly more focused on the male responses to Shechem's actions than on the hostility of the act itself. This can be seen most clearly by the fact that the narrator does not spend much time on the rape (v. 2). The majority of the story focuses on the male responses (vv. 3–31). In addition, as noted above, Dinah's response is not narrated, which focuses the reader's attention all the more on the male reactions that result from the initial sexual violence. As I will show below, the responses are varied and complicated, which is a key for understanding the progression of this narrative. In this section, however, I will first establish the nature of the rape as it is narrated in 34:1–4. The narrator describes the event in a way that emphasizes that the perpetrator and victim are from two distinct groups. The rape is narrated briefly, after which Shechem's desire to have Dinah as a wife comes into focus. When Shechem asks his father Hamor to get Dinah as a wife, the stage is set for the negotiations that follow. The male reactions and interactions dominate the narrative throughout the rest of the story.

The story begins with the characterizations and actions of two characters, Dinah and Shechem. The narrator emphasizes that they are from two different groups, namely that Dinah is the daughter of Jacob and Leah, and Shechem is from a ruling family of Hivites. Dinah is described in v. 1 as "the daughter of Leah" (בַּת־לֵאָה), "whom she bore to Jacob" (אֲשֶׁר יָלְדָה לְיַעֲקֹב). This is a more elaborate description than the expected "Dinah, the daughter of Jacob" (דִּינָה בַּת־יַעֲקֹב) in that it emphasizes Dinah's mother.[6] The only other time that Dinah is identified with her mother is in Gen 46:15. Later in chapter 34, two of Leah's sons, Simeon and Levi, are the primary instigators in the violent retaliation against Shechem and its inhabitants. Thus, the narrator's characterization of Dinah as the daughter of Leah functions in at least two ways. First, Dinah's initial characterization is placed squarely in the context of her family relations.[7] While such a characterization is common in the Hebrew

---

[6] Scholz notes that the identification of a daughter with her birth mother is rare (*Rape Plots*, 134). See Julie Kelso, however, who argues that a more pervasive suppression is at work within the Gen 34 narrative (Julie Kelso, "Reading the Silence of Women in Genesis 34," in *Redirected Travel: Alternative Journeys and Places in Biblical Studies* [ed. Roland Boer and Edgar W. Conrad; London and New York: T & T Clark, 2003], 85–109).

[7] Frymer-Kensky, *Women of the Bible*, 180.

Bible and the ANE—one would expect Dinah to be described as *baṭ* PN,[8] "the
daughter of PN"—her identity as Jacob and Leah's daughter is set in contrast to
the characterization of Shechem, who is described as the son of Hamor the
Hivite, "prince of the land" (נְשִׂיא הָאָרֶץ).

Second, the narrator's characterization of Dinah highlights the relational
connection between Dinah and her brothers, Simeon and Levi, also offspring of
Leah. This connection to a common mother foreshadows the later involvement
of her two brothers in initiating the retaliation against Shechem and its
inhabitants. Their connection to Dinah through Leah is biological and familial,
and thus they are more eager to retaliate for the crime committed against their
sister. While the characterization of Dinah emphasizes the idea that she is
Leah's daughter, the narrator also makes it clear that this indeed is a daughter of
Jacob, whom Leah bore to him (אֲשֶׁר יָלְדָה לְיַעֲקֹב). Hence, the narrator's
description of Dinah locates her within the context of her own family group,
emphasizing her connection to Leah and Jacob, and it sets the reader up to
understand the relational dynamic of the conflicts that result from Leah's sons.

The narrator also describes Dinah's action in such a way that emphasizes
that she is interacting with others outside of her family group. Verse 34:1 says,
"she went out (וַתֵּצֵא) ... to see (לִרְאוֹת) the women of the land." Dinah's
intention to see the women of Shechem suggests that she is willingly crossing a
social boundary, seeking to interact with those that the narrator characterizes as
בְּנוֹת הָאָרֶץ. Thus, Dinah's characterization as the daughter of Leah and Jacob is
juxtaposed with the Shechemite women, who are described as "daughters of the
land." These characterizations highlight the similarities and differences of the
different women. Both are described as daughters. However, Dinah is described
within the context of her family; whereas, the Hivite women are characterized
as outsiders—"daughters of the land."

The use of the verb יצא is not unusual in this context. From a narrative
point of view, Dinah's actions represent the beginning and catalyst of the story.
Her "going out" sets the plot in motion. Indeed, without her initial steps, there
is no story to tell. However, when וַתֵּצֵא is combined with the destination and
purpose of Dinah's journey—to see the daughters of the land—it signifies a

---

[8] In fact, within the book of Genesis, *baṭ* PN (father's name) occurs most frequently in the
context of marriage (Gen 11:29; 25:20; 26:34; 28:9; 41:45). The use of דִּינָה בַּת־יַעֲקֹב (34:3)
within the context of Shechem's desire to make Dinah his wife conforms to this pattern.

traversing of social space. Dinah is leaving her family to mingle with the women of the region.[9] When Dinah's actions are interpreted within the setting of the story in 33:18–20, her "going out" is consistent with Jacob's understanding of interaction with the people of the land.[10]

As my earlier comments suggest, the narrator has placed the story of Gen 34 within the setting of peaceful negotiations between Jacob and the sons of Hamor. This suggests to the reader that Dinah may be acting out of a particular understanding of social boundaries that would include interaction with the inhabitants of Shechem.[11] In this way, Dinah is following the lead of her father Jacob by seeking to extend her group's boundaries to include interaction with the people of this region. Such an understanding of intergroup dynamics would not assume a threat of danger from these particular outsiders since there is a precedent for interaction with them, especially since Dinah seeks interaction only with other women. As the reader quickly realizes through the unfolding of the story, however, Dinah's apparent sense of security does not take into account the actions of other men within the region.

The preceding understanding of Dinah's characterization is confirmed when one looks at the character of Shechem in v. 2. The narrator describes Shechem as "the son of Hamor the Hivite, prince of the land." Similar to the characterization of Dinah, Shechem is described in relation to his family, in this case his father Hamor. The designations Hivite and "prince of the land,"

---

[9] Staying with one's own kin and not mingling with outsiders was encouraged for women of the ancient world. For example, in *Midrash Tanhuma*, an interpretation of Psalm 45:14 is used proverbially to explain Dinah's going out: "'The king's daughter is all glorious within.' When a woman keeps herself secluded at home she is worthy to marry a high priest" (cited in Caspi, "Rape of Dinah," 29). Also, a passage from Ben Sira warns of the dangers of letting willful daughters out of the house (42:9–4). For more on the culturally loaded nature of Dinah's "going out," see Frymer-Kensky, *Women of the Bible*, 180–81. Fuchs also draws an interesting parallel between Dinah's going out in Gen 34 and the departure of the Levite's concubine in Judg 19. She exposes the stories' "sexual politics" by pointing out a narrative trajectory in which female movement outside of the house is constructed as danger with brutal consequences for the women (*Sexual Politics in the Biblical Narrative*, 206–13).

[10] Camp, *Wise, Strange and Holy*, 284–85.

[11] Bechtel argues that Shechem and Hamor on the one hand and Dinah and Jacob on the other model a position that is open to interaction with outsiders. Simeon and Levi, however, are threatened by outsiders and experience such social exchanges as pollution ("What If Dinah Is Not Raped?" 19–36).

however, emphasize that Shechem is from a different social group.[12] He comes from a family of privilege (נְשִׂיא הָאָרֶץ) among a group of people who are of a different ethnic designation.[13] The language of vv. 1 and 2 is also full of word plays. Dinah, the daughter of Leah (בַּת־לֵאָה), goes out "to see" (לִרְאוֹת) the "daughters of the land" (בְּנוֹת הָאָרֶץ). Then Shechem, who is the son (בֶן) of a prince of the land (נְשִׂיא הָאָרֶץ), sees (וַיַּרְא) Dinah. Dinah, the *daughter* of Leah and Jacob, begins the story as an agent, as she goes out to *see* the daughters of *the land*. In v. 2, however, she goes from subject to object when Shechem, *son* of Hamor, prince of *the land*, *sees* her. Hence, the narrator's use of language adds to the artistry of these initial characterizations and suggests a high degree of intention in the juxtaposition of these two characters and their respective social groups.

In turning to Shechem's actions, the rape itself is narrated briefly in v. 2 through a series of three verbs. Dinah becomes the object of Shechem's actions:

---

[12] Within the Hebrew Bible, the Hivites are usually listed among the other Canaanite peoples, whom the Israelites are to dispossess (Exod 3:8, 17; 13:5; 23:23, 28; 33:2; 34:11; Deut 7:1; 20:17; Josh 3:10; 9:1; 11:3; 12:8; 24:11; Judg 3:5; 1 Kgs 9:20 [= 2 Chr 8:7]). This suggests that the ethnic distinction "Hivite" was associated with conflict, a characterization that bears out in Gen 34. In addition, Josh 9:3–15 describes how the Hivites, identified with the inhabitants of Gibeon, make a treaty with the Israelites to avoid war (cf. Josh 11:19). The Hivites' cunning negotiations hark back to the shrewd bargaining of Hamor and Shechem in Gen 34.

[13] The phrase נְשִׂיא הָאָרֶץ could refer grammatically to either Shechem or Hamor. Scholz prefers to assign all modifiers to Shechem and thus, she states, "Shechem has three identifications: 'son of Hamor; the Hivite; the prince of the land'" (*Rape Plots*, 135). Scholz's point seeks to emphasize the power differential between Dinah and Shechem. That is, he uses his power and position to overwhelm Dinah. While this is possible grammatically, it is improbable contextually. The context of the narrative would suggest that נְשִׂיא הָאָרֶץ is more likely descriptive of Hamor, since he is the one who initiates negotiations with Jacob's family (v. 6). Shechem also acknowledges that Hamor must be the one who deals with Jacob's clan in order to obtain Dinah (v. 4). Both Hamor and Shechem are present when they address the men of their city (v. 20). Niehr, following Westermann's proposal that this was originally two stories combined to make a third, suggests that confusion over the identity of the נשׂיא is due to the combination of the two traditions (H. Niehr, "*nāśîʾ*," *TDOT* 10:50). Westermann, however, believes that Hamor is the נשׂיא of the city (Westermann, *Genesis 12–36*, 538). Regardless, Shechem is characterized in relation to his father, the spokesperson for the city; and thus, the narrator describes Shechem as a man who is connected to power and political leadership.

he *took* her	וַיִּקַּח אֹתָהּ
lay with her	וַיִּשְׁכַּב אֹת
and *raped* her	וַיְעַנֶּהָ

There has been much debate about this series of verbs in v. 2, in particular the meaning of the last, וַיְעַנֶּהָ, from the root, ענה, which occurs here and in the other rape texts in the Piel stem. A discussion of this issue is in order since an interpretation of Shechem's actions is crucial for understanding Gen 34.

Excursus: Was Dinah Raped?

Scholars have given much attention to the issue of whether or not Dinah is raped by Shechem in Gen 34. In her article, "What If Dinah Is Not Raped? (Gen 34)," Lyn Bechtel argues that interpretations of Gen 34 have read back modern assumptions of rape into the biblical text. She suggests that the word commonly translated as "rape" in Hebrew (ענה in the Piel) is better rendered within the context of social shaming; thus, she prefers to translate the verb as "humiliate" or "shame." A shameful sexual encounter, according to Bechtel, occurs for women, "(1) when it violates existing marital, family or community bonding and obligation or (2) when there is no prospect of its leading to marital or family bonding and obligation."[14] I have already summarized Bechtel's argument in Chapter 1. Here it is important to point out that Bechtel is arguing that Dinah is not raped, since ענה in the Piel does not refer to the forceful nature of the sexual violation but to its resulting social humiliation. Dinah, according to Bechtel, is shamed as a result of her sexual encounter with an outsider, Shechem, regardless of whether or not she consented.

Bechtel has offered some helpful insights for interpreting Gen 34. She is correct in arguing that interpreters have often read their own cultural assumptions into the text. She rightly points to cultural patterns of honor and shame, and how these dynamics might help the interpreter to understand what is going on in Gen 34. In her attempts to understand the social aspects of ענה in the Piel, however, Bechtel has minimized the violent aspects of the verb and the context of forceful sexual violence within which this verb often occurs. While ענה in the Piel certainly can mean "to humble" or "to humiliate," it often

---

[14] Bechtel, "What If Dinah Is Not Raped?" 24.

has the connotation of violence.[15] When God is the agent, it can mean "to afflict."[16] Within narrative contexts, the verb is often used to describe the oppression of a person or group of persons by another.[17] Thus, while Bechtel's argument highlights the social ramifications of ענה in the Piel, it fails to acknowledge the violent aspects of this verb, minimizing the sexual violence that is described in Gen 34.

When turning to Gen 34, most interpreters, contrary to Bechtel, assume that Dinah is raped.[18] Scholars, however, are not self-critical about their cultural presuppositions of rape, or what they mean by rape in the context of Gen 34. The arguments around the meaning of ענה in the Piel have tended to focus on definitions that are influenced by the cultural assumptions of modern interpreters. Thus, the key issue that defines the violation for most interpreters is female volition or consent. In other words, rape is defined as an act of sexual violence and aggression against the will of another person.[19] However, the problem with such a definition within the context of Gen 34 is that Dinah never speaks. The narrator never allows access to the thought of Dinah, and hence, the interpreter is left to speculate how she felt about the incident. The

---

[15] See, for example, Exod 1:11, 12; 22:21, 22; and Num 24:24.

[16] See especially Isa 64:11, where ענה in the Piel is used within the context of the destruction of Jerusalem and the temple.

[17] See Gen 15:13, 16:6; Exod 1:11, 12; Deut 26:6; 2 Sam 7:10; and 2 Kgs 17:20.

[18] For extensive bibliography on scholars who assume that Dinah is raped, see Bechtel, "What If Dinah Is Not Raped?" 19–20, n.2. See also Scholz, *Rape Plots*; idem, "Was It Really Rape in Genesis 34? Biblical Scholarship as a Reflection of Cultural Assumptions," in *Escaping Eden: New Feminist Perspectives on the Bible* (ed. Harold C. Washington, Susan Lochrie Graham, and Pamela Thimmes; Sheffield: Sheffield Academic Press, 1998), 182–98; Ronald T. Hyman, "Final Judgment: The Ambiguous Moral Question That Culminates Genesis 34," *JBQ* 28, no.2 (2000): 93–101; Stephen A. Geller, "The Sack of Shechem: The Use of Typology in Biblical Covenant Religion," *Prooftexts* 10:1 (1990): 1–15; and Graetz, "Dinah the Daughter," 306–17. See, however, Nicolas Wyatt, who argues that Gen 34 is best read in parallel to other ANE seduction stories (Nicolas Wyatt, "The Story of Dinah and Shechem," *UF* 22 [1990]: 433–58).

[19] Bechtel states, "Rape may be defined as a man's forcible, aggressive sexual intercourse with a woman who at the time *does not consent* and shows obvious resistance or vigorous struggle. It is a forceful, *nonconsensual* boundary and identity violation" ("What If Dinah Is Not Raped?" 20; emphasis mine). Scholz defines rape as "the universal physical (genital or oral) attack on a woman, a child, or a man by one or several men. Rape lacks *the consent* of the one attacked" (*Rape Plots*, 4; emphasis mine).

reader is never informed about whether or not Dinah experienced Shechem's act as a violation of her body and will.

While modern definitions of rape affect an interpreter's ability to translate and understand the meaning of ענה in the Piel, the present study suggests that a working definition of the word must be informed by evidence that is within the text itself. Thus, the word's meaning is affected by Gen 34 and the other narrative contexts where the word is used (e.g., Judg 19 and 2 Sam 13). Through a close reading of the literary conventions of the text, the present interpretation of Gen 34 will be able to examine cues that point to the dynamics surrounding rape within the text and thus could give direction to a meaningful understanding of the Piel form of ענה in Gen 34 and the rape texts in general. I contend that the dynamics in each text are different, and hence the rape signifies different things within the three stories. Thus, what is at stake in the present analysis is not a clearly formulated definition of rape in Gen 34 or the Hebrew Bible but an understanding of the narrative configurations and dynamics at play in the text around the topic of rape.

My understanding of Shechem's action against Dinah is based on two observations. The first looks at the vocabulary used to describe Shechem's actions. The second focuses upon the response from the brothers. After Shechem sees (וַיַּרְא) Dinah, his actions are described by a series of verbs: וַיִּקַּח (from the root לקח/לקח), וַיִּשְׁכַּב (from the root שכב), and וַיְעַנֶּהָ (Piel from the root ענה). The conjunction of these three verbs suggests a violent (ענה) sexual (שכב) act that is marked by seizure (לקח). All three verbs, though not necessarily representing use of force, can each have violent aspects.

לקח means "to take" or "seize." Scholars who do not see rape in Gen 34 are quick to point out that the root, in reference to women, can mean "to take a wife."[20] The idiom for "taking a wife," however, is usually לקח with the preposition לְ. In addition, within this narrative, these three verbs in v. 2 precede Shechem's desire to have Dinah as a wife (vv. 3–4). It is only after he has "taken" Dinah and raped her that he desires to marry her.

Similar to לקח, שכב, "to lie down," may or may not have connotations of violence. In the context of sexual relations, it means "to lie with" or "have

---

[20] Wyatt, "Story of Dinah," 435.

sexual intercourse with" (usually with the preposition עִם or אֶת).[21] Naturally, this definition does not exclude violent sexual interchanges. For example, in 2 Sam 13:14, the same construction וַיִּשְׁכַּב אֹתָהּ occurs with ענה in the Piel and חזק, "to be strong." This last verb, pointing to the fact that Amnon was stronger than Tamar, highlights how this half-brother uses his strength to overpower the daughter of David.[22]

In Gen 34, the combination of לקח and שכב to describe Shechem's actions makes more sense when one turns to the legal material. In Deut 22, there are a series of laws that deal with various forms of sexual offense, including rape. In two of the laws, one involving adultery with an engaged woman (22:25–27) and one addressing the rape of a virgin (22:28–29), the issue of force is operative.[23] In both cases, the act of seizing, represented in the first law by חזק and in the second by תפש, precedes the act of lying (שכב) with the woman. In fact, in Deut 22:28–29, the male is forbidden to divorce the young woman because he had raped (עִנָּה) her (v. 29). The configuration of verbs, given the context of the story in Gen 34, suggests that לקח followed immediately by שכב and the Piel of ענה is best translated as "seize," implying Shechem's use of force in his "taking" of Dinah.

I have already discussed above the violent potential within the Piel stem of ענה. When these three words are used together in staccato as in Gen 34, the implication seems clear.[24] Shechem's sexual advance on Dinah is far from

---

[21] Some have argued that שכב in Gen 34:2, which occurs with a suffixed definite direct object marker (אֹתָהּ) and not the expected preposition (אִתָּהּ), means "he laid her," thus, implying a more forced and violent sexual encounter (see Scholz, *Rape Plots*, 136; Sternberg, *Poetics of Biblical Narrative*, 446; and Gordon J. Wenham, *Genesis 16–50* [WBC; Waco: Word, 1994], 306). Other places where this construction occurs are in Lev 15:18, 24; Num 5:13, 19; 2 Sam 13:14 (the rape of Tamar), and Ezek 23:8. While the number of occurrences is significant, it is important to point out that the only cases where force seems to be implied are in Gen 34 and 2 Sam 13, both rape texts. In fact, Ezek 23:8 describes Samaria and Jerusalem, symbolized by the name, Oholah, as a whore who lusts after her lovers, and thus, she desires for men to lie *with* her. Therefore, the expression וַיִּשְׁכַּב אֹתָהּ does not mean "he laid her." The use of force in Genesis 34 is based on the roots לקח and ענה in the Piel.

[22] Hence, the NRSV translates וַיְעַנֶּהָ as "he forced her."

[23] The use of force in the context of rape is also a feature of Mesopotamian law (see MAL A §§ 12, 16, 55).

[24] Scholz, *Rape Plots*, 136.

ordinary and more than socially shameful. Shechem's sexual actions are swift and violent. He sees her. He seizes her. He lies with her. He rapes her.[25]

I use the word "rape" not to highlight that the act is without consent, as many interpreters stress.[26] One can assume that a woman would not consent to such an act. The translation, "rape," points to the violent nature of the sex act. One could just as easily translate this last verb as "he [sexually] abused her," or as the NRSV translates in 2 Sam 13, "he forced her." In Judg 20:5, the Levite uses ענה in the Piel (עִנּוּ) to describe what the men of Gibeah did to his concubine. The men's actions result in a violent death for the woman. In the preceding chapter of Judges, the verbs used to describe the horrific act are וַיֵּדְעוּ (ידע, "to know") and וַיִּתְעַלְּלוּ (Hithpael of עלל, "to deal wantonly with"). The first refers to the sexual nature of the act. The second points to the ruthlessness of it. Hence, it is clear from the immediate verbal context both here in Gen 34, and in other narrative texts where ענה in the Piel is used, that a translation of "rape" is appropriate in that it describes a forceful and violent sexual act against a woman.

However, the present analysis also suggests that a modern definition of rape, which emphasizes a woman's consent, tends to complicate understandings of ענה within Gen 34 since the reader never has access to the volition or interior process of Dinah. Dinah does not cry out; in fact, she does not say anything throughout the whole narrative. The narrator's focus is on the actions

---

[25] Scholz suggests that this threefold configuration of verbs represents a hendiadys, a syntactical construction in which more than one verb, usually two, is used to describe the same action. Thus, the three verbs all point to the same act, Shechem's violent rape of Dinah (Scholz, *Rape Plots*, 138). Ilona Rashkow also highlights the violent nature of this verbal configuration, stating that these three verbs "negate any possibility of seduction or mutual consent and imprint the act of violence" (Ilona N. Rashkow, "The Rape[s] of Dinah [Gen. 34]: False Religion and Excess in Revenge," in *The Destructive Power of Religion: Violence in Judaism, Christianity, and Islam* [vol. 3, Models and Cases of Violence in Religion; Recent Titles in Contemporary Psychology; ed. J. Harold Ellens; Westport: Praeger, 2004], 63).

[26] One could argue from the legal material that consent could be an issue in Gen 34. When, for example, a woman is seized in the country (בַּשָּׂדֶה), she is assumed to be innocent since she could have cried out without anyone hearing her (see Deut 22:25–27). The actual location of Shechem's rape of Dinah, however, is never made clear by the narrator. Though she goes out to see the daughters of the land, one cannot be certain as to whether the crime occurred within the city (which by default means consent if no cry is heard, cf. Deut 22:23–24) or out in the open country. I argue below that Dinah's silence has another narrative function within the story.

and responses of men; hence, the reader has no way of knowing Dinah's response.[27]

I will look more extensively at the brothers' response in the narrative analysis below. However, it is important to realize that a nuance to the meaning of ענה in the Piel can be seen in the response of the brothers to the event. The brothers are angered and grieved by the incident. The words used to describe what has happened to their sister are revealing. The narrator suggests that the brothers are motivated to deceive Shechem because the latter had committed נְבָלָה, "a disgraceful thing ... in Israel" by lying with Jacob's daughter. Simeon and Levi at the conclusion of the story justify their rampage on the city by saying, "Should our sister be treated like a whore?"

The narrator also provides insight into the brothers' response by adding that they are motivated by the fact that Shechem has defiled (טָמֵא) Dinah.[28] Thus, it is clear from the brothers' responses and the narrator's characterization of the brothers' motive that they experience the rape of Dinah as a defilement of their sister and breach of social space. The rape has transgressed their group boundary and norms, and therefore, they experience it as a violating act: "Such a thing should not be done" (כֵן לֹא יֵעָשֶׂה). Such an understanding of the rape is also consistent with the brothers' condition of circumcision in response to Hamor and Shechem's intermarriage proposal.[29] Though the sons of Jacob act deceitfully in these negotiations, their counteroffer suggests that marriage between the two groups is not possible because of a difference in group norms,

---

[27] In 2 Sam 13, Tamar's non-consent is narrated and emphasized within the telling of the story. In Judg 19, there is no verbal response from the concubine. While consent was a factor in determining a woman's complicity in sexual encounters within the legal material of the Hebrew Bible and the ANE (see discussion above), the issue does not appear consistently throughout the rape texts. The raped woman's response is only clear with Tamar.

[28] See especially 34:13 and 34:5. In 34:13, the narrator uses Dinah's defilement to explain the motivation for the brothers' deceitful response to Hamor and Shechem's offer. Alexander Rofé argues that biblical law does not place the seduction or rape of a virgin under the category of defilement. Gen 34 is an exception to this rule, since Dinah's brothers perceive Shechem's actions as a defiling act. Rofé understands this difference as reflecting a late, postexilic date for the story (see Alexander Rofé, "Defilement of Virgins in Biblical Law and the Case of Dinah [Genesis 34]," *Biblical* 86:3 [2005]: 369–75).

[29] Camp argues that the configuration of ideas—defilement, circumcision, and Levi's role in the retribution—is not coincidental but points to priestly themes within Gen 34 (see *Wise, Strange and Holy*, 294–302).

namely, that the Hivites are uncircumcised. Hence, within the negotiations, the brothers highlight issues of group space and definition when talking about intermarriage.

The brothers' final response is one of violent retribution on Hamor, Shechem, and their city. The brutality of the response coupled with the brothers' perception of the violation confirms that rape, as it is narratively constructed within Gen 34, has larger social implications. The brothers, especially Simeon and Levi, perceive the violence done to Dinah as a violation not only of their sister but also of their family. Thus, vengeance is carried out on the perpetrating individual and the individual's group. Such an understanding of rape makes sense within the cultural framework of honor and shame, where personality is assumed to be located not in the self but in the larger group (dyadic). Within such a cultural mindset, a violation of one's sister is a violation of one's entire clan. To rape a single member of a tribe brings dishonor on the entire tribe. Shechem's act would be perceived by the brothers as a challenge to their family honor, requiring some kind of riposte. Hence, the preceding analysis of ענה in the Piel suggests that Dinah was raped, and that this rape has larger social implications.[30]

Following the rape of Dinah, the narrator shifts emphasis from Shechem's rape of Dinah to his love for her and his desire to have her as a wife. This move by the narrator quickly turns the reader's attention from the rape to issues of marriage and intermarriage between the two groups (v. 4 ff.). As I will show below, this shift addresses her loss of virginal status but not the violence of the crime. Because of this fact, the social dynamics described above find more complicated expression as the story proceeds to the male responses. The rape becomes the impetus for further and more significant interaction between these two groups. This shift towards marriage finds initial expression in v. 3, where Shechem's post-rape response provides the reader with an interesting turn of

---

[30] Bechtel, as suggested above, has rightly pointed out that ענה in the Piel has profound social implications, though she goes on to say that Dinah was not raped. She prefers to define the word within the context of social shame or humiliation. The present argument takes into consideration the larger social implications, while not minimizing the sexual violence in this passage (see Bechtel, "What If Dinah Is Not Raped?" 19–36).

events. The rape of Dinah, which the narrator describes with three verbs, is matched by Shechem's response, again with three verbs:

And his soul *clung* to Dinah, daughter of Jacob	וַתִּדְבַּק נַפְשׁוֹ בְּדִינָה בַּת־יַעֲקֹב
he *loved* the girl	וַיֶּאֱהַב אֶת־הַנַּעֲרָ
and *spoke* to the girl's heart	וַיְדַבֵּר עַל־לֵב הַנַּעֲרָ

The violent actions of sexual aggression in v. 2 give way to the language of intimacy and affection. Shechem's initial physical and aggressive impulses, which the narrator describes with three verbs (לקח, שכב. and ענה), are countered by the narrator's threefold description of Shechem's sudden affection for Dinah (דִּבֶּר עַל־לֵב, אָהַב, דָּבַק נַפְשׁוֹ).

The first phrase, וַתִּדְבַּק נַפְשׁוֹ, "his soul clung," within the context of love, is the language of relational bonding, as found in Gen 2:24.[31] The second verb, וַיֶּאֱהַב, "he loved," confirms the emotional attachment described in the previous expression. Shechem then verbalizes his expression to Dinah—a move from the internal to the external—by "speaking to the girl's heart" (וַיְדַבֵּר עַל־לֵב הַנַּעֲרָ). These three verbs, which describe a response of relational intimacy, create a tension with the preceding verbs of violence. They do not cancel each other out, but suspend the reader in an ethical dilemma. Do the last three verbs of relational bonding tip the balance of the reader's opinion in favor of Shechem, or was the initial sexual violation, described by three verbs, too horrible a deed to overcome with affection?

Scholars are divided about how to respond to this question, the answer to which forces one's interpretation toward a certain conclusion. For Gunn and Fewell, the verbs of affection create a measure of sympathy for Shechem in the mind of the reader. They acknowledge, however, that the juxtaposition of Shechem's violent actions and post-rape "love" suspend the reader's judgment.[32] How Shechem proceeds to act on his love will determine how the reader will make his/her final determination.

---

[31] Gunn and Fewell, "Tipping the Balance," 196; Westermann, *Genesis 12–36*, 538; Fretheim, "The Book of Genesis," 577; Wenham, *Genesis 16–50*, 311; and Bechtel, "What If Dinah Is Not Raped?" 28.

[32] Fewell and Gunn, "Tipping the Balance," 197. Though Fewell and Gunn are arguing against Sternberg, they are in agreement with him about the complexity of the reader's initial

Structurally, the narrative suggests that the two sets of verbs balance each other out, creating a tension for the reader that is filled with ambiguity. The first set of verbs (לקח, שׁכב, and ענה) describes violence against a young woman. Violence against innocence, especially when a person in power is the perpetrator, creates a reaction of outrage in the reader.[33] Hence, the reader's first reaction is to judge Shechem as abusive and impulsive. The narrator complicates this reaction in the reader by describing Shechem's response to the event in terms that signify his endearment to Dinah (אָהַב, דָּבַק נַפְשׁוֹ, and דִּבֶּר עַל־לֵב). What is a reader to make of a rapist who then loves the woman that he raped? Such an idea is morally problematic, creating a dilemma for the reader.

This quandary will be compounded in two ways as the narrative progresses. First, Shechem proceeds to act in a socially appropriate way through negotiations with the brothers. His response addresses Dinah's defilement through marriage. The narrator adds the remark that Shechem was the most honored (נִכְבָּד) in his town (34:19). This incongruity presents the reader with the difficulty of how to evaluate the character of Shechem, a problem that is set up by the verbal contrasts within the structure of vv. 2–3 and by the characterization presented by the narrator.

The tension is compounded in a second way later in the story by the response of incredulity from the brothers, who view the act as a violation of their social group. Hence, the tension created in vv. 2–3 by the two clusters of verbs will become embodied in the two divergent responses of men—one from Shechem and Hamor and one from the brothers of Dinah. Shechem and Hamor are motivated to negotiation by the former's affection for the girl, emphasizing marriage and intermarriage, and hence, the last set of verbs (v. 3).

---

reaction to Shechem. They differ from Sternberg in their final evaluation of Shechem, the former arguing that the reader is sympathetic toward him and his father, the latter believing that the narrator leads the reader to side with Simeon and Levi. For Sternberg's response to Fewell and Gunn, see Meir Sternberg, "Biblical Poetics and Sexual Politics: From Reading to Counterreading," *JBL* 111, no. 3 (1992): 463–88.

[33] 2 Sam 12, in which Nathan confronts David, provides a good illustration of the appropriate response that is expected when someone in power abuses another who is vulnerable and defenseless. The rhetorical shift at the end is effective only if David's anticipated response is one of outrage.

The sons of Jacob, however, are compelled to act based on the fact that Shechem had violated their sister, stressing the first set (v. 2).

What is lacking in Shechem's response is an acknowledgment of the fact that he raped Dinah. His response, framed within the language of intimacy, does not account for the crime of his sexual violence.[34] Later in negotiation, he agrees to whatever amount Jacob and his sons propose for the bride price (v. 12). Even here, however, this gesture seems to point more to his eagerness to marry Dinah than to recognition of wrongs committed.[35] Hence, Shechem's response ignores the fact that he violated Dinah by raping her. His desire to marry her addresses the fact that she is no longer a virgin, but in his initial response of love and in his subsequent marriage negotiations that follow, he does not acknowledge the sexual violence. The narrator, by shifting the focus abruptly from the rape to Shechem's feelings of love, accentuates the tension between Shechem's response and the injustice of his acts. This tension becomes more acute when his marriage proposal does not include some form of redress for the crimes committed against Dinah. Hence, the juxtaposition of these two sets of verbs serves to highlight the dissonance between Shechem's original act of violence from his feelings of affection that follow. It also signals the transition from the initial rape to the male reactions that result.

The narrator's strategy to focus the story on the responses of men also can be seen through Dinah's lack of response. As stated above, legal texts such as Deut 22:23–27 suggest that female responses to sexual violation were socially expected, except in cases where no such response could be heard (e.g., the open country, cf. Deut 22:25).[36] The woman's crying out is important in determining

---

[34] In Deut 22:28–29, a law that implies the use of force in sexual relations with a virgin who is not engaged, the perpetrator is required to marry the woman. In addition to paying the bride price, he is prohibited from divorcing her. The redress acknowledges both the fact that the woman's marriageable status has changed and the fact that she had been violated. In Gen 34, Shechem's response acknowledges the first while ignoring the second. However, recent scholars have argued that the Deuteronomic laws work more for the protection and rights of men. See Cheryl B. Anderson, *Women, Ideology, and Violence*, 40–41; and Pressler, "Sexual Violence," 102–12.

[35] Sternberg, *Poetics of Biblical Narrative*, 456–57.

[36] In Gen 34, the narrator does not make explicit the actual location of the rape. Dinah goes out to visit with the women of the land, but it is unclear as to whether the rape occurred in the city, in the open country, or elsewhere.

whether the woman consented to the act or not.[37] For example, in 2 Sam 13, another rape text, Tamar resists the advances of her half-brother Amnon saying, "No, my brother, do not rape me, for such a thing is not done in Israel. Do not do this disgraceful thing" (2 Sam 13:12). The narrative concludes with Tamar in mourning, weeping aloud. Hence, female responses to sexual violation are not unfamiliar in the Hebrew Bible or ancient Israel.

How does one explain the absence of Dinah's response in Gen 34? For now, it is important simply to note that Dinah's reaction to the rape is absent. Though Shechem has violated the daughter of Jacob, the narrator does not show by word or deed how Dinah responds. This is different from Jacob's reaction, which is characterized by silence. The narrator makes clear (v. 5) the fact that Jacob holds his peace (וְהֶחֱרִשׁ). The key is that Jacob's response, though a silent one, is narrated explicitly. By contrast, Dinah's reaction is completely absent. This focuses the reader's attention all the more on the male responses that follow. Thus, the remainder of Gen 34 will emphasize the appropriateness or inappropriateness of the reactions of men.

In summary, the rape of Dinah is narrated in a way that suggests there are social forces at work, which complicate the initial sexual violation and will make problematic the resulting male responses. The initial descriptions of Dinah and Shechem emphasized that the characters were from two different groups. The rape itself quickly moves to an emphasis on Shechem's response of love and desire to make Dinah his wife, setting the stage for the male negotiations that follow. The abrupt transition from rape to marriage, however, creates a tension in the reader's mind since Shechem's desire to marry Dinah minimizes the fact that he has raped her. The unresolved issue of punishment anticipates the response of Simeon and Levi, who retaliate with excessive force later in the story. Hence, the rape functions as the initial catalyst, which sets in motion certain social dynamics that propel this narrative toward its complicated end.

---

[37] See Pressler, "Sexual Violence," 102–12. Pressler correctly points out that the consent aspect of these laws only determines the woman's culpability in the sex act. The woman's status, married or unmarried, is what determines the nature of the crime as well as the degree of punishment.

Male Responses to Rape: Negotiations and Retributive Violence

The second element of the rape text progression is characterized by male responses that result in excessive violence. In this section, I show how the rape provokes different responses from the male characters, leading inevitably to the conflict at the end of the story. The initial responses are played out in the negotiations between Jacob and his sons on the one hand and Hamor and Shechem on the other. Jacob's 'response—one of silence—differs from his sons' reaction of indignation. This difference anticipates the familial tension at the end of the story. The sons of Jacob respond in negotiation with deceit, which sets up the excessively violent slaughtering of Shechem. Shechem and Hamor are initially characterized as shrewd in their dealings with Jacob and his sons. When the two men address their own people in vv. 21–23, however, they propose a different motivation for the pact of intermarriage. This causes the reader to suspect that Hamor and Shechem might have an ulterior motive. In spite of this narrative judgment on the Hivites, the brothers' retributive violence is narrated in a way that accentuates the excessive nature of their retaliation on the city of Shechem.

The Response of Jacob

Throughout most of the story, Jacob remains silent about the rape of his daughter. As I will show below, his passivity contrasts sharply to his sons' violence. Verse 34:5 opens with Jacob hearing the news that Shechem had defiled (טִמֵּא) his daughter. The verb "defile," from the root טמא, is found in the book of Genesis only in chapter 34, where it occurs three times. In the Hebrew Bible, טמא is most common within Priestly terminology but is also found in Dtr (2 Kgs 23, in reference to Josiah's reform). The verb refers to ritual impurity, and therefore, Shechem's rape of Dinah has resulted in her defilement.[38] Later uses of this verb by the narrator (v. 13 and v. 27) provide motivation and/or justification for the brothers' subsequent actions in the

---

[38] Scholz incorrectly translates this verb as "oppressed" (*Rape Plots*, 143). She argues that prophetic uses of טמא suggest that defilement can result not only from cultic or ritual impurity but also from ethical "unfaithfulness." While uses in Hosea (6:10) and Micah (2:10) point to the ethical consequences of this verb, the result is the same, i.e., defilement. טמא does not suggest that Shechem "oppressed" Dinah, but his rape of Dinah led to her ritual impurity. "He defiled" her.

story. For Jacob, however, his response to Shechem's defiling of his daughter is silence: הֶחֱרִשׁ, "he kept silent."[39] Scholars differ as to how to interpret Jacob's (non)response.

Sternberg, followed by Paul Noble, argues that Jacob's silence is condemnable, reflective of his indifference to the harm done to his daughter.[40] He stresses that the narrative focus in this passage is on Jacob. In v. 6, Hamor, the father of Shechem, goes out (וַיֵּצֵא) to *Jacob*, in order to speak to him. In v. 7, "the sons of *Jacob*" come in (בָּאוּ) from the field. Thus, the narrative action in both cases—Hamor's going out and the sons' coming in—has its destination in the patriarch. The sons are characterized as "the sons of *Jacob*," which further reinforces the idea of the father as the center of attention in these verses. Sternberg argues that the reader's focal point on the patriarch serves to heighten the sense of judgment for the reader when Jacob fails to act. He states, "In the absence of the expected response on his [Jacob's] part, the device for focusing thematic attention turns into a rhetorical weapon for focusing condemnation."[41]

The structure of v. 5, according to Sternberg, also produces judgment on Jacob in the reader's mind. The beginning of v. 5, "Jacob heard that he [Shechem] defiled his daughter," demands a response of some kind. The language of defilement, coupled with the narrator's emphasis that the object of this act was "his daughter," creates anticipation in the reader. How will Jacob respond? The addition of the clause, "but his sons were with his cattle in the field," only serves to raise the tension by delaying the expected outcome. Jacob's response of "keeping silent," according to Sternberg, "lets us down with a vengeance."[42] For him, the incongruity between the first half of the verse that demands a response and the last half, which narrates Jacob's silence, causes the reader to make a moral judgment on the father's inaction.

Sternberg's interpretation of Jacob's passivity is right in pointing out that the patriarch is the textual focal point. In the end, however, his argument is made from silence. The narrative center of these verses certainly is fixed on Jacob and his non-response. To what extent this produces judgment in the

---

[39] וְהֶחֱרִשׁ, *waw* plus a perfect form, is awkward. One would expect a *waw*-consecutive imperfect (hence, the proposal of *BHS*). Such a change, however, is not required as Joüon notes (§119z). Such use of the perfect, though unusual, is not without precedent.

[40] Sternberg, *Poetics of Biblical Narrative*, 448–51; Noble, "Rape of Dinah," 179–80.

[41] Sternberg, *Poetics of Biblical Narrative*, 451.

[42] Ibid., 449.

reader's mind, however, is unknown. Neither the narrator nor the narrative context gives an unambiguous motive for Jacob's silence.

Gunn and Fewell, arguing against Sternberg, suggest another interpretation of the patriarch's silence.[43] They propose that "Jacob held his peace." In other words, the father of Dinah is keeping still in order to ponder the best course of action. Gunn and Fewell argue that Sternberg's reading betrays his preference for "action-oriented heroics." For them, "Jacob's silence derives from caution rather than apathy."[44] Gunn and Fewell's reading finds support in the interpretation of Gen 33:18–20 argued above, in which Jacob has amicable negotiations with the sons of Hamor. For Jacob to silently ponder the best course of action in a potentially volatile situation would be a sign of good diplomacy, a disposition that is consistent within a context where one might want to continue to have peaceful interchanges with the people of the land.

Similar to Sternberg's interpretation, however, Gunn and Fewell's reading of Jacob's silence is unsubstantiated. Without an unambiguous judgment from the narrator or any recourse to the thoughts of Jacob, the reader is left to ponder the significance of the father's silent response until he makes clear his concerns at the end of the story. An additional problem with Gunn and Fewell's reading is that, in the end, Jacob does nothing. If he was keeping his peace in order to discern the right course of action, he never follows through with a decision. Hence, both interpretations of Jacob's silence, Gunn and Fewell's and Sternberg's, over-read Jacob's motivation in this scene.

The reader's final evaluation of Jacob does not reach expression until the end of the story (v. 30). Gunn/Fewell and Sternberg take sides with different characters in the story, making clear what the narrator to this point has left ambiguous. While the motivation of Jacob's reaction or non-reaction is unclear, the narrative function of his silence becomes apparent in light of his sons' reaction to the news. Jacob's response of silence becomes a point of contrast with his sons' anger. As I will show below, this contrast sets up the reader for the conflict at the end.

Before I turn to the response of Jacob's sons, it is also important to point out that Jacob's response, like Shechem's post-rape love and desire for marriage, does not address the crime committed against Dinah. Jacob's silence

---

[43] Fewell and Gunn, "Tipping the Balance," 197–98.
[44] Ibid., 198.

implies that he assents to the marriage negotiations. At the very least, he does not dispute the social exchange that is made between his sons and Shechem and Hamor. Thus, both the Shechemites' proposal for intermarriage and Jacob's lack of reaction do not adequately acknowledge the wrongs committed against the injured party. This inattentiveness to the violence provokes a response from the reader, who expects that something should be done to address Dinah's situation.

I disagree with Sternberg, who argues that Jacob's silence betrays his lack of resolve with regard to Dinah. The silence is ambiguous and serves a narrative purpose of delaying the concluding familial conflict until the end of the story. The ambiguous silence keeps the reader's attention focused on the complicated negotiations between the sons of Israel and the Hivites and the inevitable clash between the two parties. Simultaneously, Jacob's passivity, when seen in contrast to his sons' anger and deception, anticipates the contention between father and sons at the end of the story.

The fact that Jacob's silence does not address his daughter's rape causes the reader to anticipate some kind of response. The unresolved issues of recompense create a tension in the reader that seeks resolution. Jacob's non-response adds to this unresolved element of the plot. Jacob's sons will eventually carry out retribution upon Shechem and his city—a response that they say is a direct result of Shechem's actions against Dinah (v. 31). The riposte, however, will be carried out in an excessively violent fashion.

The Response of Shechem and Hamor

Before I address the response of Jacob's sons—a reaction that sits in direct contrast to the inaction of Jacob—I will first examine the intervening responses of Hamor and Shechem. The two negotiate an intermarriage proposal with the sons of Jacob. The Hivite leaders show themselves to be shrewd negotiators both with the sons of Jacob and with their own people. They comply readily with the brothers' demand of circumcision, an act that the reader will realize later makes them vulnerable to attack. This sets the stage for the violent retaliation that follows.

In vv. 8–12, Hamor and Shechem make a proposal of intermarriage between the two groups. In v. 8, Hamor expresses his son's desire for Dinah and appeals to Jacob and his sons to let Shechem marry her. The father's description of his son's feelings is the language of bonding, חָשְׁקָה נַפְשׁוֹ בְּבִתְּכֶם

(literally, "his soul is attached to your daughter"), harking back to the threefold description of Shechem's affection in v. 3. Thus, Hamor appeals to Jacob and the brothers on behalf of his son's strong feelings for Dinah. The term, בְּתְכֶם, "your daughter" in the plural, suggests that Hamor's appeal is to both Jacob and his sons. The filial term, "daughter," is a clear reference to Jacob, while the second person plural possessive suffix points to Hamor's address to all the men.[45]

On the surface, Hamor's offer is marked by its mutuality and generosity. He lays out the benefits of the proposed arrangement in vv. 9–10 by offering his people's daughters for marriage and by extending the right for Jacob and his sons to settle and trade in the land. The reciprocity in the imperative, וְהִתְחַתְּנוּ, "make a marriage alliance," is made explicit in Hamor's words that follow. He says, "give to us your daughters and take our daughters for yourselves." He is also clear in his intention to allow free exchange between the people of his land and Jacob and his sons: "With us you will dwell (תֵּשֵׁבוּ), and the land will be before you; dwell and *trade in it* (סְחָרוּהָ), and *take possessions in it* (הֵאָחֲזוּ)."[46] As the last two verbs suggest, the invitation extends beyond settling in the region. Hamor encourages Jacob and his sons to do business in the land, indeed, to take property within it. The last imperative, הֵאָחֲזוּ, "take hold, take possession," is ironic and foreshadows the brothers' pillaging of the city at the end of the chapter. Hamor invites them to take property in the land not knowing that in the end, the men with whom he is negotiating will take the city's possessions as spoil. On the surface, Hamor's offer is a generous one, encouraging a mutually beneficial arrangement that will allow peaceful exchange between his people and the family of Jacob.

---

[45] Scholars have long recognized the different layers of tradition, source or otherwise, in this passage. Westermann suggests that two stories have been interwoven to create a third story (see Westermann, *Genesis 12–36*, 535–45). The seams between the two stories can be seen by the awkward expression, "our daughter," which occurs in the mouths of Jacob's sons in v. 17. Within the present narrative context, the use of the term represents the sons' usurping of Jacob's authority in negotiation. Such a move by Jacob's sons makes sense within the context of familial strife, a theme that finds more profound expression at the end of the story.

[46] The root, סחר, has the sense of travelling around as a merchant or as someone who goes around while doing their business. Hence, I am following the NRSV's translation of the verb, "to trade in." The 3fs pronominal suffix refers to the land.

In addition, Shechem adds to the offer in vv. 11–12 by allowing Jacob and his sons to set the terms of the deal. He begins by imploring their favor. The expression, אֶמְצָא־חֵן בְּעֵינֵיכֶם, "let me find favor in your eyes," is revealing given the fact that Shechem's initial act of violence began when "he saw"(וַיַּרְא) Dinah. His gaze upon Dinah was what precipitated his violent seizing of her. Now that he is negotiating to take Dinah as a wife, he appeals to the perception of Jacob and his sons, that he might find favor in their eyes (בְּעֵינֵיכֶם). Shechem is using the language of negotiation to address the issue at hand. By appealing to the favor (חֵן) of the men, Shechem submits himself to their judgment.

This does not mean that he considers himself to be a subordinate to Jacob and his sons, though his violation of Dinah has most certainly put him in their social debt. The purpose of this subordination is to entreat the men that they might find his offer satisfying. He proceeds by offering to let Jacob and the brothers set the bride price—מֹהַר ("bride price") and מַתָּן ("gift")—as high as they deem necessary (v. 12). Shechem's willingness to comply is emphasized by the similar phrases in his speech: "whatever you say to me I will give" (אֲשֶׁר תֹּאמְרוּ אֵלַי אֶתֵּן, v. 11) and "I will give just as you say to me" (אֶתְּנָה כַּאֲשֶׁר תֹּאמְרוּ אֵלָי, v. 12). He is willing to "give" whatever they ask, just as long as Jacob and the brothers "give" (תְּנוּ) Dinah to him as a wife. The use of נתן within the context of negotiation represents Shechem's willingness to bargain. Shechem, like his father Hamor, responds to the original rape by making an offer that would assume mutual exchange between the two groups. The presupposition of peaceful negotiations is consistent with Jacob's initial interaction with the sons of Hamor in 33:18–20.

On the surface, Hamor and Shechem's offer appears to be reciprocal and generous. Within the context of negotiation, however, such language is expected and does not always state directly the intention of those who are bargaining.[47] This disjunction in language is rendered ambiguous later when

---

[47] A good example of this type of negotiation is found in Gen 23. The story details Abraham's purchase of a cave for Sarah's burial. In the negotiations, honorific language is used to address Abraham (אֲדֹנִי and נְשִׂיא). Abraham offers initially to pay full price for the field. Ephron the Hittite counters by publicly offering to give Abraham the field. After Abraham emphatically states that he will pay the full price, Ephron indirectly sets the price of the field at 400 shekels of silver, saying, "between me and you, what is that?" (23:15). Such practices suggest that indirect language and generous offers have a certain rhetorical function within negotiation. They are examples of shrewd bargaining between different social groups.

Hamor and Shechem persuade the people of the city to accept the offer of Jacob and his sons by using a different motivation—the acquisition of the Israelite family's livestock and property (34:23). Within the context of the offer to Jacob and his sons, the speech of Hamor and Shechem can be seen as shrewd negotiating practices.

The original intention of the offer, as stated by Shechem in v. 4, was for Hamor to negotiate for the marriage of Dinah. Hamor offers instead the more generous proposal of intermarriage, which includes the Israelites settling in the land and taking property. Similarly, Shechem, following the lead of his father, suggests that Jacob and his sons set the bride price as high as they want. The end result of their transactions is that the brothers accept the proposal of intermarriage on the condition that every male in the city be circumcised. The only requirement that is imposed on the Hivites is circumcision. The shrewdness of Hamor and Shechem's negotiating practices becomes clearer when they proceed to address the men of their city in the following scene.[48]

Unaware of the deceit that shapes the response of Jacob's sons, Hamor and Shechem agree to the condition of the counterproposal in vv. 18 ff. Their willing acceptance of the terms accentuates the difference between the Hivites and the sons of Jacob, whose words are tainted with deceit (v. 13). Not only do the two men agree to the terms, but the words of the brothers' "were good... in the eyes of Hamor and the eyes of Shechem" (v. 18). By mentioning that the offer was good in their "eyes," the narrator highlights the perception of the two men. The offer looks good based on the face value of the brothers' words. Having already had peaceful negotiations with Jacob, Hamor and Shechem have no reason to distrust the terms of the contract. As far as they are able to see,

---

[48] I am arguing differently than Sternberg, who contends that these negotiations reveal the Hivites' "brazen disregard of antecedents" (456), that is, that Hamor neglects to acknowledge the wrong that has been done against Dinah. While Sternberg is correct in pointing out that the rape is not mentioned in the negotiation, his negative characterization of the Hivites is overstated and fails to see the larger shape of the story's development. Hamor's speech is appropriate given that it takes place within the context of marriage and intermarriage negotiations between two groups (see Sternberg, *The Poetics of Biblical Narrative*, 456–57). His interpretation becomes more problematic given the narrator's clear characterization of the sons of Jacob as deceitful in the following scene, creating a contrast with the fact that Hamor and Shechem readily comply with the terms of the agreement by circumcising every male in the city.

negotiations have gone well, with all parties leaving the bargaining table satisfied.

The narrator further accentuates Shechem's eagerness to comply by adding that "the young man did not delay to do the thing, because he delighted in the daughter of Jacob" (v. 19). The two verbal expressions in v. 19, לֹא־אֵחַר ("he did not delay") and חָפֵץ ("he delighted in"), point to his enthusiasm and motivation. He is so moved by his affection for Dinah that he wastes no time in carrying out the demands of Jacob's sons. The narrator, by highlighting Shechem's willing attitude, increases the incongruous distance between Shechem and the brothers. While Shechem eagerly seeks to fulfill his end of the bargain, the sons of Jacob have acted deceitfully (v. 13).

The narrator makes this more explicit by mentioning that Shechem was the most honored (נִכְבָּד) person in his father's house. The use of the root כבד, here in the Niphal stem, points to the fact that Shechem is an honorable man among his people. He confirms this characterization by agreeing to the terms of the contract, eagerly carrying out the demands of Jacob's sons. Though his initial act of rape put Shechem in a questionable light for the reader—one that is not easily disregarded, and one that the brothers will not forget—the narrator has complicated the characterization of Shechem through his eagerness to comply with the terms of the offer.

In vv. 20–23, the full extent of Hamor and Shechem's shrewd negotiating practices are made clear. The two men address the people at the gate of the city (v. 20). They say, "These men, they are peaceful (שְׁלֵמִים) with us." The use of the adjective שָׁלֵם harks back to 33:18, where Jacob arrives "peacefully" (שָׁלֵם) into the region of Shechem.[49] Thus, the successful transactions in 33:18–20 provide the background for Shechem and Hamor's optimism that these men are peaceable.

The two men proceed by conveying the terms of the agreement to the people of the city. Their speech reveals a motivation that differs from their earlier interactions with the sons of Jacob. Rather than a straightforward repetition of what was said in the negotiations with Jacob's family, the men emphasize some details, leaving out others. The difference between the original offer (vv. 9–10) and what the two men convey to the inhabitants of the city (vv.

---

[49] See discussion above on whether or not שָׁלֵם is best translated adverbially, "peacefully," or as a place name, "Salem."

21–23) is revealing. In the initial dealings of vv. 9–10, Hamor makes explicit what he is offering Jacob and his sons. The two peoples will intermarry, taking and giving daughters to each other (v. 9). He adds that Jacob and his family will "dwell" (יָשַׁב) in the land, "trade" (סָחַר) and "take possessions" (Niphal of אָחַז) in it (v. 10). In their speech at the gate, however, Hamor and Shechem tell the people only to let Jacob and his family "dwell" (יֵשְׁבוּ) in the land and "trade" (יִסְחָרוּ) in it. The aspect of taking possessions, represented by the Niphal stem of אָחַז in v. 10, is left out.

While the root סָחַר certainly implies business interactions between the two groups, the omission of אָחַז is significant and points to a change in emphasis. The idea of taking property within the land would have been appealing to Jacob and his sons. To the inhabitants of the land, however, it would pose a threat. Thus, Hamor and Shechem have adjusted their rhetoric to suit the context.[50] Moreover, after conveying the idea of intermarriage (v. 21) and the condition of circumcision (v. 22), Hamor and Shechem provide the inhabitants of their city with further motivation. In v. 23, they say, "Their livestock, their property and all of their animals, will they not be ours?" Commenting about this phrase, Sternberg states:

> In flagrant breach of the spirit of the agreement, this promises the Hivites (if they only ensure "accession" by "accession") such control over their future allies as extends to their very goods. And this pledge, formally given in assembly, may well reflect the hidden intentions of the speakers all along.[51]

Sternberg's comments point to the possibility that Shechem and Hamor's negotiation strategy with Jacob and his sons may have been driven by an ulterior motive—to take control of them and all of their possessions through intermarriage. Another possible interpretation is that the two men are intentionally framing the offer in a way that would be more appealing to the inhabitants of the city. It is conceivable that both could be at work in this story.

Regardless, the emphasis on acquiring the property of Jacob's family makes the omission of אָחַז all the more illuminating. By motivating both sides through

---

[50] While Sternberg misses the omission of אָחַז, he points out that the expression, "The land, behold, is large enough for them," is added in the second speech to assure the hearers that "there is little danger of overcrowding or competition" (*Poetics of Biblical Narrative*, 465).

[51] Ibid., 466.

the acquisition of property, Hamor and Shechem engage in shrewd negotiation within the context of two different groups. What they do not realize, however, is that the indirect speech, common within the context of negotiation, has also masked a hidden agenda of Jacob's sons. This element was alluded to in the narrator's characterization of the brothers' speech as deceitful (v. 13) and comes to fruition in the concluding scene. Though Hamor and Shechem assumed that they have made a shrewd deal, it will be the brothers of Dinah who have the final word.

The Response of Jacob's Sons

The sons of Jacob react differently from their father to Shechem's defiling of Dinah. In fact, their response creates a point of contrast in the story to the silent reaction of Jacob. The brothers' reaction, which culminates in an excessively violent retaliation, also moves the progression of this rape text toward the resulting social fragmentation at the end of the story.

The sons' initial response is one of outrage. In v. 7, the sons return from the field. Upon hearing the news, they respond with indignation (וַיִּתְעַצְּבוּ) and anger (וַיִּחַר). Following the sons' reaction, the narrator's words make clear the reason for such a response, "for he [Shechem] had committed a disgraceful act in Israel by lying with the daughter of Jacob, for such a thing should not be done." As stated above, the sons' outrage stands in contrast to Jacob's silence. The narrator's comment, describing Shechem's violation as a "disgraceful act" (נְבָלָה), provides a justification for the sons' reaction. The difference between the sons' response and Jacob's is significant. As the story progresses, the characters' differing responses to the initial rape will correspond to different courses of action with Hamor, Shechem, and the inhabitants of the land. As stated above, the contrasting dispositions of Jacob and his sons also foreground the conflict with which the story ends.

The sons' indignant response is the first male reaction that addresses the fact that Shechem had done something wrong to Dinah. As suggested earlier, the pattern of their responses suggest that they see Shechem's actions as a violation of their group and social norms. The narrator makes this clear by providing the reason for their angry response—Shechem had committed נְבָלָה in Israel by lying with the daughter of Jacob (v. 7). The nature and extent of the נְבָלָה becomes clearer as the negotiations unfold. Later, when the sons are negotiating with Shechem and Hamor over the issue of intermarriage, they suggest that they cannot allow Dinah to marry Shechem because he is uncircumcised (v. 14). Shechem has sexually violated their sister, and his foreskin represents a social boundary that impedes proper marriage negotiations between the two groups.

In other words, the only way that an outsider can marry their sister is if the outsider becomes an insider. Anything less for the sons of Jacob would be a disgrace (חֶרְפָּה) to them.[52] By the very fact that he is an outsider to Israel, he has violated their sister by cohabiting with her. This understanding of the brothers' rationale also helps to explain their rejoinder to Jacob at the end of the story, "Should he make our sister like a prostitute?" (v. 31). By signifying the sexual relations and potential marriage between Dinah and Shechem as "prostitution," the brothers reveal their understanding of the situation. Shechem's having sex with Dinah is socially inappropriate and equivalent to prostitution in their eyes not because of the rape itself, but because the sex/marriage is with an outsider.[53] This perception stands in contrast to Jacob's ideas of how to deal with these outsiders. As the introduction to this story suggested in 33:18–20, Jacob assumed the possibility of peaceful interaction with the people of the land. His angry response in v. 30 also suggests that he is very concerned about his reputation among the peoples of the land. Dinah's going out to visit the daughters of the land is also consistent with such a stance *vis à vis* the Hivites. These elements of the narrative suggest a particular understanding of the Israelite family with the inhabitants of Canaan, one that includes social interaction and commerce with outsiders. Such an understanding of social boundaries stands in stark contrast to the brothers' opinion. The

---

[52] It must be noted that the narrator states that the brothers responded with deceit (בְּמִרְמָה). This does not suggest that they are expressing something false about their perception of the violation. It does mean, however, that their words and intentions within negotiation cannot be trusted. Their counterproposal to Hamor and Shechem masks a hidden plot, which becomes evident only with the brothers' sacking of the city. Their perception that the Hivites are outsiders, and that marriage with such people would be disgraceful, is reinforced with Simeon and Levi's final words, "Should he make our sister like a prostitute?" Bechtel sums up this statement well by stating that the brothers understand that Dinah has become like a harlot by "pointing to the fact that she has become a marginal figure by engaging in sexual activity outside her society…For them the relationship threatens the cohesion of the tribal structure" (Bechtel, "What If Dinah Is Not Raped?" 31). Bechtel understands correctly the social significance of the brothers' language, even if she assumes incorrectly that Dinah is not raped.

[53] Bechtel, "What If Dinah Is Not Raped?" 31.

narrator, through the response of the sons in negotiation, has made the difference in perspectives between father and sons more profound, though nothing explicit is exchanged verbally between them until the end of the story.

Another aspect of the brothers' response, which is crucial to the development of the plot, is highlighted by the narrator through the characterization of their speech as deceitful. The narrator's evaluation is clear. The brothers answer בְּמִרְמָה, "with deceit" (v. 13).[54] As stated above, the motivation for the sons to respond in this manner is clarified in the last clause of v. 13, אֲשֶׁר טִמֵּא אֵת דִּינָה אֲחֹתָם, "because he [Shechem] had defiled Dinah their sister." In the brothers' minds, the initial violation justifies their deception. Hence, the narrator has shaped the perception of the reader concerning the response of Jacob's sons. They are acting deceitfully and their words and actions that follow cannot be taken at face value. Even if their counterproposal points to a real concern for the sons of Israel, i.e., their relationship to the uncircumcised outsiders (vv. 14–17), their deception suggest that the brothers cannot be trusted in negotiation. The reader will be suspicious of the counteroffer even when the brothers appear to be motivated by Shechem's defilement of their sister. This suspicion will be confirmed when the retaliation takes shape in vv. 25–29. The counterproposal of circumcision ends up disabling the males within the city, leaving it vulnerable to attack. In this way, the deceptive negotiations play a critical role in the brothers' plot of revenge.

Hence, within the plot of the story, the brothers' deception enables the movement from negotiation to retributive violence. As I will show below, the brothers' deception also contributes to the reader's sense that the retaliation is excessive. The deceitful way with which the sons of Jacob negotiate serves as a foil to their father's initial dealings with the Hivites (33:18–19). It also is contrasted with the socially acceptable dealings of Hamor and Shechem in the post-rape negotiations. This contrast serves to accentuate the deceptive nature

---

[54] Fewell and Gunn are correct in pointing out, contrary to Sternberg, that "'[d]eceit' frames the whole of the brothers' speech, so that the reader is unable to posit sincerity in any of it, whether in the specific proposal or in its ostensible socioreligious motivation. Indeed, in due course the specific proposal will turn out to be made in bad faith, and the religious custom of circumcision will have been desecrated in the process" ("Tipping the Balance," 202). Sternberg goes to great lengths to specify the rhetorical function of the brothers' deceit so that he can argue a distinction between the brothers' words and their "credo" (*Poetics of Biblical Narrative*, 458).

of the violent retribution on Shechem and the inhabitants of the city, making the plot for revenge all the more devious.

The last element of the brothers' response that I will discuss in this section is their excessively violent retribution perpetrated on Shechem and the inhabitants of his city. The brothers' deceitful words in vv. 13–16 mask a plot that comes to fruition in vv. 25–29. The narrator juxtaposes this violent scene with the Hivites' response to the negotiations in the preceding verses. Shechem, Hamor, and the inhabitants of the land unanimously agree to accept the stipulations of the agreement with the sons of Jacob, i.e., circumcision. In fact, Shechem is eager to fulfill his end of the bargain. Even though Hamor and Shechem's compliance is tainted by the possibility of an ulterior motive (v. 23)—the acquisition of property through intermarriage with Jacob's family—they have agreed to the conditions of the arrangement and fulfill their obligation in the deal by becoming circumcised.

In contrast, the sons of Jacob respond with an unexpected retaliation upon Shechem and his city. The narrator's description highlights the underhanded nature of the attack. Verse 34:25 depicts the scene: "On the third day, when they were in pain (כֹּאֲבִים), two of the sons of Jacob, Simeon and Levi, Dinah's brothers, each took his sword." By noting that the men of the city were still in pain (כֹּאֲבִים) from their circumcision, the narrator emphasizes the vulnerability of the Hivites. Coupled with the fact that circumcision was the primary point of negotiation for Jacob's sons—a deal that was made deceitfully—the nature of the attack is all the more devious. Not only have Simeon and Levi come upon the inhabitants of the city at their most defenseless and humiliated point, but they have presumably planned this from the beginning. They have waited until all the men were rendered useless for battle before putting them to the sword. The phrase, "they came upon the city securely (בֶּטַח)," is a pregnant expression describing the state of the town prior to the attack.[55] The word, from the root בטח, connotes trust. Thus, the narrator presents the Hivites as vulnerable and resting securely prior to the violent attack. The retributive act of the brothers catches the men of the city by surprise and in no state to defend themselves.

---

[55] Cf. Ezek 30:9, where בֶּטַח is used within the context of the LORD's judgment upon Egypt to describe the unsuspecting Cush. In both of these contexts, destruction comes unexpectedly, and hence, the peoples or city are caught unawares.

The detail that Simeon and Levi instigate the retaliation points to a relational dynamic at play within the violent act. As stated above, Dinah is characterized in v. 1 as the "daughter of Leah." Thus, her blood brothers are the ones who initiate the retribution against Shechem. The narrator emphasizes this in v. 25 by the additional identification of Simeon and Levi as "the brothers of Dinah" (אֲחֵי דִינָה). Previously, the sons of Jacob took negotiations into their own hands, bypassing their speechless father. Here, they act as judge and executioner as they violently make Shechem pay for his deed against their sister.

Though blood ties are clearly a factor that motivates Simeon and Levi to act, the narrator also is clear that their deeds represent the larger family. They are characterized as "two sons of Jacob" (שְׁנֵי־בְנֵי־יַעֲקֹב). Biological ties to Dinah and Leah are key in understanding the motivation of Simeon and Levi's retaliation. The violence of their actions, however, will also have lasting effects on the entire house of Jacob, as Jacob is quick to point out at the end of the story (v. 30).

Simeon and Levi are compelled to act not only because of family blood connections but also out of their desire for family purity. The last expression in v. 25, וַיַּהַרְגוּ כָּל־זָכָר, "they killed every male," harks back to earlier uses of כָּל־זָכָר. In v. 15, the sons of Jacob demand that "every male" be circumcised. The Hivites comply by circumcising "every male" in v. 24. Here, however, כָּל־זָכָר represents all of the newly circumcised males whom Simeon and Levi remove from the land by the sword. Thus, the inhabitants of the city are cut off from the possibility of becoming one people (עַם־אֶחָד) with the family of Jacob. The sword of the two brothers makes a clear divide between insider and outsider, family and foreigner.

The story comes full circle in v. 26, when Simeon and Levi take (וַיִּקְחוּ) Dinah out of Shechem's house and proceed to go out (וַיֵּצֵאוּ) with her. These two verbs (from the roots לקח and יצא) create an inclusio around Dinah's experience in the story.[56] In the beginning of the narrative, Dinah *goes out* (וַתֵּצֵא) to see the women of the land. Shechem *takes* (וַיִּקַּח) her by force and rapes her (v. 1). At the end, her brothers *take* (וַיִּקְחוּ) her out of Shechem's house, before they *go out* (וַיֵּצֵאוּ) of the city together. In both cases, Dinah is the object of male

---

[56] See Sternberg, *Poetics of Biblical Narrative*, 469–70; and Paul Kevers, "Étude littéraire de Genèse 34," *RB* 87 (1980): 38–86.

seizures, represented by the root לקח. The chiastic structure (ABB'A') focuses on the ways in which Dinah is *taken*.

Ironically, though her brothers' intentions are to bring her back into the family sphere, their actions are described in language that parallels Shechem's violation. The destination of her journey—where she *goes out*—is determined in each example by the decisions and actions of men. Dinah remains silent through these male seizures. She is the only character who does not respond to Shechem's violent deed. A story that started with Dinah *going out*—the only self-initiated action by the daughter of Jacob—results in rape, turns into negotiations of men, degenerates into violence, and in the end leaves the family in conflict (vv. 30–31).

The violent nature of the brothers' attack is made more excessive in vv. 27–29 as the sons of Jacob proceed to plunder (וַיָּבֹזּוּ) the city. The narrator adds that the motivating factor for these actions is Dinah's defilement, once again from the root, טמא.[57] Even with this motivation, however, the pillaging of the city is excessive:

> They took their flocks, their herds, their donkeys, and whatever was in the city or the field. They took captive and carried off as spoil all their wealth, all their little ones, their wives, and all that was in the houses (vv. 28–29).

The grammar of v. 28 and v. 29 highlights the disproportionate nature of the brothers' riposte. Both sentences begin with a series of direct objects, emphasizing the extent of the spoil that is taken from the city. The excessive amount of property (and people) that the brothers steal brings an ironic fulfillment to Hamor's words in v. 10, where he invited the brothers and Jacob to "take possessions" (הֵאָחֲזוּ) in the land—words that were curiously missing from the speech at the gate. What Shechem and Hamor left out when addressing their people, the brothers have seized through their pillaging. Once

---

[57] As early as Wellhausen, scholars have noticed the doublet in this text describing two violent acts committed by the sons of Jacob. The verb, טִמְּאוּ, "they defiled," is awkward since all previous references (v. 5 and v. 13) are singular and refer to Shechem as the perpetrator. The plural use of טמא represents an editor's attempt to harmonize the doublet represented in vv. 25–26 and vv. 27–29. The motivation of their sister's defilement helps to connect the plundering with the retributive slaying in vv. 25–26. The use of the plural points to the fact that every male (כָּל־זָכָר, v. 25) is held accountable for Dinah's defilement. For a good discussion, see Westermann, *Genesis 12–36*, 532–45.

again, the sons of Jacob have taken matters into their own hands. Jacob's earlier silence and Hamor and Shechem's proposal of intermarriage did not adequately address the rape of Dinah, creating a sense of anticipation in the reader. While the retaliation on Shechem is motivated by what happened to Dinah (v. 31), the brothers' response is excessive in its premeditated violence and, in the end, is an unsatisfactory solution to the situation at hand. Dinah is led out from the house of Shechem, but she remains desolate and defiled.[58] The punishment certainly does not fit the crime; indeed it inadequately addresses the rape. The sons of Jacob have taken vengeance into their own hands and have done so in extreme fashion.[59] This excessively violent retaliation on the Shechemites becomes a point of contention between Jacob and his sons, a point to which I now turn.

Social Fragmentation: Severed Ties and Family Dissension

The third element in the rape text progression, social fragmentation, takes shape in two ways within this narrative. The first can be seen within the context of the relationships between Jacob's family and the inhabitants of Canaan, specifically the Hivites. The second aspect of social fragmentation is found within the Israelite family itself in the contention between Jacob and his sons, specifically Simeon and Levi. The brothers' excessively violent retaliation cuts off a group who sought to negotiate a pact of intermarriage with them. Simultaneously, the brothers' actions anger the once silent Jacob, who rebukes his sons for their reckless behavior.

---

[58] By "defiled," here I mean that she is no longer marriageable. Shechem's rape not only violates her through the violence of the act, but also by the fact that it changes her status. Dinah is no longer marriageable. Hence, Shechem's actions, even without the rape, constitute her defilement since the sexual relations occur in a socially inappropriate context among outsiders (c.f., Gen 34:14). Most uses of טמא occur in Priestly material, assuming a cultic context. There are cases, particularly in the book of Ezekiel, where טמא is applied specifically to a woman's defilement (Ezek 18:6, 11, 15; 23:17; 33:26; see Westermann, *Genesis 12–36*, 534). In each of these cases, the woman's defilement assumes socially unacceptable sexual relations. Ezek 23:17 is an especially pertinent parallel since it occurs in a context that uses language of prostitution for Oholibah, a symbolic representation of Jerusalem. This configuration is strikingly similar to the narrator's use of the language of defilement in Gen 34 and the brothers' final words that suggest that Shechem's actions were equated with treating their sister like a prostitute (v. 31). Bechtel makes a similar argument in relation to the culture of honor and shame ("What If Dinah Is Not Raped?" 32–34).

[59] Rashkow, "The Rape(s) of Dinah," 57.

The excessive premeditated violence of Jacob's sons has consequences for their social interaction with other groups. As was argued earlier, the narrator emphasized the fact that the rape of Dinah brought together two distinct social entities—the family of Jacob and the Hivites. It is clear that both groups intended different outcomes from the negotiations—the sons of Jacob deceived Hamor and Shechem with the intention of killing them, and Hamor and Shechem sought to benefit their people from the intermarriage of the two groups (v. 23). Regardless, the agreement held the possibility of future interactions and social exchanges. The brothers' violent actions destroy the ties between the two groups through violent retribution and represent a severe breach of contract.

Jacob's silent observance of these negotiations suggests that he consented to the proceedings. Such a position would be consistent with his earlier interactions with the Hivites in Chapter 33. The excessively violent retribution on the Shechemites, initiated by Simeon and Levi, decimates and humiliates the people with whom the family of Israel had made a pact. Such an action could have serious consequences for Jacob and his family in future interactions with the inhabitants of Canaan—a point that Jacob is quick to point out. In v. 30, Jacob states, "You have stirred up trouble (עֲכַרְתֶּם) for me by making me odious (לְהַבְאִישֵׁנִי) to the inhabitants of the land." The first verb, from the root עכר, "to stir up, to trouble," has the connotation of making something taboo.[60] This is coupled with the Hiphil infinitive construct from the root באש, "to stink." Thus, Jacob accuses his sons of making his name a stench in the land. His reputation has become an unbearable smell among the Canaanites and Perizzites.

The consequence of such a situation is that he and his family are now vulnerable to attack, the results of which could mean destruction for his entire family: נִשְׁמַדְתִּי אֲנִי וּבֵיתִי, "I shall be destroyed, I and my house." As the story progresses, Jacob's specific fear—that the people of the land will attack him— turns out to be unfounded. In 35:5, the narrator states that the "terror of God" fell upon the cities. This comment from the narrator suggests that God was protecting Jacob and his family.

---

[60] See Westermann, *Genesis 12–36*, 533–34, who cites Josh 6:18; 7:25; Judg 11:35; 1 Sam 14:29; and 1 Kings 18:17ff. as examples.

The need for protection, however, confirms that the sons' reckless behavior had consequences on their interactions with other peoples of the land. What began as peaceful navigation and negotiations in the land (33:18–19) now has become a journey that requires the "terror of God" for protection. The brothers' retaliation against Shechem resulted in a reinforced social distance between insiders and outsiders, between the family of Israel and the inhabitants of Canaan. The result of Simeon and Levi's violent breach of contract is a more pronounced separation between the family group and foreigners—one that must be enforced with fear and terror.

The second form of social fragmentation occurs within the family of Jacob in the conflict between the father and his sons. Similar to the fragmentation described above, this social fracturing is a direct consequence of the sons' violent retribution on the inhabitants of Shechem. Jacob, who had been silent to this point in the story, speaks out angrily against Simeon and Levi. As stated above, Jacob rebukes his sons for their reckless behavior. Their actions have given the family a bad name (לְהַבְאִישֵׁנִי) and have opened up the potential for further violence from the inhabitants of the land. The reasons for Jacob's reprimand are obvious given the turn of events. The brothers had made a pact with Shechem and Hamor that involved intermarriage. By deceiving the Hivites, Jacob's group has proven that they cannot be trusted in social exchanges. Such a reputation would make future interactions with the people in the land problematic. In addition, the sons' retribution could provoke further hostilities from the peoples of the land. Because of their small numbers, any concerted attack from other Canaanite peoples would result in the destruction for the family of Jacob. While his intentions and care for Dinah are not explicit throughout the story, Jacob's disappointment toward Simeon and Levi is clear. Jacob will not forget what these two sons have done to his reputation, not even at the end of his life. At the conclusion of the book of Genesis, the blessings of Jacob make clear that Simeon and Levi will be remembered as reckless and violent men (Gen 49:1–27).[61]

---

[61] Gen 49, "the blessing of Jacob," is more a tribal list than a blessing in the proper sense. Many scholars assume it is an early poetic text. The present narrative context, however, frames the poem as a deathbed blessing by the patriarch. For discussion on the date and language of Gen 49, see David Noel Freedman, "'Who is Like Thee Among the Gods?' The Religion of Early Israel," in *Ancient Israelite Religion: Essays in Honor of Frank Moore Cross* (ed. Patrick D. Miller, Paul D. Hanson, and S. Dean McBride; Philadelphia: Fortress, 1987), 315–35; and David Noel

The two brothers respond to their father's criticism in v. 31 by justifying their sister's need for retribution—the need to restore her reputation. They say, "Should he make our sister like a prostitute?" Thus, they defend their behavior by appealing to the wrong that Shechem committed against Dinah and the social stigma that resulted from the rape. The reader, while sympathetic to the notion that Dinah deserves justice, is skeptical of the brothers' rationalization due to the excessive violence and plundering in vv. 25–29. To what extent have their actions made right the wrong that was done to Dinah? The narrator's characterization of the violence as premeditated and excessive suggests that the punishment that the brothers' have brought upon the Hivites is disproportionate to the crime. In addition, the detailed description of the spoil adds to the inappropriateness of the retaliation. At the end of this story, the justice that the rape of Dinah demanded has degenerated into her brothers' deceitfully planned massacre and plundering of the city of Shechem.

The rhetorical question "Should he make our sister like a prostitute?" at the end of this story functions in two ways. First, the question itself, with its expressed concern for Dinah, causes the reader to ponder how this story addresses or does not address the wrong done to her. The rape of Dinah deteriorates into the negotiations and wars of men. Second, the question points to a divide in the family of Jacob—a rift between Jacob and his sons. The initial rape has created divergent responses from the men in Jacob's family. These differences have caused divisiveness between the brothers and their father, marking a fracture in the family unit. While familial conflict is nothing new to the stories in Genesis, this theme finds particular expression within Gen 34. Within this narrative context, the dissension between Jacob and his sons is seen as a social/familial fragmentation that results from the initial rape and excessively violent male responses to that rape.

Conclusion

The rape of Dinah in Gen 34 shares a family resemblance to the other rape narratives. The story follows a progression of rape to excessive male violence to social fragmentation. Each of these elements is crucial to the plot of the story. In addition, the three characteristic traits of this rape narrative flow and

---

Freedman and Frank Moore Cross, *Studies in Ancient Yahwistic Poetry* (2nd ed.; Grand Rapids: Eerdmans, 1997), 46–63.

interrelate in a particular way. As I have shown, the rape of Dinah embodies the rape progression within a specific context, namely, the negotiation of Jacob and his family among the Hivites, a specific group of peoples in the land of Canaan. Throughout the story, the narrator uses language that highlights the issues involved in navigating the space between two different groups. The rape of Dinah complicates these interactions, especially when Shechem desires to have Dinah as a wife. The negotiation of intermarriage between these groups is made problematic by the deceit of Jacob's sons, which is motivated by their understanding of how to relate to the uncircumcised Hivites. The deception of the brothers also is set in contrast with Jacob's silence on the one hand and with the Shechemites eagerness to fulfill their obligations (circumcision) on the other. The excessively violent retaliation that follows results in two kinds of social fragmentation, one that is external to Jacob's family and one that is internal. Israel's relationship to other peoples in the land has become more problematic with the possibility of further of violence (v. 30); and the story ends in familial conflict between Jacob and Simeon and Levi.

Why does this text move from an initial rape to excessive male violence? I have argued, following Bechtel and others, that the brothers retaliate against Shechem because they perceive that their group's boundaries and norms have been violated through the rape of their sister Dinah. Hence, their deceptive plot of revenge is motivated by a particular view of how to maintain their family's integrity.[62] The brothers' actions, however, complicate further encounters with other peoples of the land, a point that Jacob makes at the end of the story (34:30). The conflict between the brothers and their father persists to the end of the book of Genesis. Thus, internal and external social dynamics determine the shape of the rape, excessive violence, and social fragmentation in Gen 34.

---

[62] Bechtel, "What If Dinah Is Not Raped?" 32–34; and Tikva Frymer-Kensky, "Law and Philosophy: The Case of Sex in the Bible," *Semeia* 45 (1989): 95.

CHAPTER THREE

Judges 19: The Rape of the Nameless Concubine, Hospitality Gone Awry and the Decline of a Nation

Introduction

Judges 19 depicts the rape of a nameless concubine. In this chapter, I show how this story demonstrates its family resemblance to the other rape texts by moving through a progression of rape → male responses of excessive violence → social fragmentation. However, Judg 19, which is structured through the juxtaposition of two hospitality scenes, embodies the rape text progression in a particular way.[1] I argue that the rape itself is a catalyst within the forces of social decline that are already at work within the story. In the last chapters of the book (Judg 17–21), the narrator characterizes this period as being a time without a king, when "every man did what was right in his own eyes" (Judg 17:6, 21:25). For the narrator, the consequences of such a situation are that the social order moves progressively toward chaos.[2] Within this movement toward disorder, the rape functions within the narrative to illustrate how Israel has reached a moral

---

[1] For a discussion of hospitality as it relates to two different scenes, see Victor H. Matthews, "Hospitality and Hostility in Genesis 19 and Judges 19," *BTB* 22, no. 1 (1992): 3–11.

[2] The narrator's refrain, which occurs in 17:1 and 21:25, and in abbreviated form in 18:1 and 19:1, are clear evaluative frames for the reader. Jacqueline Lapsley, however, in a very insightful reading of Judg 19–21, shows the subtleties of the narrator's craft at the conclusion of the book of Judges. See Jacqueline E. Lapsley, *Whispering the Word: Hearing Women's Stories in the Old Testament* (Louisville: Westminster John Knox, 2005), 35–67.

low point. The narrative accomplishes this through an allusion to the Sodom and Gomorrah legend. Thus, within this topsy-turvy world,[3] good hospitality cannot fully protect the guests within; in fact, the host's hospitality contributes to the eventual rape of the Levite's concubine.

The rape also ignites male responses that are excessively violent, provoking a civil war that almost leads to the complete decimation of the tribe of Benjamin. In the post-war scene, the situation continues to degenerate, leading to the killing of men, women, and children at Jabesh-gilead and the abduction of more virgin women to repopulate Benjamin. The final picture at the end of the book of Judges is one of social and moral disintegration. In the case of this rape narrative, the rape of a woman ignites a civil war within Israel. Chaos results, and the social order moves increasingly toward moral, communal, and religious decline.

Scholars, interested in the narrative study of the book of Judges, have recognized that Judg 19 is situated within the larger conclusion of the book found in chapters 17–21. Such interpretations seek to read these chapters as an integrated, if not complex, unit that brings the book of Judges to a chaotic end. This trend within scholarship challenges the proposal of those who would see these five chapters as a mere appendix or series of appendices that were later put at the end of the book.[4] Many scholars have shown that Judg 17–21 is well-integrated thematically into the preceding material and the book of Judges as a whole, suggesting that later redactors or editors intended these chapters to be

---

[3] For discussion on the topos of the topsy-turvy or inverted world in biblical texts and the ANE, see Raymond C. van Leeuwen, "Proverbs 30:21–23 and the Biblical World Upside Down," *JBL* 105 (1986): 599–610 (see esp. 602–6 and n. 13); and Stuart Lasine, "Guest and Host in Judges 19: Lot's Hospitality In an Inverted World," *JSOT* 29 (1984): 37–59. As van Leeuwen and others have pointed out, the inverted world motif is found within Egyptian pessimistic literature such as "The Prophecies of Neferti" (*AEL*, vol. 1, ed. Miriam Lichtheim [Berkeley: University of California Press, 1973]: 139–45). See also Seow, who discusses Egyptian literature in his interpretation of Eccl 10:5–15 (Choon-Leong Seow, *Ecclesiastes: A New Translation With Introduction and Commentary* [AB 18C; New York: Doubleday, 1997], 325). Themes of the topsy-turvy world also can be found in images found on ostraca and papyri from the Ramesside period. See Flores, who argues, however, that such images are not necessarily satirical or socially critical (Diane Flores, "Topsy-Turvy World," in *Egypt, Israel, and the Ancient Mediterranean World: Studies in Honor of Donald B. Redford* [ed. Gary N. Knoppers and Antoine Hirsch; Leiden: Brill, 2004], 233–55).

[4] For example, see J. Alberto Soggin, *Judges: A Commentary* (trans. John Bowden; OTL; Philadelphia: Westminster, 1981), 5, 263–305.

read as a conclusion to the book rather than as simple afterthoughts.[5] Scholars also have argued that these chapters, or portions of them, at an early stage in their development and/or in their final placement here at the end of the book of Judges, had a sociopolitical function as a polemic against northern shrines or against the Saulide monarchy. Such issues have been argued well in other places.[6] The focus of the present discussion, however, is on the narrative movement of Judg 17–21, in particular, its function as the literary context of Judg 19.

The Context of Rape

The rape of the Levite's unnamed concubine is set within a specific context that shapes the reader's understanding of the sexual violence. In this section, following the work of other literary scholars, I will show how Judg 17–21 provides a larger narrative context within which to understand the rape. The rape is situated within a setting of social and moral collapse at the end of the

---

[5] See David W. Gooding, "The Composition of the Book of Judges," *Eretz-Israel* 16 (1982): *70–*79; Barry G. Webb, *The Book of Judges: An Integrated Reading* (JSOTSup 46; Sheffield: JSOT Press, 1987); Lillian R. Klein, *The Triumph of Irony in the Book of Judges* (JSOTSup 68; Sheffield: Almond, 1989), 141–92; Alexander Globe, "Enemies Round About: Disintegrative Structure in the Book of Judges," *Mappings of the Biblical Terrain* (ed. V. L. Tollers and J. Maier; Lewisburg: Bucknell University, 1990), 233–51; Robert H. O'Connell, *The Rhetoric of the Book of Judges* (VTSup 63; Leiden: Brill, 1996), 229–67; Marvin A. Sweeney, "Davidic Polemics in the Book of Judges," *VT* 47 (1997): 517–29; Dennis T. Olson, "The Book of Judges: Introduction, Commentary, and Reflections," *NIB* 2:863–66; and Marc Zvi Brettler, *The Book of Judges* (Old Testament Readings; London: Routledge, 2002), 80–91.

[6] See in particular Martin Noth, "The Background of Judges 17–18," in *Israel's Prophetic Heritage* (ed. Bernhard W. Anderson and Walter Harrelson; New York: Harper & Row, 1962), 68–85; Marc Brettler, "The Book of Judges: Literature as Politics," *JBL* 108, no. 3 (1989): 395–418; Yairah Amit, "Literature in the Service of Politics: Studies in Judges 19–21," in *Politics and Theopolitics in the Bible and Postbiblical Literature* (JSOTSup 171; ed. Henning Graf Reventlow, Yair Hoffman and Benjamin Uffenheimer; Sheffield: JSOT Press, 1994), 28–40; Sweeney, "Davidic Polemics," 517–29; and Andrew D. H. Mayes, "Deuteronomistic Royal Ideology in Judges 17–21," *BibInt* 9, no. 3 (2001): 241–58. While some scholars locate the date of the Gibeah rape story early to the period of the monarchy, Amit and others have argued for a post-exilic setting. In this case, the polemic against Saul's kingdom is more literary than actual, reflecting group tensions in Yehud rather than an actual attempt to revive a Saulide dynasty. See Yairah Amit, "The Saul Polemic in the Persian Period," in *Judah and the Judeans in the Persian Period* (ed. Oded Lipschits and Manfred Oeming; Winona Lake: Eisenbrauns, 2006), 647–61.

period of Judges. As I will show later, the rape itself is a catalyst that propels the story toward increasing male violence and depredation.

Within Judges 19, the rape's more specific meaning is structured through the juxtaposition of two hospitality scenes. These two scenes function as a point of contrast with the inhospitable town of Gibeah. The second scene also serves to show how hospitality can go horribly wrong within a context of moral and social decline. The final hospitality scene provides an allusion to the Sodom and Gomorrah story (Gen 19). The differences between the two narratives provide the reader with a specific understanding of the rape. Gibeah's rape of the Levite's concubine suggests that Israel's wickedness has become worse than the legendary evil of Sodom and Gomorrah.[7]

The Narrative Context of Judges 17–21: Social and Moral Decline

Judges 17–21 provides the larger framework for Judg 19 and gives the reader a specific context—one of moral and social decline—in which to view the rape. With the death of Samson in Chapter 16, the tales of individual judges give way to a series of stories that portray Israel in a state of deterioration prior to the rise of the monarchy. The narrator characterizes this period with the phrase, "In those days, there was no king in Israel; every man did what was right in his own eyes." The complete refrain occurs in 17:6 and 21:25. Abbreviated forms of the theme occur in 18:1 and 19:1. Hence, the narrator makes an explicit value judgment on this era at key points throughout the end of the book of Judges. The shape of this judgment will develop for the reader as the story progresses.

The phrase, "every man did what was right in his own eyes," summarizes the disintegration and social chaos that is characteristic of this period—a time in which "there was no king in Israel." In Judg 17–21, the people resort to the worship of idols, priests and their families have become corrupt, hospitality is forsaken, a woman is raped and killed, and Israel commits acts of holy war against itself. Hence, the refrain echoes throughout this narrative, reminding the reader of the narrator's judgment through repetition.[8] Within this context of

---

[7] Sodom and Gomorrah's depravity is legendary in Israelite traditions (see esp. Jer 23:14), making the two cities paradigmatic examples of God's wrath and judgment (see, for example, Deut 29:22; Isa 1:9, 13:19; Jer 49:18; Amos 4:11).

[8] Most scholars recognize the negative connotations of this refrain and seek to argue for the correct historical context of it. The larger narrative movement toward social disintegration

moral decline, I will show that the rape functions as a catalyst that propels the tribes of Israel toward a cycle of increasing violence and social fragmentation.

Chapters 17–21 divide into two sections. Chapters 17–18 depict the deterioration of the cult, whereas chapters 19–21 point to a larger social chaos, indeed a breaking down of the very fabric of Israel's tribal society.[9] As scholars have noted, there is significant thematic overlap between these two sections. Olson makes the following connections between Judg 17–18 and 19–21:

- Both stories involve a Levite as one of the main characters.
- In the first section, the Levite travels from Bethlehem of Judah to Ephraim; in the second, the Levite reverses the direction of travel, going from the hill country of Ephraim to Bethlehem of Judah.
- The actions of both men are "implicitly condemned" by the narrator.
- The stories begin with family issues of the Levite and progress to larger tribal concerns.
- Both stories end with the preservation of an individual tribe; the survival of the tribe is secured through violent means.[10]

Olson, following Crüsemann, suggests that the social chaos that results at the end of each section—where "innocent victims suffer with no mechanism for accountability or redress"—is a direct result of the lack of political leadership within Israel.[11]

---

suggests that a positive take on this phrase is forced (but see William J. Dumbrell, "'In Those Days There Was No King in Israel; Everyman Did What Was Right in His Own Eyes': The Purpose of the Book of Judges Reconsidered," *JSOT* 25 [1983]: 23–33). For a good summary of this issue, see Olson, "Book of Judges," 864–65.

[9] Klein, *Triumph of Irony*, 141–92; Gale A. Yee, "Ideological Criticism: Judges 17–21 and the Dismembered Body," in *Judges and Method: New Approaches in Biblical Studies* (ed. Gale A. Yee; Minneapolis: Fortress, 1995), 158–67; and Olson, "Book of Judges," 863. Olson also rightfully points out that the twofold conclusion at the end of the book of Judges corresponds to the twofold introduction in which Israel experiences "social fragmentation (1:1–2:5) and religious deterioration (2:6–3:6)." Hence the introduction and conclusion form a chiastic frame (ABB'A') around the book of Judges.

[10] Olson, "Book of Judges," 864.

[11] Ibid., 864; cf. Frank Crüsemann, *Der Widerstand gegen das Königtum* (Neukirchen-Vluyn: Neukirchener Verlag, 1978), 157–58.

Hence, both stories, through the development of plot, prove to the reader what the narrator makes explicit: "In those days there was no king in Israel; every man did what was right in his own eyes" (21:25). When the first part of this refrain is used in Judg 19:1, it serves as a cue to the reader of what type of events will follow. The events within Judg 19 will exemplify the socially and morally chaotic world of life without strong political leadership—a narrative theme that began in Judg 17–18.[12] As I will show below, the rape will serve as a catalyst to the excessive violence and social fragmentation that result. The rape itself and the post-rape responses provide an example of how things go wrong in Israel without a king.

Framing the Rape: Two Hospitality Scenes

Within Chapter 19, the rape is set specifically within the context of two hospitality scenes. The first describes an excessive and extravagant display of hospitality from the woman's father that results in the Levite and his concubine leaving the house as the night approaches. The second involves the hospitality of an old Ephraimite man. Both scenes, in which different forms of hospitality are shown, serve as a contrast to the lack of hospitality of the men of Gibeah. This contrast produces a judgment in the reader's eyes on the people of the town.

In my discussion of rape below, I will show how the meaning of the rape in Judg 19 is shaped through an allusion to Sodom and Gomorrah. The difference in outcome between these two stories causes the reader to view this period and

---

[12] In addition to framing the judgments of the reader, the first verse introduces the two main characters: a Levite and a woman who is designated as פִּילֶגֶשׁ. The Levite is characterized in terms of place, "sojourning" (גָּר) in "the hill country of Ephraim" (הַר־אֶפְרַיִם). He takes a wife for himself from Bethlehem of Judah. The geographical configuration of this relationship draws the reader's attention to the preceding story in Judg 17–18, in which a Levite from Bethlehem of Judah comes to Ephraim. The confluence of geographical terms—Bethlehem, Judah, and Ephraim—in addition to the designation of one of the key characters as a Levite connects these two stories in the reader's mind. The outcome of the previous story left the reader with a negative image of the tribe of Dan as an idolatrous tribe, and the Levite as a weak religious figure with shifting loyalties. Therefore, the reader, when confronted again with a similar configuration of Levite, Ephraim, Bethlehem, and Judah, is set up to expect a negative outcome in Judg 19. See Olson, "Book of Judges," 875.

the events within Gibeah as more terrible than the deeds of the infamous cities. The difference, of course, is that such evil has happened within Israel.

Thus, the framing of the rape within two hospitality scenes serves the function of providing a critical assessment of the period of Judges generally and the town of Gibeah specifically. Both scenes provide examples of a host taking care of his guest. Within the topsy-turvy world at the end of the book of Judges, however, displays of welcoming and protecting visitors lead to the giving up of the guest's concubine to be raped. Hence, even the important social custom of hospitality is distorted when social and moral chaos is in the land. Such an assessment of the story affirms the narrator's judgment of this period as being a time without a king when "every man did what was right in his own eyes."

Hospitality Scene One: The Father's Excessive Hospitality

The first hospitality scene occurs within the house of the concubine's father.[13] Within this first episode, the father provides excessive hospitality for his son-in-law, though the narrator does not make clear the motivation for this excess. The scene functions in two ways within the larger context of the narrative. First, it provides an example of extreme hospitality, which will be contrasted later in the story with the lack of hospitality, indeed the eventual hostility, from the town of Gibeah. Second, this scene serves the narrative function of delaying the

---

[13] The woman is identified as פִּילֶגֶשׁ. Though she is the only wife in the story, her characterization as a concubine points to the fact that she is a wife of secondary status. Hence, Trible states, "Legally and socially, she is not the equivalent of a wife but is virtually a slave, secured by a man for his own purposes" (*Texts of Terror*, 66). However, see Mieke Bal, "Dealing/With/Women: Daughters in the Book of Judges," in *The Book and the Text: The Bible and Literary Theory* (ed. Regina M. Schwartz; Oxford: Basil Blackwell, 1990), 25–28. Bal argues that the term, *pilgesh*, when examined within the context of its narrative structure, refers not to her status as a secondary wife, but points to where she lives after marriage, i.e., if the marriage is patrilocal (living with the father) or virilocal (living with her husband's family). Bal, and later Exum (*Fragmented Women*, 176–77), chooses to name the woman in an attempt to counter the text's tendency to distance the reader from the woman. However, both the woman's secondary status and her anonymity are crucial elements of the story; therefore, I choose to stay with the translation of "concubine." For an examination of the narrative function of the anonymous characters within Judg 19, see Don Michael Hudson, "Living in a Land of Epithets: Anonymity in Judges 19–21," *JSOT* 62 (1994): 49–66. See also Alice Bach, who chooses to keep the woman anonymous by referring to her through the transliterated word "*pilgesh*" ("Rereading the Body Politic: Women and Violence in Judges 21," *Biblical Interpretation* 6, no. 1 [1998]: 2 n. 2).

Levite and his concubine at the father's house.[14] This delay, coupled with the Levite's decision not to stay in Jebus, lands the travelers in Gibeah as the night approaches. The growing darkness provides the dangerous setting for the final hospitality scene within which the rape will occur. The elements of night combined with issues of hospitality set the stage for the story's comparison/contrast with the Sodom and Gomorrah incident.

The scene also leads the reader to a negative assessment of the Levite. The priest's original intention is to "speak to the heart" of his concubine. As the scene unfolds, however, the visit to the father results only in the "making glad" of the Levite's own heart through the experience of the father's hospitality. The father's excessive display has the Levite as its object. The Levite's concubine vanishes from the narrative's focus as the two men participate in this social exchange. Throughout this scene the husband fails to address his concubine at all.

The episode begins when the Levite arrives at his father-in-law's house in an apparent attempt to reconcile with his wife, i.e., to "speak to the heart" (לְדַבֵּר עַל־לִבָּהּ) of his concubine.[15] At the beginning of the story, the woman had left her husband and returned to her father's house.[16] The Levite's arrival to Bethlehem initiates the extravagant display of hospitality from the father-in-law.

---

[14] Matthews identifies these two functions of the first hospitality scene in his summary of the episode ("Hospitality and Hostility," 7). He is following Lasine in his observation that the hospitable actions of the father delay the Levite from departing (see Lasine, "Guest and Host," 56–57 n. 34).

[15] On the Levite's coming to the father's house, the MT reads וַתְּבִיאֵהוּ, suggesting that the woman took initiative to meet the man and "brought him" to her father's house. Other interpreters, following some textual witnesses (LXX^AL and the Syriac), suggest that it is the man who "comes" (וַיָּבֹא). Burney, citing Moore, correctly assumes that the MT is influenced by וַתִּזְנֶה, "she played the harlot," in v. 2. Since the MT suggests that the woman is at fault, she is the one who must initiate reconciliation in v. 3. Hence, וַתְּבִיאֵהוּ, "she brought him back" (Charles F. Burney, *The Book of Judges: With Introduction and Notes; and The Hebrew Text of the Books of Kings: With an Introduction and Appendix* [New York: KTAV, 1970], 461).

[16] There is much debate about what the concubine does before she leaves. In v. 2, the MT describes the actions of the Levite's concubine through the verb וַתִּזְנֶה, from the root זנה, which points to sexual infidelity. However, Robert Boling, followed by many others, suggests that such a meaning within this narrative context makes little sense. He argues that it would be strange for a woman to prostitute herself and then flee home in response. For a thorough discussion of the issues, including the text-critical elements involved, see Robert G. Boling, *Judges: A New*

The hospitality within the first scene is described in such a way that emphasizes its excess. The extreme nature of the father's hospitality is stressed through the story's wording and repetition. The father greets (לִקְרָאתוֹ) the Levite with joy (וַיִּשְׂמַח) in v. 3, and prevails over (וַיֶּחֱזַק) his son-in-law to stay in v. 4. For three days, they, presumably the two men, eat (וַיֹּאכְלוּ) and drink (וַיִּשְׁתּוּ). The warm greeting, the persuading to stay, and the eating and drinking are all signs of good hospitality. However, the use of the verb חזק at the beginning of the scene is instructive in that it suggests that the father prevails over his son-in-law by persuading him to remain in his house longer than the Levite desires.

Each time that the Levite gets up to leave, the father makes another offer for him to stay (19:5, 7, 8, 9). Almost two days pass within vv. 5–9, but the situation and location remain the same. Each day the man arises early in the morning, expressed through the Hiphil of שׁכם (vv. 5, 8), and he gets up to go (וַיָּקָם לָלֶכֶת). The recurrence of these verbs points to the repeated desire of the Levite to journey back to his home. In each case, however, the father persuades his son-in-law to stay longer into the day, asking him to strengthen his heart with food (vv. 5, 8).

With each exchange, the father's requests get longer.[17] As the stay approaches the fifth day, the repetition and the increasing length of the father's

---

Translation with Introduction and Commentary (AB 6A; New York: Doubleday, 1975), 273–74, and Soggin, *Judges*, 284. In order to make sense of the MT's use of זנה, some scholars have suggested that the very act of leaving her husband would be understood as an act of sexual infidelity, especially since women were forbidden from initiating divorce within Israelite law (see Boling, *Judges*, 274; Exum, *Fragmented Women*, 178–80; Danna Nolan Fewell and David M. Gunn, *Gender, Power and Promise: The Subject of the Bible's First Story* [Nashville: Abingdon, 1993], 133; Ken Stone, "Gender and Homosexuality in Judges 19: Subject-Honor, Object-Shame?" *JSOT* 67 [1995]: 90–91; and Olson, "Book of Judges," 876). There is evidence in other legal materials of the ANE, however, that suggests that women were permitted to initiate divorce, even if such actions were atypical. See Annalisa Azzoni, "The Private Life of Women in Persian Egypt" (Ph.D. diss., Johns Hopkins University, 2000), 85–106. Even if the concubine's actions were illegal or socially unacceptable, such actions could make sense within the present narrative context. The woman's initiation of divorce would be a cue to the reader that something is wrong with the social order of things. Throughout Judg 17–21, characters act in ways that are atypical, depicting the religious, moral, and social decline during this period. The woman's actions would be another indication that things are amiss in this time without a king.

[17] Trible, *Texts of Terror*, 69.

persuasion move this tale of hospitality into excess. Olson is right in suggesting that the father practices "exaggerated hospitality."[18] Thus, the repetition and increasing length of the father's plea serves to frustrate the reader in that the father's controlling generosity slows the plot into an increasingly absurd repetitive dialogue.

The father's social control and centrality in this narrative is also structurally reinforced through the language that describes him. In v. 4, the narrator depicts the father through a double characterization: חֹתְנוֹ אֲבִי הַנַּעֲרָה, "his father-in-law, the father of the girl."[19] These two terms, bound up in one character, point to the dual position of the host's role as father-in-law to the Levite and father to his daughter.

This double identification also frames the first hospitality story, occurring at the scene's beginning in v. 4 and its end in v. 9, where the master of the house is once again described as חֹתְנוֹ אֲבִי הַנַּעֲרָה, "his [the Levite's] father-in-law, the father of the girl." Thus, the host's dual identity, situated socially between his son-in-law and daughter, is also represented structurally in the narrative. Hence, the narrative's structure conveys what the story tells—the Levite will not be able to leave with the host's daughter without first being subjected to the father-in-law's hospitality. Thus, the initial action of the father, in which he prevails over his son-in-law (וַיֶּחֱזַק), reinforces through explicit vocabulary the inclusion of the host's social control over the situation.

The father-in-law dominates and controls this scene with his hospitable acts and urgings. By itself, the father's insistence that the Levite stay is representative of good hospitality. However, the repetition of his persistence day after day, in spite of his guest's desire to leave, moves this show of generosity into the realm of excess. It is certainly expected that a host should shower his guest with extravagant displays of hospitality. When it is carried to a point of excess, however, such displays can be viewed as excessive and shameful.[20]

---

[18] Olson, "Book of Judges," 876.

[19] Freedman, in a private communication to Boling, suggests that the double-identification is due to the ambiguity in the term חֹתֵן, which can refer equally to father-in-law or son-in-law. The additional reference of אֲבִי הַנַּעֲרָה resolves the ambiguity (Boling, *Judges*, 274).

[20] Abou-Zeid makes this observation in his discussion of hospitality codes in honor/shame societies. See Ahmed M. Abou-Zeid, "Honour and Shame Among the Bedouins in Egypt," in *Honour and Shame: The Values of Mediterranean Society* (ed. Jean G. Peristiany; London: Weidenfeld & Nicolson, 1965), 259.

The excessive hospitality of the father-in-law serves as a contrast to Gibeah's lack of hospitality in the scenes that follow. Here, it is important to point out that the father's actions are not necessarily viewed as examples of poor hospitality. In fact, he is overly hospitable. His actions are depicted as excessive because of the overbearing and repetitive ways with which he shows his generosity. Such displays of excessive generosity make Gibeah's lack of hospitality later in the story all the more egregious. The contrast is stark and extreme. Over-hospitality in the house of the father-in-law is juxtaposed with a complete lack of reception in Gibeah's town square. In the topsy-turvy world without a king, however, both contribute to the calamity at the end of the story.

The second function of this first hospitality scene is that it delays the departure of the Levite and his concubine. Thus, the travelers begin their journey late in the day, as the evening approaches. The impending darkness will provide the backdrop for the allusion to the Sodom and Gomorrah story. It also leads the reader to the conclusion that the excessive hospitality within the father's house contributes to putting the travelers in danger.[21]

Verse 19:9 signals the transition out of the father's house in that it breaks the repetition of the host's pleading and the Levite's acquiescence. The Levite's departure seems more certain in that his concubine (פִּילַגְשׁוֹ) and his servant (נַעֲרוֹ) join in his preparations to leave. The reintroduction of these two characters signals a breaking up of the cyclical giving and receiving of hospitality. The father, yet again, proceeds to entreat his son-in-law to stay. His words in this final speech, however, are more specific in describing the environment outside of his house. Twice in v. 9 the father points to the fact

---

[21] The narrator also makes explicit the number of days that the Levite stays. The use of the numbered days three, four, and five, also point to the possibility that something is wrong. The Levite remains initially for three days (v. 4). He gets up to leave on the fourth day, but his father-in-law persuades him to stay. Finally, the priest leaves later on the fifth day (v. 8). The numbers three and four can have symbolic meaning within the Hebrew Bible. Both numbers represent wholeness or completeness. See, for example, Amos' use of the phrase, "for three transgressions… and for four," in the oracles against the nations, suggesting the complete nature of the LORD's judgment (Amos 1:3–2:16). Hence, leaving on the third or fourth day could evoke for the reader the sense that the Levite's stay was complete. By leaving on the fifth day, the travelers have stayed longer than they should have. For a survey of the meaning of different numbers in the Hebrew Bible and the ANE, see Marvin H. Pope, "Number, Numbering, Numbers," *IDB* 3:561–67; and Bruce C. Birch, "Number," *ISBE* 3:556–61.

that the day is ending through the particle הִנֵּה. The expressions, "the day has waned" (רָפָה הַיּוֹם) and "the closing of the day" (חֲנוֹת הַיּוֹם)[22] both are followed by imperatives to "spend the night" (from the root לוּן). The repetition of the father's speech emphasizes for the reader that the day is spent and that night is approaching. The waning day and the coming of night create an ominous setting for the narrative as the travelers prepare to leave. With the coming of darkness, the character's environment moves into a liminal space— the boundary between day and night, safety and danger. The threat of peril increases with the coming dark.[23]

As others have shown, the need for hospitality within the context of evening brings to mind echoes from the story found in Gen 19, depicting the evil of Sodom and Gomorrah (see discussion below). Beyond providing this setting, the end of this first hospitality scene also contributes to putting the travelers in danger. The father's extended speech in v. 9 emphasizes the fact that the day is quickly passing and the evening is approaching. The narrator echoes this detail in v. 11. This repeated element highlights the fact that the Levite, by failing to refuse his father-in-law's persistent offers, has lingered in Bethlehem too long. Hence, one of the results of the excessive hospitality is that the travelers leave at a time that makes them vulnerable to the coming night. When this scene is viewed within the larger context of Judg 17–21, a more profound meaning emerges. In this kingless era, even when hospitality is practiced in excess, it has the potential to contribute to endangering the safety of the travelers—something that hospitality is supposed to protect.

Before moving to the second hospitality scene, it is important to note a theme that will be useful for understanding the male responses to rape discussed below. Throughout this first scene, the Levite is viewed as a weak man, who never accomplishes what he originally sets out to do: "speak to the heart" of his concubine. The reader's perception of the Levite diminishes through the repetition of the father's excessive hospitality. The son-in-law

---

[22] The infinitive construct, from the root חנה, "to decline," is synonymous with the previous idiom. The repetition serves to emphasize the fact that the day is passing and that night is approaching.

[23] For a discussion of the association of danger with night, see Weston W. Fields, "The Motif 'Night as Danger' Associated with Three Biblical Destruction Narratives," in *"Sha'arei Talmon": Studies in the Bible, Qumran, and the Ancient Near East, Presented to Shemaryahu Talmon* (ed. Michael Fishbane and Emanuel Tov; Winona Lake: Eisenbrauns, 1992), 17–32.

clearly desires to go home, since each morning begins with the guest getting up early to leave. However, he is not able to refuse the father-in-law's urgings until late into the fifth day. Thus, the reader views the Levite as a man with a weak will.[24] He is unable to decline the excessive hospitality of his overbearing father-in-law.

In addition, twice the father appeals to the Levite to "sustain" his heart (vv. 5, 8) and to "let [his heart] be glad" (vv. 6, 9). The language of the *heart* brings the reader's attention back to the Levite's initial reason for going to the house of his father-in-law, which was "to speak to the heart" of his concubine (לְדַבֵּר עַל־לִבָּהּ). In this way, the father's speech alerts the reader to the fact that the Levite's original intention for reconciliation—speaking words to his concubine's heart—has digressed into an excessive and prolonged display of drinking, eating, and merrymaking. The son-in-law sustains and makes glad his own heart, neglecting the heart of the woman for whom he came. This negative characterization is confirmed as the story progresses and later serves to distance the reader from the Levite's post-rape response.

Hospitality Scene Two: Gibeah and an Old Ephraimite Man

The excessive hospitality of the first scene is contrasted with Gibeah's inhospitable reception of the Levite in v. 15. Gibeah's actions begin with neglect, but turn quickly hostile. A second act of hospitality takes shape when an old Ephraimite man invites the travelers into his house. Later in the scene, the demands of an unruly mob compromise the host's protection of his guests, leading to the objectionable solution of handing over the Levite's concubine to be raped.

As I will show, the two displays of hospitality are contrasted with the actions of the men of Gibeah. This produces a critical assessment from the reader. Such a judgment also provides the proper context within which to understand the meaning of rape in Judg 19. This second hospitality scene, as many scholars have shown, bears striking similarity to Gen 19, the story of Sodom and Gomorrah. The differences between the two stories serve the function of producing judgment in the reader's mind on the town of Gibeah.

---

[24] Olson, "Book of Judges," 876.

Thus, the two hospitality stories will prove to frame the rape in a particular way, shaping its meaning within the context of an "inverted world."[25]

A Brief Interlude: Setting the Stage for Gibeah. The reader's understanding of the contrast between the two hospitality scenes is set up through a brief interlude (vv. 11–14) in which the Levite, his concubine, and his servant journey toward home. This break between the two hospitality scenes cues the reader into the Levite's perceptions about where he feels safe to stay, and provides an ironic contrast between Jebus, "a city of foreigners," and Gibeah of Benjamin. The Levite's decision to choose Gibeah will prove to be disastrous. It also cues the reader into the fact that the town in which the evening hostilities occur is Israelite.

The interlude functions as a narrative boundary between Bethlehem and Gibeah, day and night, safety and danger. The closing of the day—a time that stands between daylight and nightfall—marks this in-between space. Upon the group's arrival at Jebus, the narrator adds the description הַיּוֹם רַד מְאֹד, literally, "the day had gone down much." The approaching dark casts an ominous shadow over the narrative, leaving this band of travelers vulnerable to the uncertainties of the night.[26]

The servant, recognizing the potential danger, suggests that the group of travelers turn aside and go to "this city of the Jebusites" (עִיר־הַיְבוּסִי הַזֹּאת) and "spend the night in it" (נָלִין בָּהּ). The mention of this place as belonging to the Jebusites flags the reader to the ethnic composition of the city. In addition, the earlier narratorial comment in v. 10, which ties the city of Jebus with Jerusalem, creates an ironic tension for the reader. The reader knows that the approaching city will eventually be known as the capital of Judah. It is marked in this period, however, by the foreign designation, "this city of the Jebusites."

The Levite, characterized as the servant's master (אֲדֹנָיו), decides against staying in Jebus because it is a "city of foreigners" (עִיר נָכְרִי). A further

---

[25] Lasine uses the idea of an "inverted world" to describe what is taking place in Judg 19. He says, "Comparison of Judges 19–21 with Genesis 19 and 1 Samuel 11 allows the reader to recognize that a world in which there is no king in Israel and every man does what is right in his own eyes (Judg. 19.1; 21.25; cf. 17.6) is an 'inverted world' where actions are often ludicrous, absurd, and self-defeating." He is drawing from the works of literary critics to describe an anti-world where things are reversed (Lasine, "Guest and Host," 37, 50 n. 1).

[26] Fields, "Motif," 23–25.

clarification of what constitutes the foreignness of this place is added in the next phrase, "who are not from the children of Israel" (אֲשֶׁר לֹא־מִבְּנֵי יִשְׂרָאֵל). This description is thick with irony and serves to distance the reader from the perspective of the Levite. The latter is living in a time when foreigners inhabit the future capital of Judah, a perspective that the reader does not share. The Levite refuses to stay there, preferring to confront the threat of night rather than stay in a city inhabited with Jebusites. He assumes that his party will be better off traveling further to Gibeah in Benjamin.[27] Within an Israelite city, the Levite expects that he will receive better hospitality. This decision, and the assumption that governs it, proves to be in error. In fact, as will be shown below, the Levite and company are heading straight for another Sodom and Gomorrah.[28]

The Inhospitality and Hostility of Gibeah. Gibeah's initial neglect of the travelers (v. 15) is set in contrast to both the preceding scene of excessive hospitality and an Ephraimite's reception of the visitors into his home. In v. 15, the group of travelers arrives at the city of Gibeah in order to lodge there for the evening. The Levite wanders into the town and sits down in the square of the city because no one will take them in for the night. The picture at the beginning of the scene is one of isolation. The night is closing in on the travelers, and no one is offering them a place to stay. Thus, the man has become a sojourner (cf. 19:1) within an Israelite city. In this city, rather than facing foreigners, he is confronted with isolation.

The actual neglect of the travelers is described briefly. The brevity of this depiction stands in stark contrast to the extended urgings of the father-in-law in the previous scene. In addition, the picture of the travelers sitting in the square in the evening serves to highlight their pitiful circumstance and vulnerability as visitors within the town. The last phrase, "But no one took them into their house to stay the night," makes explicit Gibeah's neglect and accentuates the

---

[27] Gibeah was an additional 5 km north of Jebus/Jerusalem. Ramah was further, just less than 9 km north of their location.

[28] Daniel Block summarizes this well: "By patterning the following climactic scene after Genesis 19, the narrator serves notice that, whereas the travelers had thought they had come home to the safety of their countrymen, they have actually arrived at Sodom" (Daniel I. Block, "Echo Narrative Technique in Hebrew Literature: A Study in Judges 19," *WTJ* 52 [1990]: 336).

fact that they are all alone with no offer of hospitality from the inhabitants of the city.

Gibeah's neglect in v. 15 is also contrasted with the hospitality of the old Ephraimite man, who extends them an offer to stay in his house in vv. 16–22. The old man is described in such way that emphasizes his commonness and hospitality. The Ephraimite's characterization resembles many features of the Levite's description. The old man is "from the hill country of Ephraim" (מֵהַר אֶפְרַיִם), and he is "sojourning" (גָּר) in Gibeah. This depiction of the man corresponds to the characterization of the Levite in v. 1, who was sojourning (גָּר) in "the hill country of Ephraim" (הַר־אֶפְרַיִם). Such a connection provides a point of contact for the two journeyers. For the Levite, this old man (אִישׁ זָקֵן) represents a familiarity that he has yet to experience in this Israelite city. At the end of v. 16, the narrator adds in passing an ironic and condemning remark, "and the men of the place were Benjaminites" (בְּנֵי יְמִינִי). The Levite is unable to find a place to stay within this town of Benjamin. It is only an old Ephraimite man, who happens to be sojourning in Gibeah, that offers the Levite the hospitality that should be shown to other Israelites.

The initial encounter between the Levite and the old man that follows (vv. 17–18) accentuates more the narrator's implicit judgment on the Benjaminites. In v. 17, the old man lifts his eyes (וַיִּשָּׂא עֵינָיו) and sees "the traveler" (הָאֹרֵחַ) sitting in the city square (רְחוֹב).[29] The term "traveler" highlights the fact that the Levite is in an unfamiliar place, that he is an outsider to the inhabitants of the city. By focusing the reader's gaze through the eyes of the old man, the narrative continues to emphasize the vulnerability of the Levite in this inhospitable town. He is a sojourner alone in the square of a city whose inhabitants do not receive him.

The Levite proceeds to give the old man a detailed description of his journey (v. 18), suggesting to the reader that the priest is travel weary. After his long circuitous trip, the Levite finds himself with no place to stay at the end of the day. This initial exchange between the Levite and the old man highlights the

---

[29] Matthews notes that the רְחוֹב is an undesirable place to seek shelter for the evening. This term also is used in the Gen 19 story of Sodom and Gomorrah. The angels suggest to Lot that they will stay in the רְחוֹב (Gen 19:2), which prompts Lot to urge them to stay in his house. Matthews also states that it reflects poorly on the hospitality of the city's inhabitants if visitors have to resort to staying in the רְחוֹב ("Hospitality and Hostility," 7).

pathetic situation in which the travelers find themselves. They have been on a long journey, and they have bypassed the city of the Jebusites in order to find an Israelite town. However, when they arrive in Gibeah at the end of the day, no one is willing to take in the weary group. The narrator's depiction of the Levite as being in a pitiable state serves all the more to cast a negative shadow on the inhabitants of Gibeah and their lack of hospitality. Hence, even in the initial meeting between the Levite and the Ephraimite, a contrast has been developed between the old man and the inhabitants of Gibeah

The Ephraimite's offer to stay the night further distances the old man's hospitality from Gibeah's neglect. After the Levite suggests to his potential host that he will not be a difficult guest (v. 19), the old man responds in kind by extending a generous offer of hospitality. Two phrases, expressed as conditions, emphasize the generosity of the old man. Both expressions begin with רַק, "surely, only," and point to the terms of this social contact. The old man says:

Surely, all of your needs will be upon me	רַק כָּל־מַחְסוֹרְךָ עָלָי
Only in the square do not stay the night	רַק בָּרְחוֹב אַל־תָּלַן

Hence, the conditions for the Levite are that he let the old man take care of his needs by providing the travelers with a place to stay for the evening. The Ephraimite does not allow his guest to provide anything for himself, something that the Levite offered in v. 19. By making himself responsible for the Levite's needs, the old man proves to be a willing and hospitable host.

The transition into the Ephraimite's house begins with the old man making good on his offer. In v. 21, he brings the travelers to his house and provides for his guests in a threefold expression of hospitality—he feeds their animals, the guests wash their feet, and they proceed to eat and drink (וַיֹּאכְלוּ וַיִּשְׁתּוּ) with him. The latter phrase, repeated from v. 4, recalls what the Levite and father-in-law did in the first hospitality scene. In addition, the expression, "they were making their hearts glad" (v. 22), was used in the former hospitality scene on the lips of the father (vv. 6, 9). These expressions in vv. 21–22, which are directly tied to hospitality, echo the previous episode, in which the father-in-law was overly hospitable. The old man's welcome at the beginning of this second scene and the excessive generosity displayed in the house of the father-in-law provide the reader with two examples of hospitality that are contrasted with the inhospitality of Gibeah (v. 15). As stated above, the identification of this city as being within Benjamin (vv. 14, 16) makes the contrast more significant in that it is an Israelite city that has become inhospitable to this sojourning Israelite.

Within this last scene, a final point of contrast exists between the old man's protection of his guest and the hostile demands of the men of Gibeah later in the story. The hospitality within the house of the old man is juxtaposed with the violent mob that shows up on the other side of his door. This is made clear through the wording that describes the events within the house and the debauchery outside. As stated above, vv. 21–22 describe the hospitable atmosphere of the old man's house. The host and his guest eat and drink as they are "making glad their hearts" (הֵמָּה מֵיטִיבִים אֶת־לִבָּם). The festivities in the scene are interrupted when a mob comes to the door. Explicit and implicit characterizations mark the rest of v. 22. The "men of the city" (אַנְשֵׁי הָעִיר), described as "worthlessness men" (בְּנֵי־בְלִיַּעַל), surround the house and "beat violently" (מִתְדַּפְּקִים) on the door. The term "worthless" (בְלִיַּעַל) points to the depraved character of this group of men. Their repetitive beating on the door, represented by the Hithpael participle מִתְדַּפְּקִים, confirms to the reader that these men are not only inhospitable but have no respect for social boundaries. The hospitality of the old man, which to this point in the narrative has been set over against the Benjaminites' disregard of the Levite, now comes to an alarming point of contrast with the men of Gibeah's hostility. The two participles (מֵיטִיבִים and מִתְדַּפְּקִים) within v. 22 mark this difference. The first represents the joyful eating and drinking that is taking place within the old man's home. The second describes the disgraceful behavior of the men who wait outside of the house. The door, here signified by the noun דֶּלֶת, represents the border that divides inside from outside, merriment from debauchery, hospitality from hostility.[30]

What the narrator has already conveyed to the reader about this mob through the term בְלִיַּעַל, the men verbalize by saying, "Bring out the man who came to your house that we might know him" (v. 22b).[31] Thus, the men's words

---

[30] For a good discussion of the domestic/public dichotomy and the complexity of this binary in Judg 19, see Karla G. Bohmbach, "Conventions/Contraventions: The Meaning of Public and Private for the Judges 19 Concubine," *JSOT* 83 (1999): 83–98.

[31] Stone has argued persuasively that the crowd's request, when viewed within the cultural perspective of honor and shame, represents the men of Gibeah's desire to humiliate the Levite sexually. By having sexual relations with the Levite, the men are attempting to feminize him, subduing him through sexual penetration ("Gender and Homosexuality," 87–107). Michael

show implicitly what the narrator has already made explicit—these men are a worthless and immoral group. Their desire both to humiliate this outsider (violate his social space) and "to know" him sexually (violate his body) shows the group's utter disregard for social boundaries. Hence, the contrast between hospitality and inhospitality has reached an apex in this concluding scene. The only thing that separates hospitality from violence is the door (דֶּלֶת) and the host's words (vv. 23–24).

As I will show below, the mob's persistent demands will serve to complicate issues of hospitality. This complication is most noticeable in the old man's suggestion that the men take his daughter and the Levite's concubine and rape them (v. 24). The clear allusions to Sodom and Gomorrah within this text will provide yet another contrast between the old man's actions and the hospitality of Lot in Gen 19. The configuration of narrative elements—issues that complicate hospitality at night, a mob outside that desires to sexually humiliate visitors, and a host that seeks to protect his visitor—produce a clear echo to the story of Sodom and Gomorrah in Gen 19. As I will show below, this intertextual allusion helps define the meaning of rape within Judg 19. It is to the topic of rape that I now turn.

The Rape Text Progression

The contrasting issues of hospitality and inhospitality/hostility, which provide the context for this scene, collide at the rape of the Levite's concubine. In this section, I will show how these particular narrative trajectories shape the understanding of rape in Judg 19, a text with clear allusions to the story of Sodom and Gomorrah. As in the previous chapter, I will show how this rape narrative moves through the progression—rape to excessive male violence to

---

Carden criticizes Stone's reading of Judg 19 and Gen 19, suggesting that Stone's reading serves to reinforce "Christian homophobic discourse" about these texts and the Bible in general (Michael Carden, "Homophobia and Rape in Sodom and Gibeah: A Response to Ken Stone," *JSOT* 82 [1999]: 83). Carden recommends "a reading perspective that foregrounds homosexuality in the reader's experience rather than as an issue in the narratives" (p. 85). Carden's argument is misleading. In "Gender and Homosexuality," Stone attempts to describe issues within the text through the lens of honor and shame in order to foreground modern assumptions of homosexual contact (see also his published dissertation, *Sex, Honor, and Power*). Carden mistakenly assumes that Stone's textual analysis is informed by a concealed ideological readerly bias—a bias that Stone is consciously trying to make clear through his methodology.

social fragmentation—that is characteristic of these stories' family resemblance. Judg 19 bears the marks of its family connection to the other rape texts, while embodying the traits in a particular way.

The Rape of the Unnamed Woman

The issues and themes discussed in the preceding section shape the particular expression of rape within Judg 19. The rape of the Levite's concubine is simultaneously the result of how hospitality goes wrong in a topsy-turvy world without a king and the catalyst for escalating violence and social fragmentation in Israel at the end of the book of Judges. Allusions to the Sodom and Gomorrah story provide a particular meaning for the rape within the context of hospitality. In this section, I will discuss the nature and meaning of the rape within this particular narrative trajectory. I will show that the rape provides an illustration of the narrator's characterization of this time when "there was no king in Israel" and "every man did what was right in his own eyes" (Judg 17:6, 21:25). This strategy aligns the reader with the narrator's perspective, particularly through the neglect of the woman and the violence committed against her.

As suggested above, the second hospitality scene has clear intertextual allusions to the Sodom and Gomorrah story of Gen 19.[32] These echoes have an important effect upon the interpretation of rape and the events leading up to the rape in Judg 19. The mob's unruly behavior in Judges alludes to the actions of another group of base men from Sodom and Gomorrah in Gen 19. Many scholars have detailed the similarities and connections between these texts.[33] On

---

[32] For a discussion of the meaning of "intertextuality" in biblical literature, see George Aichele and Gary A. Phillips, "Introduction: Exegesis, Eisegesis, Intergesis," *Semeia* 69/70 (1995): 1–18; and, Timothy K. Beal, "Ideology and Intertextuality: Surplus of Meaning and Controlling the Means of Production," in *Reading Between Texts: Intertextuality and the Hebrew Bible* (ed. Danna Nolan Fewell; Louisville: Westminster/John Knox, 1992), 27–39. The present understanding of intertextuality is informed by what Lasine calls "literary dependence." Rather than an author-centered, historical notion of borrowing, he explains, "I mean that Judges 19 presupposes the reader's awareness of Genesis 19 in its present form, and depends on that awareness in order to be properly understood" ("Guest and Host," 38).

[33] See Susan Niditch, "The 'Sodomite' Theme in Judges 19–20: Family, Community, and Social Disintegration," *CBQ* 44 (1982): 365–78; Lasine, "Guest and Host," 37–59; Block, "Echo

the issue of literary dependence, most have understood the Gen 19 text to be primary.[34] The parallels and differences between the stories produce a meaning that gives significance to the rape.[35]

Two differences are worth noting for the purposes of this argument. First, and most noticeably, while both hosts offer up women to the mobs outside their doors, it is only the men of Gibeah who act out their lustful violence. While the characterizations of both crowds are negative in the eyes of the reader, it is only the men of Gibeah who wantonly rape the woman. Hence, the rape in Judg 19 goes beyond the evil of Gen 19. Second, the old man's words are more explicit than the words of Lot in that he implores the men to "rape" (עַנּוּ) his daughter and the Levite's concubine (v. 24). While both hosts suggest that the mob "do what is right in [their] eyes" with the women (Gen 19:8, Judg 19:24), it is only the old man who explicitly tells the mob to rape them. This difference in detail suggests to the reader that the Ephraimite's generosity has overstepped the bounds of hospitality and has moved into the realm of the absurd.[36] In both scenes, the host's hospitality is compromised by the angry mobs' demands for sexual relations with the male guest(s). Lot's decision to offer his daughters is a problematic response to the situation, but one that is

---

Narrative," 325–41; Stone, "Gender and Homosexuality," 87–107; and, Brettler, "Literature as Politics," 395–418 (also see Brettler's more recent discussion in *Book of Judges*, 85–89).

[34] A clear piece of textual evidence that supports the position that Judg 19 is dependent on Gen 19 is found in the narrative detail of two women. In Gen 19, Lot offers his two virgin daughters to the angry mob outside his door (v. 8). In Judg 19, the old man also offers two women, his guest's concubine along with his virgin daughter (בְּתוּלָה). The host's daughter is an extraneous detail. She is mentioned only in v. 24. She is not cast out to the crowd with the Levite's concubine. Her only function within the Judg 19 story seems to be to fulfill the quota of two women—a thematic motif that assumes the dependence of Judg 19 on Gen 19. See Lasine, followed by Matthews (Lasine, "Guest and Host," 38–39; and Matthews, "Hospitality and Hostility," 9; also see Brettler, *Book of Judges*, 87). For an opposing opinion, see Niditch ("Social Disintegration," 365–78), who argues that the Judges account is not dependent on Gen 19. She argues less convincingly that the Judges account is primary. Penchansky seeks to go beyond the issue of literary dependence, preferring a particular understanding of intertextuality (see David Penchansky, "Staying the Night: Intertextuality in Genesis and Judges" in *Reading Between Texts: Intertextuality and the Hebrew Bible* [ed. Danna Nolan Fewell; Louisville: Westminster/John Knox, 1992], 77–88).

[35] Lasine, "Guest and Host," 39–41. See also Matthews, "Hospitality and Hostility," 10.

[36] Lasine, "Guest and Host," 39.

clearly seen as an attempt to protect his guests. In Judg 19, however, the old man's explicit suggestion to rape the women goes beyond Lot's response, casting the Ephraimite's actions in a more critical light in the eyes of the reader.

The implication is clear. Within the topsy-turvy world of Judges, attempts to protect the guest degenerate into both the host's suggestion to rape the women, and the actual carrying out of this violence by the mob. Hence, the allusions to Sodom and Gomorrah within this second hospitality scene serve to show how bad things have become in Israel during this period of the Judges. The old man's hospitality, in contrast to Lot's, results in a more problematic and inhospitable act—his guest's concubine actually gets handed over to the hostile men of the city and is raped. The addition of the host's suggestion to rape the women makes the old man's actions all the more questionable.

Within the context of these strong literary allusions, the rape signifies a marked difference between the worlds of Gen 19 and Judg 19. The prompting from the Ephraimite host, coupled with the actual rape of the concubine, leads the reader to the conclusion that the deeds in Gibeah resemble, if not exceed, the evil events of Sodom and Gomorrah.[37] Such an assessment provides a concrete literary example of the lawlessness of this period without a king and provides an illustrative meaning of the phrase, "every man did what was right in his own eyes."[38] In such a topsy-turvy world, the "good" in these men's eyes is characterized as the epitome of evil.

In turning to the description of the rape itself, the act is marked by the seizing of the woman and by appalling acts of sexual violence (v. 25). As I showed in the previous chapter, the use of force is a key factor for understanding rape in Israel and the ANE. Ironically, in Judg 19, it is the concubine's husband who "seizes" the woman and hands her over to the crowd

---

[37] For a comprehensive discussion of the Sodom and Gomorrah motif as it relates to Judg 19, see Weston W. Fields, *Sodom and Gomorrah: History and Motif in Biblical Narrative* (JSOTSup 231; Sheffield: Sheffield Academic Press, 1997).

[38] The old man's use of the phrase, "do to them the good in your eyes" (v. 24) brings to the reader's mind the theme that has characterized this last section of the book of Judges (17–21). From the narrator's point of view, the period of the Judges was a time when there was no king and hence, degenerated into a period that was marked by chaos and lawlessness (17:6 and 21:25; see discussion above). Thus, the mob's behavior will become an illustration of the phrase, "every man did what was right in his own eyes."

to be sexually violated. In an act of desperation, the Levite grabs (וַיַּחֲזֵק) "his concubine" (פִּילַגְשׁוֹ) and "puts *her* out" (וַיֹּצֵא) to them. The abrupt shift in character focus from the old man to the Levite in v. 25 suggests the haste with which the Levite "seizes" his concubine. The term פִּילַגְשׁוֹ, "his concubine," designates the object of his grasp. When push comes to shove, with the mob threatening to invade the old man's house, the Levite sacrifices his concubine to the violent crowd in order to save his own skin. His concubine is the object of his "seizing" (חזק) so that he does not become the object of the crowd's "knowing" (ידע). As suggested in the earlier hospitality scene, the Levite has lacked concern for his concubine, which has made the reader critical of this character. Now, in a situation where his safety is threatened, he offers up his concubine to the violent mob to protect himself. Such an act further confirms the reader's critical judgment of this character. I will return to this theme later when addressing the Levite's shockingly inappropriate response to the rape. Moreover, the negative characterization of the Levite throughout this story serves later to distance the reader from further male responses that follow.

The rape itself is narrated in v. 25b. Both the duration of the violence and the woman's battered state after the rape align the reader with the victim. This meaning of the rape simultaneously reinforces the reader's judgment on the men of this story. The action of the mob is described through two verbs:

they knew her	וַיֵּדְעוּ אוֹתָהּ
they wantonly abused her	וַיִּתְעַלְּלוּ־בָהּ

The first verb, וַיֵּדְעוּ, describes the sexual nature of the mob's violence. The second, וַיִּתְעַלְּלוּ, points to the ruthlessness of it. The length of the act, highlighted in vv. 25–26, emphasizes the cruelty and duration of the gang rape. Though the narrator's description is brief, the elapsed time in the narrative cues the reader into the lengthy nature of the sexual violence. The phrase כָּל־הַלַּיְלָה עַד־הַבֹּקֶר, "all night until morning," encompasses the entire span of the event. After the mob releases her (וַיְשַׁלְּחוּהָ), the narrator reiterates that a new day has come (בַּעֲלוֹת הַשַּׁחַר). In v. 26, when the woman struggles to the door, the narrator again mentions the morning (הַבֹּקֶר) and coming light (הָאוֹר). With these references to the breaking of the day, the narrator emphasizes that the woman's sexual torture has lasted all night. Such information reinforces the reader's horror concerning the depravity of the preceding night. It also appeals to the reader's sense of compassion for the victim, who was subject to the mob's violence for such a long duration.

In a similar way, the narrator's focus on the woman's struggle to the door in v. 26 produces additional pity, aligning the reader's sympathies even more with the victim. At the break of morning, she struggles to the door out of which she was cast. At the boundary between night and day, i.e., the dawn, she returns to the door—the margin between safety and danger, hospitality and hostility, inside and outside. There she "falls" (תפל), collapsing at the entryway to the old man's house. Thus, the narrator's elaborate description of the woman's attempt to return to the old man's house highlights for the reader the devastating effects of the preceding night's events, emphasizing her desolate state. The woman's raped and exhausted body becomes a symbol of the wrong that is committed when "every man did what was right in his own eyes." The image of this woman struggling to the door demands a response from the participants in the story. The male reactions that transpire, however, complicate this narrative further.

Male Responses to Rape

The second element of the rape text progression—excessively violent male responses—finds its expression through the Levite's problematic reaction to the rape and collective Israel's excessively violent retribution on the tribe of Benjamin. In this section, I will show how the rape serves as a catalyst for the excessive violence that spirals out of control at the end of the book of Judges, even when the male responses obscure the clear connection between rape and retaliation. Hence, the rape leads to a series of problematic male responses that are excessively violent and misguided. Such responses are characteristic of this period without a king, when every person does what is right in their own eyes.

The Levite's Response

The Levite's response to the rape confirms the reader's critical assessment of this character. His initial response, consistent with his neglect of his concubine in the first scene, is calloused and indifferent. He proceeds to respond to the violence of the rape with the brutal carving up of the concubine's body, sending out the pieces to the different tribes as a call to war (19:29–30). He later justifies this summons with an equally problematic explanation of the events at Gibeah to the gathered tribes (20:4–7). The total effect of these responses is to further distance the reader from the civil war and violence that result. The rape remains a catalyst for the violent male reactions that follow. However, the characters' convoluted and conflicted responses obscure the reason for the punishment on Gibeah.

The initial response of the Levite at the end of Chapter 19 is startling in its indifference. As stated above, the narrator, in v. 26, describes the rape's effects upon the woman when she goes back and falls (וַתִּפֹּל) "at the door of the man's house, where her master was" (פֶּתַח בֵּית־הָאִישׁ אֲשֶׁר־אֲדוֹנֶיהָ שָּׁם). Exhausted and left for dead by the crowd, the woman acts as a subject for the last time in this story, arriving back at the house at which "her master" (אֲדוֹנֶיהָ) was a guest. She returns only to fall at the door. When her master arises (וַיָּקָם) in the morning, he prepares to leave. He is on his way out the door when his departure is interrupted by the discovery of her body:

וְהִנֵּה הָאִשָּׁה פִילַגְשׁוֹ נֹפֶלֶת פֶּתַח הַבַּיִת וְיָדֶיהָ עַל־הַסַּף

And there was the woman, his concubine, lying at the door
of the house, and her hands were upon the threshold (v. 27).

The Levite's actions just prior to this discovery show disregard for his concubine. The narrator makes this explicit through the phrase, "he went out to go on his way" (וַיֵּצֵא לָלֶכֶת לְדַרְכּוֹ). Either the Levite assumed that the mob killed his wife, or he planned to leave without her. He is surprised to find her at the door, conveyed through the particle הִנֵּה. The phrase that follows this particle interrupts his plans to leave, describing once again the devastating effect of the gang rape upon the woman. The narrator repeats the use of the verb נפל to remind the reader that she had fallen at this spot in front of the door, but adds וְיָדֶיהָ עַל־הַסַּף, "and her hands were upon the threshold." This last phrase further describes the woman's pathetic state and evokes pity from the reader, as she is literally hanging on to the threshold of the house. The narrator's graphic description of the woman's position juxtaposed with the Levite's disregard leads the reader into a critical evaluation of the male character, a criticism that will grow as the Levite's response to the rape takes shape through his words and actions. Lasine is correct in labeling the Levite's behavior as absurd and ludicrous.[39]

---

[39] Lasine, "Guest and Host," 44–45.

The Levite's reaction to the sight of his "fallen" concubine goes from bad to worse in v. 28. The master callously addresses his concubine with words קוּמִי וְנֵלֵכָה, "Get up, let's go." The Levite had set out originally to "speak to the heart" of his concubine. His final and only words to her, however, do not convey feelings of affection but betray his utter disregard for the woman.[40] When she does not answer, presumably because she is unconscious or dead, the Levite puts her on his donkey and continues with the action that he had begun in the previous verse, i.e., he arises (וַיָּקָם) and goes to his place (וַיֵּלֶךְ לִמְקֹמוֹ). The Levite's determination to leave in spite of what has happened to his concubine stands in stark contrast to his inability to leave in the former hospitality scene at the father-in-law's house. The indifference and callousness of the Levite's response, combined with the narrator's description of the concubine's pathetic post-rape condition, pushes the reader's assessment of this character into further condemnation.

The Levite's response is also characterized by its excessive violence and incongruity. After he returns home, he proceeds to take a knife and dismember his concubine into twelve pieces (v. 29), sending her body throughout Israel as a message. This act, which is gruesome on its own, has the potential of becoming more terrible when one considers the fact that the narrator has not made explicit the woman's death.[41] Regardless of the woman's state, the Levite's

---

[40] Trible, *Texts of Terror*, 79.

[41] The language of "fall," expressed through the verb נפל, may suggest the concubine's death. The woman, however, just as likely could have fallen out of exhaustion due to the trauma. The language is ambiguous, as scholars have pointed out, suggesting that perhaps it is the Levite who kills the woman in the next verse. See Robert Polzin, *Moses and the Deuteronomist: Deuteronomy, Joshua, Judges* (vol. 1 of *A Literary Study of the Deuteronomic History*; Indiana Studies in Biblical Literature; ed. Herbert Parks and Robert Polzin; Bloomington: Indiana University Press, 1993), 200–202; and Trible, *Texts of Terror*, 79–80. Lasine, however, argues that reading such information into this omission stretches the meaningfulness of the text since it would require the reader to believe that the woman was alive for the trip home and that the Levite "cold-bloodedly murdered her, for reasons unexpressed" ("Guest and Host," 56 n. 29). I would argue that both interpretations—the woman is already dead or the Levite kills her—are possible and that the narrator uses this double potential to create a certain effect upon the reader. To this point in the narrative, the Levite has shown little if no regard for his concubine and has been insensitive to the point of being absurd. For him not to recognize that she is dead is consistent given this characterization. What most commentators miss in interpreting the omission of the woman's death is the effect of the narrated language on the reader. The ambiguity of whether or not the

actions are at least a grisly display of his handling of the corpse. The explicit mention of the instrument (הַמַּאֲכֶלֶת) used for the dismemberment, combined with the expression that he divided (וַיְנַתְּחֶהָ) her by her limbs (לַעֲצָמֶיהָ), provides a detailed description of the macabre deed.

In addition, as many scholars have shown, the Levite's dividing up of his concubine into twelve pieces is a gruesome enactment of a custom in which an animal was cut up to summon different tribes to battle (cf., 1 Sam 11:7).[42] Rather than an animal such as an ox, however, here the message is sent through the dismemberment of the woman. Her fragmented body has become writing.[43] The gruesome form of this message and the descriptive way in which the narrator depicts the Levite's authoring of it moves the characterization of the Levite and his actions into the category of grotesque.[44]

---

woman is alive or dead is intentional; but it remains a possibility only for a brief amount of time in the reader's mind. The story time at this point in the text speeds up tremendously, moving from direct discourse at the beginning of 19:28, which the reader experiences as "real" time, to miles of terrain being covered in the space of a few words at the end of v. 28 and the beginning of v. 29: "He went to his place. When he came into his house" (וַיֵּלֶךְ לִמְקֹמוֹ: וַיָּבֹא אֶל־בֵּיתוֹ). The Levite has taken (וַיִּקַּח) a knife, seized (וַיַּחֲזֵק) his concubine, and divided her (וַיְנַתְּחֶהָ) before the reader has time to ponder seriously whether or not the woman is dead. These actions, which are narrated quickly and decisively, do not give the reader time to determine exactly how the concubine has died. The explicit mention of her death is left out, leaving open a brief window of ambiguity for the reader before the narrator slams it shut by removing forcefully and gruesomely any doubts as to whether or not the concubine was dead. The effect on the reader is shock at the suddenness of such resolution and horror at the gory detail of it. It is only after this startling end that the reader has time to ponder whether or not the woman died earlier. For scholars who maintain the ambiguity in this passage concerning the concubine's death, see Mieke Bal, "Body of Writing," 89–93; and Olson, "Book of Judges," 877–78.

[42] Brettler takes this a step further and argues that the comparison to the Saul material is intentional and is used here as a polemic against a faction who continued to favor the Saulide kingship over the Davidic at a later point in Israel's history ("Literature as Politics," 412–15).

[43] Some feminist scholars, drawing off the work of Derrida, see the woman's dismemberment, which contains a message to the tribes, as a violent and problematic form of discourse. See Peggy Kamuf, "Author of a Crime," in *A Feminist Companion to Judges* (ed. Athalya Brenner; The Feminist Companion to the Bible 4, Sheffield: Sheffield Academic Press, 1993), 187–207; and Bal, "Body of Writing," 208–30.

[44] By "grotesque" I am referring to the use of exaggeration and incongruous elements within literature and art to create a desired effect upon the audience. For further discussion of the use of the grotesque in literature, see Wolfgang Kayser, *The Grotesque in Art and Literature* (trans. Ulrich Weisstein; New York: Columbia University Press, 1981); and, Mary Russo, *The Female Grotesque:*

Thus, when the Levite announces his case against Gibeah in 20:4–7, the reader hears the words within the context of the Levite's actions in the preceding episodes. The reader, having seen the Levite's disregard and callousness toward his concubine, perceives his words of indignation as incongruous. Moreover, within his accounting of what happened, there are significant points of departure between his telling of the events and the narrated details of Judg 19. The most significant differences in the Levite's tale is that he omits both the fact that the mob originally wanted to "know" him, and that it was he who cast his concubine out to the crowd.[45]

He says of the men of Gibeah, "They intended to kill *me*, and they raped *my concubine*, and she died" (20:5). He distorts the intentions of the mob, changing their desire to have sexual relations with him to "they intended to *kill* me." In addition, he leaves out his significant role in the woman's death by failing to mention that he seized her and handed her over to the men. Thus, the Levite's incongruous speech serves to vilify the men of Gibeah and to distance himself from any wrongdoing.[46] Lasine is correct in pointing out that the reader is "intended to notice the blatant contradiction between the two accounts, in order to conclude that the Levite is an irresponsible liar."[47]

Hence, the Levite's finals words serve to confirm a critical judgment upon the character. This assessment of the Levite calls into question his righteous indignation, and, hence, the appropriateness of his call to battle. While the men of Gibeah are certainly deserving of punishment—the parallel with the Sodom and Gomorrah story prepares the reader for the judgment of the evil men—the Levite's incongruous words taint the rationale for the retribution with impropriety. Later in the story, the tribes' excessively violent retaliation on Benjamin, including their bizarre attempt to repopulate the tribe, will serve to tarnish further the male reactions to rape.

Risk, Excess, and Modernity (London: Routledge, 1994). For an introduction to this topic, including a discussion of the theological significance of the grotesque, see Wilson Yates, "An Introduction to the Grotesque: Theoretical and Theological Considerations," in *The Grotesque in Art and Literature: Theological Reflections* (ed. James Luther Adams and Wilson Yates; Grand Rapids: Eerdmans, 1997), 1–68.

[45] For further discussion, see Trible, *Texts of Terror*, 82; Lasine, "Guest and Host," 48–49; Exum, *Fragmented Women*, 186; and Olson, "Book of Judges," 884–85.

[46] Olson, "Book of Judges," 884–85.

[47] Lasine, "Guest and Host," 48.

Throughout the Levite's incongruous response, the rape is used to fuel the outrage against Gibeah. In this way, the rape continues to function within the story as a catalyst for the excessive violence that follows. However, the Levite's negative characterization, including his skewed account of the events in 20:4–7, obscures the easy movement from rape to retaliation for the reader. The Levite's statements emphasize that the "lords of Gibeah" raped (עָנּוּ) his concubine, after which she died. Thus, the rationale for the retribution that follows continues to be the rape of the woman. However, the incongruity of the Levite's actions in this story—his indifference, his callousness, and his deceit—serves to distance the reader from the character's version of the story and creates suspicion concerning the Levite's motivation for calling the tribes to war. While the Levite's tale of rape and death motivates the tribes to seek retaliation, his incongruous words serve to distance the reader from the retributive acts of violence that follow. This reaction from the reader helps to establish the perspective of the narrator that this is an evil period of social and moral decline. Even the horrible acts of a riotous mob of men, which in Israel's memory brought about the judgment of God (Sodom and Gomorrah), creates a retaliatory response that is from its inception tainted with morally questionable speech and behavior.

The Tribes' Response

The gathered tribes of Israel respond to the Levite's incongruous story of rape and death with a retaliation on Gibeah and Benjamin that is excessively violent and absurd. The tribes of Israel decide to make Gibeah pay for the crimes committed. They adopt the language of outrage that was indicative of the Levite's distorted characterization of the violation. The tribes will carry out vengeance upon the inhabitants of Gibeah for "all of the disgrace which they did" (כָּל־הַנְּבָלָה אֲשֶׁר עָשָׂה, v. 10). The unity of their resolve takes shape in 20:11 through the language of "all the men of Israel" acting as "one man." By adopting the Levite's sense of indignation, the tribes have made the Levite's cause their own. Gibeah's act of disgrace now becomes an issue for all of Israel. As stated above, the reader experienced the words of the Levite as incongruous with the narrated events of the story, and, hence, his recounting of the deed was viewed negatively. The tribes' unconditional acceptance of the Levite's version of the story sets the reader up to see the retaliation that follows in a similarly critical light.

Excessive violence characterizes Israel's post-rape response. Collectively, the tribes demand that Benjamin give up the wicked men of Gibeah (20:13). When the Benjaminites refuse, war ensues. Over the course of three days, approximately 25,000 Benjaminites and 40,000 other Israelites fall in battle. The end result of the conflict leaves only six hundred men left from the tribe of Benjamin. The narrator's description of the massive amount of casualties and the near extinction of an entire tribe points to the extent of the war's violence. When the battle is put within the full context of Judg 19, the excessive nature of the violence becomes more appalling. The rape and murder of a woman has ignited a retaliation that leads to the killing of over 65,000 warriors in Israel and the near extinction of Benjamin. In addition, as stated above, the outrage that caused the civil war was fueled by the Levite's distorted recounting of the events at Gibeah. In the end, there is no appropriate response to the woman's rape, and 65,000 men are killed in battle based on the distorted words of one Levite.

The aftermath of the holy/civil war in Chapter 20 breeds more absurdity and violence in Chapter 21. In response to the near extinction of the tribe of Benjamin, the other Israelites, who were responsible for the tribe's decimation, return to Bethel and again lift their voices in weeping to the LORD. This time, however, their reason for appealing to Yahweh is due to the fact that one of their tribes, Benjamin, is "lacking" (לְהִפָּקֵד, v. 3). The irony of this plea is obvious to the reader. In this absurd, inverted world, not only does the nation war with itself, but the Israelites proceed to weep for the very tribe that they put to the sword. The first verse of Chapter 21 complicates their request further since the Israelites had vowed not to give their daughters in marriage to Benjamin. Hence, the quandary that is before Israel is doubly self-imposed.

If the Israelites' request to Yahweh is absurd, their solution moves the reader even further into the realm of the unbelievable. In 21:8, after offering burnt offerings and sacrifices to the LORD, the Israelites determine that Jabesh-gilead is deserving of death since they failed to answer the call to battle at Mizpah. The tribes had earlier sworn הַשְּׁבוּעָה הַגְּדוֹלָה, "a great oath" (21:5), that whoever did not respond to the battle call at Mizpah would be put to death.[48] 12,000 Israelite men march on Jabesh-Gilead to attack it with the order

---

[48] The language of swearing oaths in conjunction with the location of Mizpah recalls an earlier scene in Judges where Jephthah swears a vow (נָדַר) at Mizpah in order to secure victory

that they are to put to the sword the inhabitants, including "the women and children" (v. 10). This last phrase, which points to the most vulnerable part of the social group, highlights the extent of the destruction and the inhumanity of the violence. In v. 11, the narrator uses the language of holy war through the verb חָרַם ("devote to destruction" in the Hiphil), so that the reader is aware of the irony of this battle. Holy war among Israelites almost wiped out Benjamin, and holy war on an Israelite city (Jabesh-gilead) will help to replenish the decimated tribe. 400 virgins are found within Jabesh-gilead, and they are given to the Benjaminites as an offering of peace.

These 400 women, however, were not enough. Hence, the elders of the congregation and the people instruct the Benjaminites to lie in wait and abduct (וַחֲטַפְתֶּם, from the root חטף, "seize") the daughters of Shiloh when they come out to dance for their annual festival (vv. 20–21). The Benjaminites heed the Israelites' plan and the tribe is saved from extinction. Thus, the Israelites are successful in their attempts to replenish the tribe of Benjamin. The means by which they obtain this success, however, stretches the reader beyond the limits of reason. Trible summarizes well the reader's incredulity toward the men in this story:

> Entrusted to Israelite men, the story of the concubine justifies the expansion of violence against women. What these men claim to abhor, they have reenacted with vengeance. They have captured, betrayed, raped, and scattered four hundred virgins of Jabesh-gilead and two hundred daughters of Shiloh. Furthermore, they have tortured and murdered all the women of Benjamin and all the married women of Jabesh-gilead. Israelite males have dismembered the corporate body of Israelite females. Inasmuch as men have done it unto one of the least of women, they have done it unto many.[49]

Hence, in Judg 20–21, the original incongruous outrage of the Levite escalates into civil war and further retributive violence. In the end, the rape of one woman leads to further excessive violence against other men, women, and

---

over the Ammonites (Judg 11:29–31). He promises to offer up as a sacrifice whoever comes out of his house to meet him. After the battle, his only child, his daughter, comes out of his house first. Jephthah tragically makes good on his vow, and his daughter is sacrificed. Hence, the association of vows at Mizpah within the context of holy war recalls to the reader's mind the potential disaster of this configuration of narrative elements. This echo of details sets the reader up for the absurd turn of events that follow (See Olson, "Book of Judges," 886).

[49] Trible, *Texts of Terror*, 83–84.

children. At the end of the book, the topsy-turvy world of Judg 17–21 needs no further comment. The judgment of the reader is clear. The narrator, however, seals this tomb with a final inscription, "In those days there was no king in Israel; every man did what was right in his own eyes" (21:25).

Social Fragmentation: Social and Moral Collapse in a Time without a King

The third element of the family resemblance, social fragmentation, can already be seen in much of the preceding discussion. The division of Israel against itself, as seen in the civil war with Benjamin, is a prominent example at the conclusion of Judges of how this period without a king fails, resulting in moral and social erosion. The fragmentation of Israel, the roots of which begins earlier in the book, is exacerbated by the excessive male violence that results from the rape of the Levite's concubine.

The narrator makes this idea clear through an allusion to earlier themes in Judges. The language of Judg 20:18 ff., like the language of Judg 1:1–2, describes holy war that is justified through the word of Yahweh. However, at the beginning of the book of Judges, Israel's holy war is against the Canaanites within the context of Israelite settlement. Israel inquires of the LORD, and Judah is chosen as the first tribe to go up against the Canaanites. They are successful as predicted. Thus, Judah is singled out for specific honor. Chapter 20 has similar elements but departs in noticeable ways from Judg 1. The Israelites go to Bethel to inquire of the LORD (20:18). Their inquiry, however, is about which tribe should go up against Benjamin. Hence, their request is thick with irony. Holy war against the Canaanites has become holy war within Israel. Like the first story, Judah is chosen to go up first against the Benjaminites. Unlike Judges 1, they are routed, with 22,000 killed. The battle continues for three days, with the tribes of Israel suffering heavy losses. After each defeat to the Benjaminites, the Israelites cry out to Yahweh, which is typical of their response throughout the book of Judges when their enemies oppress them.[50] Again, the irony within these closing chapters is that the enemy is from within Israel. The LORD does not insure victory to the Israelites until the third day, after which Benjamin is defeated almost to the point of

---

[50] See 3:9, 15; 4:3; 6:6; and 10:10.

extinction. Hence, Israel's attempt to vindicate the Levite leads to a retaliation that almost wipes out an entire tribe from among Israel.

The ironic perspective created by the narrator allows the reader to see that this holy war is, in fact, a gross exhibition of self-mutilation. Israel has become divided against itself. In this way, the woman's divided body has become a symbol of the divided tribes. Alice Keefe summarizes well this idea:

> The dismembered body of the concubine stands contiguous with the civil war, a metonym for a bloody and divided Israel. The point of the war narrative emerges as it is refracted through the image of the woman's tortured and broken body, so that the rape becomes the interpretive key for assessing the meaning of Israel's internecine violence. Rape, which marks not only the beginning, but also the end of this final narrative in Judges, frames the civil war in images which expose the reality of such a war as the brokenness of the body and life of the Israelite community.[51]

At the end of the book of Judges, Israel is warring against itself, raping and killing many others to replenish a tribe that was decimated through the excessively violent holy war that was a civil war. The end of this period is marked with social and moral decline. Social fragmentation has resulted from an initial retaliation that was based in one man's outrage against Gibeah. As scholars have recognized, the narrated setting in the closing chapter of Judges describes "an 'inverted world' where actions are often ludicrous, absurd and self-defeating."[52]

Conclusion

The rape of a Levite's concubine in Judg 19 follows the progression of an initial rape that leads to excessive violence and results in social fragmentation. Thus, this rape story bears its family resemblance to the other rape narratives in the Hebrew Bible. Forces and themes of religious, moral, and social decline within

---

[51] Keefe, "Rapes of Women," 86. Keefe's argument that the raped women's bodies in the rape texts serve as a metonym for Israel's larger social body works well within the context of the book of Judges. The concubine's divided body is clearly a symbol for divided Israel within this narrative. In the other rape texts, however, especially Gen 34, the symbolic function of the raped women within the narratives is less clear (see my discussion of Keefe's article above in Chapter 1). The symbolization of "woman" for larger social bodies in the Hebrew Bible is well attested (for examples, see Bird, *Missing Persons*, 64–65).

[52] Lasine, "Guest and Host," 37.

the larger narrative context determine the shape of this particular text. Judg 17–
21 describes a period of increasing chaos, a time when "there was no king in
Israel" and "every man did what was right in his own eyes" (17:6, 21:25). The
rape narrative of Judg 19 is set within the context of two contrasting hospitality
scenes. Allusions to the Sodom and Gomorrah legend show how even the
custom of protecting and providing for a guest go awry in an inverted world.
The rape itself acts as a problematic catalyst for the civil war that ensues—a
battle that nearly destroys the entire tribe of Benjamin. The post-rape violence,
which is narrated as a holy war of Israel with itself, degenerates into further
violence and abduction of women in order to repopulate the decimated tribe.
The concluding scene at the end of the book of Judges is one of religious,
moral, and social demise. Forces of chaos within the topsy-turvy world at the
end of the period of Judges cause this story to move from the initial rape to
excessive violence of Israel with itself. The social disintegration that results
confirms the explicit judgment of the narrator upon this period (17:6, 21:25)
and brings this tale to its dramatic end.

CHAPTER FOUR

2 Samuel 13:1–22: The Rape of Tamar and the Fragmentation of a Kingdom

Introduction

2 Sam 13:1–22 describes the rape of Tamar, daughter of David, at the hands of her half-brother Amnon. In this chapter, as in the previous chapters, I will show how this text moves through the progression of rape to excessive male violence to social fragmentation. Forces that are already at work within the narrative, however, determine the movement of this text through the characteristic progression of its family resemblance. The story is framed within the complicated issues of royal succession that run throughout 2 Sam 9–20. Nathan's oracle of judgment on David and his house begins to take shape through the rape itself and in its aftermath. Hence, the rape serves to ignite forces of rivalry and contention that are implied within a context of succession and foretold through Nathan's oracle. The paradigmatic king of Israel and his family are marked with violence, conflict, and social fragmentation. The narrative analysis below highlights how the rape contributes to these dynamics by fueling the relational hostilities assumed within the story. The post-rape responses lead to a sibling rivalry that is marked by violent retaliation. The resulting social fragmentation is represented through the royal family's discord and strife, culminating in Absalom's rebellion against David. As Nathan had prophesied, the sword will end up dividing David's house against itself.

Scholars have long recognized the literary unity of certain sections within the books of Samuel, especially the so-called Succession Narrative or Court

History. Modern scholarship on this topic has been heavily influenced by the work of Leonhard Rost, who recognized royal succession as being a central and unifying theme for large segments of 2 Samuel and the first two chapters of 1 Kings.[1] Following the lead of Rost, most scholars have treated 2 Sam 9–20 and 1 Kgs 1–2 as a literary unit, though there has been disagreement on where the unit begins and ends.[2] More recent scholarship has emphasized literary and narrative approaches to these texts. Such interpretations have highlighted additional themes beyond succession such as David and the sons of Zeruiah, the judgment-eliciting parable, the woman and the spies, the two messengers, and the letter of death.[3] Numerous articles and books have provided narrative and literary-critical readings of 2 Sam 13 in particular.[4] The present

---

[1] See Leonhard Rost, *The Succession to the Throne of David*, (trans. Michael D. Rutter and David M. Gunn; introduction by Edward Ball; Historical Texts and Interpreters in Biblical Scholarship 1; ed. John W. Rogerson; Sheffield: Almond, 1982), which is a translation of *Die Überlieferung von der Thronnachfolge Davids* (BWANT 3/6; Stuttgart: Kohlhammer, 1926), later reprinted in *Das kleine Credo und andere Studien zum Alten Testament* (Heidelberg: Quelle und Meyer, 1965), 119–253.

[2] For scholarly discussion on the Succession Narrative see R. N. Whybray, *The Succession Narrative: A Study of II Sam. 9–20 and I Kings 1 and 2*, SBT² 9 (Naperville, IL: Allenson, 1968); James W. Flanagan, "Court History or Succession Document? A Study of 2 Sam 9–20 and 1 Kings 1–2," *JBL* 91 (1972): 172–81; David M. Gunn, *The Story of King David: Genre and Interpretation* (JSOTSup 6; Sheffield: JSOT Press, 1978), 19–34; Charles Conroy, *Absalom Absalom! Narrative and Language in 2 Sam 13–20* (AnBib 8; Rome: Biblical Institute, 1978), 1–13; P. Kyle McCarter, Jr., "'Plots, True or False.' The Succession Narrative as Court Apologetic," *Int* 35 (1981): 355–67; idem, *2 Samuel: A New Translation with Introduction, Notes and Commentary* (AB 9; New York: Doubleday, 1984), 9–16; Arnold A. Anderson, *2 Samuel* (WBC 11; Waco: Word, 1989), xxv–xxxvi; Harold O. Forshey, "Court Narrative (2 Samuel 9–1 Kings 2)" *ABD* 1:1172–79.

[3] Gunn, *King David*, 37–62. Literary and narrative critical approaches to this material are numerous. See also George P. Ridout, "Prose Compositional Techniques in the Succession Narrative (2 Sam. 7, 9–10; 1 Kings 1–2)" (Ph.D. dissertation, Graduate Theological Union, 1974); Conroy, *Absalom Absalom!*; J. P. Fokkelman, *King David (II Sam. 9–20 and I Kings 1–2)*, vol. 1 of *Narrative Art and Poetry in the Books of Samuel: A Full Interpretation Based on Stylistic and Structural Analyses* (Assen: Van Gorcum, 1981); Robert Polzin, *David and the Deuteronomist:2 Samuel* (vol. 3 of *A Literary Study of the Deuteronomic History*; Indiana Studies in Biblical Literature; ed. Herbert Marks and Robert Polzin; Bloomington: Indiana University Press, 1993).

[4] See George Ridout, "The Rape of Tamar: A Rhetorical Analysis of 2 Sam 13:1–22," in *Rhetorical Criticism: Essays in Honor of James Muilenburg* (ed. Jared J. Jackson and Martin Kessler; Pittsburgh Theological Monograph Series 1; Pittsburgh: Pickwick, 1974), 75–84; Trible, *Texts of Terror*, 37–63; Fokkelien van Dijk-Hemmes, "Tamar and the Limits of Patriarchy: Between Rape and Seduction (2 Samuel 13 and Genesis 38)," in *Anti-Covenant: Counter-Reading Women's Lives in the*

interpretation will build off the work of other scholars who have explored the literary features of this text. This narrative analysis, however, will emphasize the particular ways in which this text moves through the progression of rape → violent male responses → social fragmentation.

The Context of Rape: Judgment and Succession

Forces of prophetic judgment and royal succession shape the meaning of rape in 2 Sam 13:1–22. The rape of Tamar finds its larger literary context within the events that precede and follow the story. Scholars have recognized a shift in emphasis within the stories about David in 2 Sam 11–12, which describes David's twofold sin of adultery with Bathsheba and murder of Uriah, her husband.[5] The consequences of David's actions result in Yahweh's explicit judgment of the king. This judgment finds expression in the parable of Nathan and the prophet's subsequent oracle (12:1–14). Because David had killed Uriah "with [the] sword" (בְּחֶרֶב) and taken (לקח) Bathsheba, "the sword will not depart" (לֹא־תָסוּר חֶרֶב) from the king's house forever (12:10). In addition, Yahweh will take (לקח) David's wives and give them to another (12:11). Hence, what David has done unto others, Yahweh will now do unto the king.[6]

Yahweh's judgment casts an ominous shadow over the events that will follow. The paradigm of prophetic word/fulfillment, characteristic within the Deuteronomistic History, causes the reader to anticipate this oracle's realization in the ensuing chapters. Thus, the reader is prepared to see how the sword (חֶרֶב), i.e., violence and murder, will divide David's family against itself and

---

Hebrew Bible (ed. Mieke Bal; JSOTSup 81; Bible and Literature Series 22; Sheffield: Almond, 1989), 135–56; William H. Propp, "Kingship in 2 Samuel 13," *CBQ* 55 (1993): 39–53; and, Mark Gray, "Amnon: A Chip Off the Old Block? Rhetorical Strategy in 2 Samuel 13.7–15, The Rape of Tamar and the Humiliation of the Poor," *JSOT* 77 (1998): 39–54.

[5] Rolf A. Carlson, *David, the Chosen King: A Traditio-Historical Approach to the Second Book of Samuel* (Stockholm: Almqvist & Wiksell, 1964), 140–162; Alter, *Art of Biblical Narrative*, 119; Walter Brueggemann, *David's Truth in Israel's Imagination and Memory* (2nd ed.; Minneapolis: Fortress, 2002), 39–43.

[6] MAL A § 55, which details punishment for the rape of an unattached girl, allows for the father of the girl to rape the perpetrator's wife. Hence, Yahweh's judgment on David's house has overtones of *lex talionis*, a corresponding act of sexual offense and violence as punishment for crimes committed.

how other men will forcibly take the women of the royal house. 2 Sam 13:1–22 narrates the first such occurrence of these events.

The rape of Tamar, an act of sexual violence of Amnon on his half-sister, points to the intra-familial nature of the violation. The rape sets off family dynamics of sibling rivalry that lead to Absalom's retaliation against Amnon. As I will show below, Absalom's revenge is bound up in issues of royal succession and revenge. Thus, the reader is able to see clearly how this rape narrative sets in motion elements of Nathan's oracle. David's house divides through issues of sex and violence, which corresponds to David's sins of adultery and murder. His future line is fraught with sibling rivalry. Hence, issues of royal succession have been complicated. Yahweh's judgment exposes the shame that marks David's house.[7] What is made explicit through prophetic utterance is fulfilled implicitly through the narrator's artful crafting of the events that follow.[8]

Before I examine how this text moves through the progression of rape → violent male responses → social fragmentation, some comments on the structure of this passage will prove helpful. Within the narrative's careful shaping of the events, themes of love and hate emerge that will prove important for understanding the relational dynamics that move this narrative from the rape to its post-rape responses and intra-familial conflict. The structure of 2 Sam 13 is intricate in its thematic details, though the plot follows a simple

---

[7] Matthews and Benjamin say the following about rape: "Rape declares a household to be insolvent or shamed, and, therefore, unable to fulfill its responsibilities to the village. It confirms that the father of a household has left its mothers and virgins in harm's way, and, therefore, must be impeached" (Matthews and Benjamin, "Amnon and Tamar," 346). While shame is a good descriptor of some of the cultural dynamics at work in this specific text, it does not take into full account the "honor," with which Yahweh and the Dtr editors have characterized David's house within the larger literary context (e.g., 2 Sam 7:16).

[8] Gerhard von Rad has provided an excellent study that examines the hidden quality of God within the succession narrative. He argues that this narrative emphasizes human freedom or the "secular," but that God continues to work in and through the narrative. Von Rad states, "God's activity is not experienced now as something miraculous and intermittent, as in the old 'holy wars'. It is hidden to the natural eye, but is understood to be more continuous and all-embracing. God works in every sphere of life, public as well as private, in profane matters no less than in religious ones" ("The Beginnings of Historical Writing in Ancient Israel," in *The Problem of the Hexateuch and Other Essays* [trans. E. W. Trueman Dicken; Edinburgh: Oliver and Boyd, 1966], 202).

progression of pre-rape desire, rape, and post-rape response. There are three scenes:

Scene One (vv. 1–9a)	Amnon's Love for Tamar and the Scheme to Seduce Her
Scene Two (vv. 9b–17)	The Crime of Amnon: The Rape of Tamar (Love Turns to Hate)
Scene Three (vv. 18–22)	Post-Rape Responses—Tamar's Mourning, David's Passive Anger, Absalom's Silent Hatred of Amnon

The actual act of rape is at the center of the narrative and provides the fulcrum point between the pre-rape and post-rape actions and exchanges.[9] Shimon Bar-Efrat, by studying the ways in which characters enter and exit this story, adds a more relational dimension to the structure provided above.[10] The story moves according to the encounter of different pairs of characters. The second character in each pair becomes the first in the next sequence of characters:

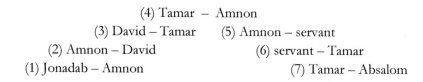

Bar-Efrat notes that Tamar and Amnon meet at the central event in the story, the rape. Amnon occurs in the first two pairs of exchanges, whereas Tamar

---

[9] Ridout, followed and modified by Fokkelman and van Dijk-Hemmes, has proposed a convincing structure for 2 Sam 13 that suggests the story's elaborate and well-organized symmetry of themes (See, Ridout, "Rape of Tamar," 81; Fokkelman, *King David*, 100; and, van Dijk-Hemmes "Limits of Patriarchy," 138. Note, however, that Fokkelman's proposal is working from Ridout's 1971 dissertation, which Ridout modifies in his later article).

[10] It should be noted that Bar-Efrat also proposes a different structure for the story: the exposition (vv. 1–3); Jonadab and Amnon (vv. 4–5); Amnon and David (v. 6); David and Tamar (v. 7); Tamar and Amnon (vv. 8–16); Amnon and the servant (v. 17); the servant and Tamar (v. 18); Tamar and Absalom (vv. 19–20); and conclusion (vv. 21–22). See Bar-Efrat, *Narrative Art*, 278. Though Bar-Efrat and Ridout propose different divisions for the narrative structure, Fokkelman suggests that the two are complementary in that they both direct the reader's attention to the symmetry of the passage (*King David*, 102).

appears in the last two. Hence, leading up to the rape, Amnon and his desire dominate the narrative. After the rape, however, the narrator's focus is on Tamar and the post-rape responses.

Fokkelman notes within Bar-Efrat's scheme the emotive movement in the story. At the beginning of the chapter, the narrator describes Amnon's *love* (וַיֶּאֱהָבֶהָ) for Tamar. At the end of the narrative, Absalom is described in terms of his *hate* (שָׂנֵא) of Amnon. The meeting of Tamar and Amnon marks the transition from *love* to *hate* in Amnon's pre-rape and post-rape state. Hence, Fokkelman suggests that the movement of emotion within the text can be diagramed: *love* ➔ *love/hate* ➔ *hate*.[11] When one takes into consideration the relational configurations in the text, the emotive movement is suggestive of the dynamic that propels the story toward the retributive violence that ensues later in the chapter. The following progression emerges:

Amnon *loves* Tamar/Absalom's sister (v. 1)
Amnon *loves/hates* Tamar (vv. 8–16)
Absalom/because of his sister Tamar (v. 22) *hates* Amnon

Hence, it is Absalom's tie to his sister that brings him into the dynamic of love/hate, fueling his revenge. This tie is made explicit by the narrator's characterization of Tamar in v. 1 and v. 22 as Absalom's sister. Thus, the structure of this well-crafted narrative provides the meaning that the content makes clear through the story's telling. Though the form of the narrative provides symmetry between the pre-rape desire and post-rape responses, the plot's progression moves forward toward retribution and conflict. What begins as a plan hatched by Jonadab and Amnon eventually leads to Absalom's angry but silent resolve to avenge the rape of his sister.

The Rape Text Progression

The narrative context described above provides the thematic and relational dynamics that propel this story through the progression of rape ➔ male response of violence ➔ social fragmentation. Amnon's rape of his half-sister Tamar leads to the further retributive violence of Absalom, Tamar's brother. Themes of intra-familial violence and rivalry, within the context of royal

---

[11] Fokkelman, *King David*, 102.

succession, are made clear throughout the story. The characterization of the different parties involved, including their motivations of love and hate, paint a picture of a family in conflict.

Within the context of prophetic judgment, this scene points to the fulfillment of Nathan's oracle. David's house will divide against itself with brother killing brother and son rebelling against father. The precipitating event, the rape of Tamar, suggests how love and hate are intermingled in the royal family. Love is expressed in a perverted and exploitative way, displaying the violence of one of David's sons on his daughter. In this twisted and judged kingdom, love translates into the rape of a virgin in the king's house. Sexual misconduct and violence bring conflict into the family of David, providing the roots to Absalom's revenge and eventual rebellion against his father. The sword (חֶרֶב) with which David slew Uriah the Hittite has now come back to divide his house. As in the previous rape narratives, the plot progresses to further male violence, leading to social, and in this case, familial fragmentation.

The Rape of Tamar

Within 2 Sam 13, the narrator sets up the relational configurations of the sexual violation through the initial characterizations of the parties involved. These portraits shape the reader's understanding of the complex relational dynamics within the story and provide the background to the different characters' love and hate for each other. Amnon's deceitful planning prior to the rape and his revulsion of Tamar after the act, coupled with his sister's extended pleas of resistance, serves to condemn Amnon in the eyes of the reader and anticipates the male responses that follow the sexual violation. David's role in the plotting of Tamar's seduction is one of unknowing complicity. The reader concludes that David's authority is wavering, a judgment that is confirmed when he is conflicted in his response to the rape. Thus, Absalom's angry reaction becomes a point of contrast with his father's lack of resolve to do anything to Amnon. In the end, Tamar is left desolate in her brother Absalom's house, leading the reader to the conclusion that her rape only serves as a pretext to the forces of rivalry and succession that dominate this story.

The Relational Dynamics of Rape in David's House

The narrator's characterizations at the beginning of 2 Sam 13 set the stage for the conflict that results and point the reader to the relational dynamics that

serve to complicate the rape. Each of the characters within vv. 1–2 is described
in terms of his/her relationship to others within the family. Absalom is
described as David's son (בֶּן־דָּוִד). He is also linked possessively, through the
preposition לְ, to his sister, Tamar (לְאַבְשָׁלוֹם...אָחוֹת). Tamar, however, is
characterized in terms of her appearance, i.e., she is beautiful (יָפָה). Though
most of Chapter 13 will focus on Tamar, the narrator makes explicit that she is
related to her brother Absalom—a connection that foreshadows the conflict
resulting from the rape. This opening characterization suggests that when
Amnon commits a crime against Tamar, his actions will have consequences on
her brother Absalom.

Similar to his half-brother, Amnon is also described in relation to his father
(בֶּן־דָּוִד). Hence, Amnon and Absalom share the title "son of David," making
them both potential successors to the throne, though Amnon is the firstborn (2
Sam 3:2). The brothers' relationships to Tamar, however, differ. Whereas
Absalom is the brother of Tamar, Amnon is described in terms of his feelings
for his half-sister. In 13:1b, the narrator says that Amnon "loved her" (וַיֶּאֱהָבֶהָ).
Thus, right from the beginning, the narrator has set up a tension that will
continue throughout this story. Amnon is in love with his half-sister, Tamar,
and this love will have a direct effect upon her brother Absalom. Tamar's
characterization as a beautiful woman comes between the narrator's comments
about Absalom and Amnon. Hence, structurally the sister stands between these
two brothers.[12] As the plot unfolds, she becomes a point of rivalry between the
men.

The narrator adds to the tension that is created through these initial
characterizations by further describing Amnon's love for Tamar. Amnon is
distressed to the point of making himself sick "on account of Tamar his sister"
(בַּעֲבוּר תָּמָר אֲחֹתוֹ). The first two verbs—וַיֵּצֶר, "he was distressed," and
לְהִתְחַלּוֹת, from the root חלה, "make oneself sick"—point to the extent and
intensity of Amnon's love. The phrase "his sister" highlights the fact that his
love is endogamous, within the bounds of his own family.[13] Thus, Amnon's

---

[12] Trible, *Texts of Terror*, 38; Bar-Efrat, *Narrative Art*, 241.

[13] Most scholars do not think that incest is the issue. For discussion of this topic, see
Matthews and Benjamin, "Amnon and Tamar," 351; Propp, "Kinship in 2 Sam 13," 39–53; Bar-
Efrat, *Narrative Art*, 239–40. See, however, McCarter, *2 Samuel*, 323–24.

love will be complicated within the nexus of family relationships described in 13:1.

The narrator further characterizes Tamar by her status, i.e., she is a virgin (בְּתוּלָה). Her identity, therefore, is described in terms of her sexuality and status in relation to marriage.[14] While Tamar's virginity characterizes her as available for marriage, the description of Amnon's feelings in 13:2, points to her inaccessibility: "it was too difficult in the eyes of Amnon to do anything to her." The narrator does not make explicit why Amnon finds it "too difficult" to act on his passion. This last phrase, which immediately follows Tamar's description as a virgin, has caused some commentators to argue that Amnon sees Tamar as unattainable due to her pre-marital status. Unmarried women within the royal house were often well protected, and contact with men was closely monitored.[15] This explanation, however, is contradicted by the ease with which David sends Tamar to Amnon later in the scene (v. 7). Given the fact that v. 1 describes Tamar as Absalom's sister, a more likely explanation is that the narrator has chosen to frame Amnon's difficulty within the complex web of family relationships. That is, Amnon sees it as impossible to do anything about his feelings because of Tamar's relationship to others within the family, namely, her blood-ties to Absalom. Since Absalom and Amnon are rival successors to the throne, Amnon's "love" for Tamar is all the more complicated, if not impossible. Thus, when Amnon is confiding to Jonadab about his problem later in v. 4, he says, "I love Tamar, my brother Absalom's sister." Hence, for Amnon, his love is impossible to act on since the object of his desire is the sister of his half-brother. Any action directed at Tamar will produce a reaction

---

[14] Matthews and Benjamin emphasize the economic connotations of virginity within the culture of honor and shame. See "Amnon and Tamar," 342–46.

[15] See McCarter (2 Samuel, 321) following Peter R. Ackroyd, The Second Book of Samuel (CBC; London: Cambridge, 19770, 321. See also Hans Wilhelm Hertzberg, I and II Samuel: A Commentary (trans. J. S. Bowden; OTL; London: SCM, 1964), 323; Arnold A. Anderson, 2 Samuel, 174; Gordon J. Wenham, "bᵉtûlāh: A Girl of Marriageable Age," VT 22 (1972): 326–48; Matthews and Benjamin, "Amnon and Tamar," 345–46. For more general discussion of bᵉtûlāh, which means "woman of marriageable age," see Frymer-Kensky, "Virginity in the Bible," 79–96; and Day, "From the Child Is Born the Woman: the Story of Jephthah's Daughter," in Gender and Difference, 58–60. See also Walls' discussion about "liminal" young women in the ancient world, who are labeled as either "virgin" or "whore" because of their deviation from the social norm (Neal H. Walls, The Goddess Anat In Ugaritic Myth [SBLDS 135; Atlanta: Scholars Press, 1992], 21–26).

from her brother Absalom, especially when situated within the complex and competitive issues of royal succession.

The issues of family tension and royal succession that hover around Amnon's distorted love for Tamar will be important for understanding the reactions of David and Absalom following the rape. It also points to the fact that the rape is internal to the family of David, occurring between half-brother and half-sister. Viewed within the larger narrative context of Yahweh's judgment in 2 Sam 12, the rape becomes the first example of how רָעָה, "calamity," arises within the house of David (12:11). Sexual misconduct and violence characterize David's sin and judgment, as Nathan's oracle makes clear. The rape of Tamar represents a type of sexual violation that exemplifies how sex and violence divide David's house. It also anticipates the future strife within the family since the rape ignites hostilities between two rival brothers.

Setting the Stage for Rape: The Plot to Seduce Tamar

The rape of Tamar is set within the context of Amnon's larger plan, conceived by Jonadab, to seduce his half-sister. Before turning to the meaning of the rape itself, conclusions can be drawn from Amnon's scheming that are helpful for the purposes of the present interpretation. First, Jonadab constructs a plan that uses ambiguous speech in order to deceive David into letting Tamar attend to the supposedly sick Amnon. This deceptive plan will contribute to a particular characterization of Amnon that will be important for understanding the rape and the male responses that follow.

In 13:3, with the entrance of Amnon's friend, Jonadab, a plan is formulated that will alleviate Amnon's frustration by helping him to act on his obsession. Jonadab's counsel takes shape in v. 4. He asks Amnon about the source of his trouble. The friend's question contrasts Amnon's present state with his position of status. Jonadab asks, "Why are you so downcast (דַּל), son of the king (בֶּן־הַמֶּלֶךְ)?" Amnon's condition, i.e., his sickly state, does not befit the potential heir to the throne.[16] The king's son responds with what the narrator had made clear in v. 1—Amnon is sick on account of his love for his sister. As suggested earlier, the words of Amnon's response suggest the familial complications of this "love":

---

[16] Bar-Efrat, *Narrative Art*, 251.

אֶת־תָּמָר אֲחוֹת אַבְשָׁלֹם אָחִי אֲנִי אֹהֵב

I love Tamar, my brother Absalom's sister (v. 4b)

Tamar, the object of Amnon's self-described "love," is emphasized through word order. She is modified by the phrase, "the sister of Absalom, my brother," which syntactically distances Amnon (אֲנִי) further from the object of his desire. Hence, the inaccessibility of Tamar described in v. 2 is reinforced through the wording of Amnon's response to Jonadab. Each term that modifies this relational chain complicates the love of Amnon through familial ties—Tamar is Absalom's sister and Absalom is his brother. It is an understatement to suggest that the object of Amnon's "love" is relationally complex.[17]

Jonadab responds to the confession of Amnon with detailed advice in v. 5. He conceives a plan that will help Amnon to address his obsession. The friend advises the prince to "lie down" (שְׁכַב) on his bed and pretend to be sick (הִתְחָל, literally, "make yourself sick"). The verb, from the root חלה, "be weak, sick," draws the reader's attention back to the characterization of Amnon in v. 2, where he is described as being distressed to the point of making himself ill (לְהִתְחַלּוֹת). Hence, the crafty Jonadab begins his plan by using Amnon's current condition within the scheme itself. He will use Amnon's sick-love state to appeal to the compassion of David, the prince's father.

Jonadab continues by telling Amnon to wait until his father comes (בָּא) to see (רֹאה) him. He then instructs Amnon to say to David, "Let my sister Tamar come" (תָּבֹא נָא תָמָר אֲחוֹתִי). Hence, as Trible notes, Amnon will "use the coming (bô᾿) of his father to request the coming (bô᾿) of *his* sister" (her emphasis).[18] In this way, as I will show below, David unknowingly plays a key role in the plan to seduce Tamar. By using the term, "my sister" (אֲחוֹתִי) within the request, Jonadab instructs Amnon to use familial language, which is intended to alleviate David's concern about this visitation. Rather than calling Tamar, "Absalom's sister," as the narrator emphasized in v. 1, Jonadab identifies the daughter of David in relation to Amnon (אֲחוֹתִי), minimizing the politics of fraternal rivalry. Thus, Jonadab has framed the request in language of family obligation and hospitality.

---

[17] Ibid., 252.

[18] Trible, *Texts of Terror*, 41.

Moreover, the use of the root רָאה, which initially characterizes David's coming "to see" Amnon, becomes a point of emphasis for Tamar's visit in Jonadab's plan. She will come and feed Amnon bread and make it before his eyes (לְעֵינַי) so that he can see it (אֶרְאֶה). Hence, the language of sight marks the occasion of this visit and appeals to Amnon's true intention—to see his sister Tamar. In this way, Jonadab crafts a planned speech that is ambiguous enough so that David suspects nothing and specific enough so that Amnon can see how the scheme will be successful in fulfilling his desires.

The last phrase in v. 5 also carries a double meaning. וְאָכַלְתִּי מִיָּדָהּ, which translates "and I will eat from her hand," would suggest to David that Amnon is too sick to feed himself. For Amnon, however, eating from his sister's hand brings Tamar close enough to touch.[19] Hence, Jonadab's elaborately devised scheme appeals to both parties involved. It utilizes Amnon's present condition while alleviating the potential suspicion of David. The narrator's description of Jonadab is fitting; he was "a very crafty man" (v. 3).[20] The detailed elements of the scheme point to Jonadab's cunning nature.

Hence, Jonadab gives Amnon the advice that his friend needs to act upon his desire. The reader is critical, however, of this plan since the elaborate plot is tainted with deception. The request for a visit pretends to be one thing, when Amnon's intention is another. Amnon is sick, but food is not what he wants. His desire is for his virgin half-sister who is preparing the meal. Therefore, Jonadab's well-crafted advice provides Amnon with the opportunity to act out his desire through a plan intended to deceive David and his daughter. The friend does not advise Amnon to seduce his sister, though his words provide the latter with the means for doing so. When Amnon's characterization is seen within the context of the full narrative, this initial plot to seduce Tamar sets up the reader to see his actions more negatively. Rape by itself is a punishable crime, but such sexual violence, when narrated as part of a deceitful plan to seduce an unmarried maiden, makes the sexual violation all the more egregious.

---

[19] Ibid.

[20] The term "wise" (חָכָם), as many commentators point out, is morally neutral. In other words, wisdom here means that Jonadab has the intellectual capability to help Amnon out of his dilemma for good or for evil. For an excellent discussion of this topic, see Bar-Efrat, *Narrative Art*, 247–50. See also Whybray, *Succession Narrative*, 58; McCarter, and *2 Samuel*, 321; Arnold A. Anderson, *2 Samuel*, 174.

A second conclusion that can be drawn from Amnon's pre-rape scheme is tied to David's role within his son's plot. David, unsuspecting of Amnon's intention, goes along with the plan that leads to the seduction of his daughter. This plot element is important because it develops a picture of David that will contribute to the post-rape dynamics toward the end of this rape text. In v. 6, David, who is described as הַמֶּלֶךְ, responds according to the planned script— "he comes" (וַיָּבֹא) "to see" Amnon. This echoes Jonadab's initial plan, in which the coming of David (בָא) is used to ask that Tamar come (תָבֹא) to feed her brother (v. 5). The use of בוא is not unusual within these contexts. However, throughout v. 6, the vocabulary of Amnon's deeds and speech corresponds closely with Jonadab's advice. Thus, when the king comes (וַיָּבֹא), reiterating the use of בוא, the effect of this repetition suggests that Jonadab's advice is working just as he had planned. David, unaware of his oldest son's plot, concedes to Amnon's request in v. 7. Hence, the king unwittingly plays a role in Amnon and Jonadab's deceptive scheme to seduce Tamar.

Moreover, David instructs his daughter to go to "her brother Amnon's house" (בֵּית אַמְנוֹן אָחִיךְ) and "make him food" (עֲשִׂי־לוֹ הַבִּרְיָה). The use of the verb עשה, along with the noun הַבִּרְיָה, harks back to Jonadab's original advice in truncated form (cf. v. 5). Again, this echo of vocabulary confirms to the reader that the plan is going as expected. David does not know what forces he has set in motion by sending his daughter Tamar to the allegedly sick Amnon. His role in this scheme, however, is done willingly and according to plan.

Hence, David is the unknowing contributor to Jonadab and Amnon's plot. The king has agreed to fulfill his son's wishes, commanding his daughter to visit her sick brother. This fact alone does not cause the reader to think unfavorably of David since Amnon has deceived his father. However, David's unwitting participation in the seduction of his daughter, when combined with his later failure to punish Amnon after the rape, leads the reader to the conclusion that David's control over his family is waning. Amnon dupes David into helping him seduce Tamar. After the rape, David, though angry, fails to do anything. David's lack of resolve points to the weakening of the king's authority and resolve within his own house.[21] In addition, David's response, or lack of it, anticipates

---

[21] In biblical law the crime of rape is perceived as a crime against the father of the household (see Pressler, *Family Laws*, 35–43; and Cheryl B. Anderson, *Women, Ideology, and Violence*, 87–91).

the actions of Absalom, who will seek vengeance on his half-brother and rival to the throne since his father has done nothing. These dynamics—David's diminishing control over his family and Absalom's resolve to address what his father has neglected—point to the fragmenting of David's family according to the word of Yahweh. I will address these ideas further below.

Rape and Resistance

Amnon's scheme to seduce Tamar results in her rape. The scene is comprised of four key elements: Tamar's resistance to Amnon's advances; the rape itself; Amnon's post-rape response of hatred; and Tamar's plea for Amnon not to put her away. The events of this scene, including Tamar's pleadings before and after the rape and Amnon's post-rape loathing, are narrated in great detail. These elements of the story produce an important effect upon the reader that will set up the post-rape responses that follow. The combination of Tamar's pleas with Amnon's hatred of his half-sister after the violation aligns the reader with the victim and produce scorn toward the perpetrator. The detailed narration of the rape and post-rape responses of the two characters makes this crime more deplorable. As stated above, the intentional scheming and deception that preceded the rape adds further to the reader's sense of condemnation. The effect of such an assessment of Amnon's actions causes the reader to anticipate a response to address the crime. Such an outrageous offense, especially when it is described in elaborate detail, cannot go unpunished. Hence, the rape anticipates the responses of David and Absalom that follow.

Tamar's Initial Resistance. Amnon's initial attempt to lie with Tamar is met with resistance that marks her as a wise young woman in contrast to her impetuous half-brother.[22] In v. 11, as Tamar draws near (וַתַּגֵּשׁ) to feed her brother, Amnon seizes (וַיַּחֲזֶק) her, unveiling his true intentions through a double imperative: בּוֹאִי שִׁכְבִי עִמִּי אֲחוֹתִי, "Come, lie with me, my sister!" The narrator has shown previously in the story that Amnon is a man who

---

Hence, David's refusal to punish Amnon shows the father/king's growing weakness. His conflicting family loyalties complicate his royal duty to act as the administrator of justice.

[22] Of course, in a legal sense, Tamar's resistance is clear narrative evidence that she does not consent to the rape. For discussion on the issues of consent in the legal materials about rape, see Chapter 1 above.

commands people with his words. In fact, after his request to David in v. 6, imperatives shape the rest of Amnon's speaking to the end of the scene (cf. vv. 9, 10, 11, 15, and 17). Amnon, being a son the king, knows how to order people around. He does not possess, however, the ability to use or listen to reasonable speech when his passion is involved, as the rest of this scene will show. By completing his command with the relational term, "my sister" (אֲחוֹתִי), he claims for his own this member of his family's house.

Tamar responds to her brother's advances with an elaborate argument, speaking words of resistance and wise counsel in vv. 12–13. Prior to this point in the story, Tamar had been silently obedient both to David and Amnon. With her half-brother's aggressive attempt to lie with her, however, she fights back with words. Tamar's speech is emphatic in its attempt to negate Amnon's intentions. Negative particles abound. She says:

No, my brother!	אַל־אָחִי
Do *not* rape me	אַל־תְּעַנֵּנִי
for such a thing is *not* done in Israel	כִּי לֹא־יֵעָשֶׂה כֵן בְּיִשְׂרָאֵל
Do *not* do this disgraceful thing	אַל־תַּעֲשֵׂה אֶת־הַנְּבָלָה הַזֹּאת

The first phrase, "No, my brother!" is an immediate appeal to Amnon. Tamar uses the language of family (אָחִי, "my brother") to counter her attacker's forceful address (אֲחוֹתִי, "my sister"). She responds to his double imperative with two negative commands: "Do not rape me" and "Do not do this disgraceful thing."

The first command, אַל־תְּעַנֵּנִי, refers to the intended act itself and is followed by a rationale: "for such a thing is not done in Israel." Hence, Tamar appeals to larger social norms in an attempt to dissuade her aggressor. The second prohibition points to the shamefulness of the act that Amnon wants to commit—"Do not do this disgraceful thing" (הַנְּבָלָה). As discussed in earlier chapters, the term הַנְּבָלָה, "disgraceful thing," is found in all three rape narratives (Gen 34:7, Judg 19:23, 20:6). In each case, though the contexts vary, the word connotes an explicit judgment from the narrator (Gen 34:7) or the characters in the story (Judg 19:23, 20:6) on the act or intended act of rape. Within the present story, Tamar's use of הַנְּבָלָה provides moral judgment on Amnon's command, a perspective that the reader shares.

In 2 Sam 13:13, Tamar develops her case further by presenting the ramifications of Amnon's proposed act on both parties involved.[23] For herself, Tamar states that she will have no place to put her humiliation (אָנָה אוֹלִיךְ אֶת־חֶרְפָּתִי, "where would I take my shame?").[24] Hence, she uses the language of disgrace in an attempt to dissuade her brother from such a vile act (הַנְּבָלָה). Similarly, she suggests to Amnon that he will become "like one of the disgraceful fools in Israel" (כְּאַחַד הַנְּבָלִים בְּיִשְׂרָאֵל). By committing הַנְּבָלָה הַזֹּאת, Amnon will become כְּאַחַד הַנְּבָלִים בְּיִשְׂרָאֵל. Thus, Tamar shapes the consequences of Amnon's intended action within the language of social humiliation. In the culture of honor and shame, Amnon's desire to lie with Tamar will result in a loss of face for her, her brother, and the entire family. Tamar will be disgraced with nowhere to put her shame, and Amnon's reputation will be associated with foolishness and dishonor. Matthews and Benjamin correctly identify Tamar's response to Amnon as "shaming speech," which they describe as follows:

> Unlike insults and taunts, which are components of aggressive behavior and may or may not be rationally based, shaming speech is a social control mechanism designed through reasoning or the "vocabulary of embarrassment" to make the prodigal or the enemy rethink his plans. It calls on him to behave honorably, with prudent actions, not in the manner of a fool who acts in the height of passion, without considering the consequences of his act.[25]

Hence, Tamar uses shaming language in an attempt to make Amnon reevaluate his suggestion. Tamar proves herself to be an honorable woman. She is also a wise maiden of Israel, who is able to see the consequences of actions, even in the midst of a crisis situation.[26] In this way, she counters Amnon's obsessive passion with wisdom and reason.

Tamar concludes her plea with a pragmatic solution. She advises Amnon to "speak to the king, for he will not withhold me from you" (v. 13b). The daughter of David appeals to the justice of their mutual father, whom she calls

---

[23] Bar-Efrat, *Narrative Art*, 263.

[24] McCarter, *2 Samuel*, 315.

[25] Matthews and Benjamin, "Amnon and Tamar," 356. See also Bechtel, "Shame as a Sanction," 47–76.

[26] Matthews and Benjamin add that shaming speech is often used in the context of wisdom arguments ("Amnon and Tamar," 356–57).

here "king" (הַמֶּלֶךְ), in order to direct the attention of her half-brother to the one who can provide proper resolution for this situation. She argues that David would allow their union if Amnon would only ask. Her advice is practical and would avoid shame by receiving the blessing of their mutual father.[27]

Hence, Tamar has resisted the advances of Amnon by naming the act for what it is (נְבָלָה); she has utilized "shaming speech" that emphasized the consequences of Amnon's intended actions in an attempt to dissuade him; and she has offered a pragmatic solution that would receive the blessing of their father, enabling both parties to save face. In the midst of a traumatic situation, Tamar is able to articulate a persuasive argument in response to her attacker. Trible's description of Tamar as a personification of Dame Wisdom is appropriate.[28] Facing an abusive act against her person, Tamar reasons with her perpetrator, hoping that he will see the wisdom of her words.

The structure of this passage and the above characterization of Amnon confirm that such an outcome is not possible. Within this episode, the narrator juxtaposes Amnon's short imperatives, "Come, lie with me," with Tamar's lengthy and rational appeal in order to produce judgment in the mind of the reader against David's oldest son. Amnon is deceptive and impulsive, refusing to listen to reason and wisdom. Tamar uses different rhetorical strategies of survival in an attempt to dissuade Amnon from committing "this disgraceful thing" (הַנְּבָלָה הַזֹּאת). This prince, however, is unwilling to listen to the voice of wisdom (לִשְׁמֹעַ בְּקוֹלָהּ). Within Israel's traditions, Amnon would be considered a fool.[29] He heeded the advice of his friend Jonadab and was willing to carry out his plan to completion. Here, however, Amnon can hear nothing but the

---

[27] While one must take into account that Tamar's suggestion is framed within a context of potential rape, her response to this point has been well articulated within the framework of a "wisdom argument" (Matthew and Benjamin, "Amnon and Tamar," 357). It would be incongruent with her speech and disrupt the rhetorical force of the passage if she were to suggest something unseemly or foolish. As many commentators note, Tamar's advice makes the most sense within the context of endogamous marriage. Therefore, Amnon's crime cannot be considered to be incest, but must be tied to the act of rape and/or the subsequent defilement that results. For discussion see Bar-Efrat, *Narrative Art*, 239–40; Matthews and Benjamin, "Amnon and Tamar," 351; and Propp, "Kinship in 2 Samuel 13," 39–53.

[28] Trible, *Texts of Terror*, 55–57.

[29] Cf. Prov 1:7, 23:9.

screaming of his passion. As a character, he knows only how to command; and when words fail, Amnon resorts to force.

Amnon's Rape of Tamar: Love Turns to Hate. The rape of Tamar is at the center of this scene and the narrative as a whole.[30] It highlights the violence of Amnon against his sister and the resulting desolation for Tamar. The sexual violation also represents a turning point in the narrative in that Amnon's love turns into hate. This shift adds to Tamar's humiliation and heightens the reader's sense of condemnation for David's oldest son. In 2 Sam 13:14b, Amnon, having ignored Tamar's advice, proceeds to overpower his sister. The narrator describes Amnon as "stronger than her" (וַיֶּחֱזַק מִמֶּנָּה), using vocabulary that is similar to Amnon's initial seizing (וַיַּחֲזֶק) of Tamar in v. 11. The first use of the root חזק points to Amnon's attempt to physically control Tamar. The second use in v. 14b shows that he is able to force himself upon Tamar by overpowering her. The recurrence of the root before and after Tamar's verbal resistance brackets Tamar's speech within the strength (חזק) of her half-brother. Amnon literally and literarily overpowers his sister.

The rape itself is narrated with a quick succession of two verbs: "He raped her" (וַיְעַנֶּהָ) and "lay" (וַיִּשְׁכַּב) with her.[31] The deed is done in an instant. The events and planning that led up to the crime were described with great detail. Tamar's speech also provided a lengthy interruption of Amnon's intent to lie with her. When it comes to the actual rape, however, the incident is over quickly, but with devastating effect.

The Post-rape Responses of Amnon and Tamar. The devastation of the rape for Tamar is compounded by Amnon's post-rape response. The impulsive half-brother adds to the humiliation of his sister's sexual violation by hating her. The narrator describes the chorus of this deep hate:

> Amnon *hated* her (וַיִּשְׂנָאֶהָ) with a very great *hatred* (שִׂנְאָה)
> Indeed, greater was the *hatred* (הַשִּׂנְאָה) with which he *hated* her (שִׂנְאָה)
> than the love with which he loved her. (v. 15)

---

[30] See Ridout, "Rape of Tamar," 81; Fokkelman, *King David*, 100; van Dijk-Hemmes, "Limits of Patriarchy," 138; and Bar Efrat, *Narrative Art*, 278.

[31] Reading the suffixed preposition, אֹתָהּ, rather than accusative particle. For discussion see McCarter, *2 Samuel*, 317.

The contrast could not be starker. Amnon was characterized initially as being in love with his half-sister to the point of being sick (v. 2). It was his obsession with Tamar that caused Amnon to adopt Jonadab's detailed plan, deceiving both his father and his sister in the process. Having now acted out his desire sexually, Amnon's love has turned into a very great hatred (note the double use of גְּדוֹלָה in v. 15). In retrospect, the reader realizes what the narrator has shown through the telling of this story—Amnon's "love" is better described as lust. The commanding prince has added more disgrace to the initial humiliation by hating his sister. Hence, the reader's judgment echoes Tamar's earlier warning—Amnon has become כְּאַחַד הַנְּבָלִים בְּיִשְׂרָאֵל "like one of the disgraceful fools in Israel" (v. 13).

Amnon's hatred expresses itself through rejection in 15b. He says to Tamar, "Get up, go!" (קוּמִי לֵכִי). The insensitivity of these words echoes the Levite's absurd response to his raped concubine in Judg 19:28 (קוּמִי וְנֵלֵכָה, "Get up, let's go!"). In both cases, the men in the narratives are judged as callous. The Levite's command was cruel in that his concubine was either dead or too injured to get up. In the case of Amnon, however, his heartless words land on living ears and command Tamar to leave alone (the Levite's last words are the cohortative "let's go"). Amnon's harsh double command compounds the injury and desolation of his victim. In addition, the prince who gives this order through a double imperative is also the perpetrator of the crime. Such insensitivity is outrageous to the reader, evoking an even greater awareness of the wrong committed. This sense of appalling injustice anticipates the male responses that follow the rape. Such a hostile crime must be addressed by the males associated with Tamar.

Tamar's final plea serves to distance the reader further from Amnon and aligns the reader with the plight of the victim. Amnon's command prior to the rape was met with a lengthy verbal response from Tamar. In v. 16, she answers her brother's demand to leave with another appeal. She implores him not to rape her, telling him that this evil (הָרָעָה), i.e., sending her away (לְשַׁלְּחֵנִי), is greater than the other that he had committed against her. The last word of her response, לְשַׁלְּחֵנִי, "to send me away," comes from the root שלח, which is a technical term for "the dismissal of a divorced wife."[32] Hence, though the two

---

[32] McCarter, *2 Samuel*, 324.

are not married, Tamar appeals to legal language in an attempt to prohibit Amnon from sending her away.[33]

In a similar response to Tamar's first appeal, however, Amnon "would not listen" to his sister's voice (לֹא אָבָה לִשְׁמֹעַ לָהּ). The narrator uses identical language to describe Amnon's reaction to both of Tamar's pleas (cf. v. 14). The brother acts predictably. He does not hear the cry of this young maiden of Israel before or after the rape. Rather than listen to reason or an appeal from the law, Amnon commits the greater evil (הָרָעָה) of which Tamar spoke. He chooses to send her away (שׁלח). Amnon says to his servant, "Send this one (זֹאת) from me outside and bolt the door after her." Amnon's last command in the story is direct and abrupt. He asks his servant to take Tamar from his presence, referring to the former object of his "love" with the impersonal demonstrative זֹאת, "Take *this* away from me!" (v. 17). Thus, after the rape, Amnon adds more humiliation to Tamar's shame by failing to recognize her humanity.

As the servant escorts Tamar out of the room, the reader has only contempt for the domineering half-brother. Bar-Efrat states:

> The deliberate degradation of Tamar which accompanies her expulsion draws the reader's opinion of Amnon down to even lower depths. This man has deceived his father, raped his sister, cast her out of his presence and on top of it all humiliated her too. This kind of behaviour cannot fail to arouse intense revulsion, which increases as the narrative progresses.[34]

Having completely rejected Tamar's pleadings, the reader's judgment of Amnon moves toward disgust. Amnon has deceived David and Tamar in order to seduce his half-sister. He has persistently refused to hear her appeals before and after the rape. He has forced himself sexually upon Tamar and raped her. Finally, his initial love has turned into hate, which causes him to throw out his sister in spite of her pleas. Amnon's actions and words are deplorable. Such a violation and disgrace (נְבָלָה), especially when narrated with the detail found in this story, requires a response from the men associated with Tamar. Before the narrator turns to these responses, however, increased pity is evoked from the reader through an explicit description of Tamar's response to the rape.

---

[33] McCarter, following Conroy, is correct in asserting that the rape has caused Amnon to forfeit his right to dismiss her (ibid.). Cf. Conroy, *Absalom Absalom!* 33 n. 59). See also Bar-Efrat, *Narrative Art*, 267.

[34] Bar-Efrat, *Narrative Art*, 269.

After a digression in v 18, in which there is an elaborate explanation of Tamar's coat (כְּתֹנֶת פַּסִּים),[35] the narrator evokes additional pity for Tamar in v. 19 by describing in detail her mourning. Tamar's reaction is immediate and spontaneous. She puts ashes (אֵפֶר) on her head, tears (קָרְעָה) her royal robe (כְּתֹנֶת פַּסִּים), and puts her hand on her head. All three actions are expressions of mourning. The second phrase, "the long-sleeved robe, which she was wearing, she tore," has additional significance given the narrator's earlier description of the garment. The gown itself is placed first in word order to emphasize the symbolic nature of the item. By tearing up the royal garb worn by virgins, Tamar expresses particular grief about the humiliation of the rape. The gown, which was a symbol of her honor and purity, has been rent.[36]

---

[35] Scholars have debated the nature of כְּתֹנֶת פַּסִּים, which occurs only here and in Gen 37. While the explanation of the meaning of כְּתֹנֶת פַּסִּים varies among modern and ancient interpreters, the narrator makes clear the significance of this garment with the next clause, suggesting that only "virgin daughters of the king" (בְּנוֹת־הַמֶּלֶךְ הַבְּתוּלֹת) wore such robes. This intrusion to the narrative is most certainly an ancient misplaced gloss, intended to explain the significance of the robe that Tamar tears in v. 19. In the present literary context, however, the narrator's comments illumine a contrast between Amnon's hostile treatment of Tamar with her former status as a virgin daughter of David. By digressing into an explanation of כְּתֹנֶת פַּסִּים, the narrator highlights for the reader the meaning of this garment, i.e., it was only worn by virgin daughters of the king. The conflation of these terms, בְּנוֹת־הַמֶּלֶךְ הַבְּתוּלֹת, is thick with significance. Tamar's virginal status has been shattered by her half-brother. Hence the term בְּתוּלָה is ironic in this description of the coat. Tamar is wearing a garment that is intended for virgins within the house of David, but the coat cannot cover the defilement of the rape. The first two terms in the description, בְּנוֹת־הַמֶּלֶךְ, point to the fact that women of royalty wore this type of clothing. Once again, the use of this language to describe the coat is ironic. Amnon refused to listen to Tamar after the rape and has sent her away. Hence, he has treated this royal daughter of the king like a prostitute. This frock of honor cannot cover the humiliation of Tamar. Hence, though the narrator's description of the coat interrupts the action of the story, the meaning of the כְּתֹנֶת פַּסִּים functions rhetorically to fuel even further the reader's judgment of Amnon's crime. The royal robe is set in stark contrast to both the humiliation that Tamar experienced at the hands of her half-brother and the shame that she now feels as she is being escorted out by one of his servants. For more discussion on this topic, see McCarter, *2 Samuel*, 325–26. For additional discussion, see Ephraim A. Speiser, *Genesis: A Translation with Introduction and Commentary* (AB 1; New York: Doubleday, 1964), 325; George E. Mendenhall, *The Tenth Generation: The Origins of the Biblical Tradition* (Baltimore: Johns Hopkins University Press, 1973), 54–55; and Bar-Efrat, *Narrative Art*, 270.

[36] Bar-Efrat, *Narrative Art*, 270.

The narrator describes the severity of her grief by adding, "she went away, crying continuously as she went" (וַתֵּלֶךְ הָלוֹךְ וְזָעָקָה, v. 19). The elaborate description of Tamar's mourning highlights the intensity and duration of her distress and evokes compassion from the reader. The pity that the narrator elicits from the reader stands in stark contrast to the contempt that has been generated for Amnon. These contrasting feelings, which the narrative evokes simultaneously, align the reader with Tamar and distance the reader from Amnon. Also, as suggested earlier, this juxtaposition of post-rape reactions fuels the need for a response to this appalling crime against the unmarried daughter of David.

Male Responses to Rape: Dynamics of Love and Hate

The complex relational elements that have been present throughout this story complicate and motivate the male responses that follow the rape. As stated above, the narration of 2 Sam 13 has led the reader to anticipate a response to Amnon's sexual violation of Tamar. The initial male reactions to the rape do not lead immediately to retaliation. Instead, the narrator refocuses the reader's attention on the relational consequences of Amnon's actions, i.e., how the rape of Tamar affects Absalom and David. As I will show, the dynamics within these initial post-rape responses anticipate the future conflict of Absalom with his half-brother Amnon and point to the future rebellion of Absalom from David.

Absalom's eventual revenge on Amnon displays the excessive male violence that characterizes the family resemblance of the three biblical rape narratives. Moreover, the initial reactions of David and Absalom to the rape provide a further trajectory for the social fragmentation that results. The brother's initial response is directed to Tamar, in which he silences his mourning sister. The narrator proceeds to juxtapose David's angry response with the comment that Absalom refuses to say good or bad against Amnon on account of his hatred for his half-brother. The exchange between the first pairing of characters, Absalom and Tamar, is best explained within the context of a secret plot to kill Amnon—a plan that is revealed over time. The responses of the second pair of characters, David and Absalom, are contrasted with each other, highlighting the growing differences between father and son, the king and a potential successor. David's reaction will result in him doing nothing to punish his firstborn son. Absalom's silent response of hatred is a pregnant expression that looks forward to his eventual revenge on Amnon later in the chapter.

Initial Responses to Rape: Absalom and David

The initial response to the rape produces thematic trajectories that will move this rape text toward retaliatory male violence and the fragmenting of David's family. In vv. 20–22, Absalom's initial response is directed to Tamar. He addresses his sister's grief by silencing her and by encouraging her to make light of the incident. In v. 20, Absalom tells his sister to be silent (הַחֲרִישִׁי) for "he [Amnon] is your brother." The use of the root חרשׁ in the Hiphil recalls Jacob's silent response to the rape of Dinah. In Gen 34:5, Jacob holds his peace (וְהֶחֱרִשׁ) about the rape of his daughter, not wanting to make a decision while his sons were away. In the Gen 34 passage, Jacob's silence is ambiguous, causing the reader to suspend the meaning of this phrase until Jacob's true feelings are revealed at the end of the story (cf. Gen 34:30). In the present text, however, Absalom tells Tamar how she should respond to the rape. She should be silent about it.

The key to understanding Absalom's advice lies in the expression אָחִיךְ הוּא, "he is your brother," which follows the imperative הַחֲרִישִׁי. This does not mean, as some scholars have argued, that Tamar should be quiet about the rape because she has had sexual relations with her brother, i.e., incest. This position is difficult to maintain given the fact that the context assumes endogamous marriage as seen most clearly in Tamar's plea (v. 13; see also nn. 13, 27 above). Absalom's use of the kinship term "your brother" suggests that, on the surface, he is appealing to issues of family reputation and relationship in order to silence his sister. That is, his words suggest that his sister should not make such a public display of mourning for the sake of the family name.

In addition to silencing his sister, Absalom concludes his words to Tamar by attempting to "soften" the blow for her.[37] He suggests that she should not take this thing to heart (לִבֵּךְ?), literally, "do not set your mind on this thing" (v. 20b). His words amount to "don't worry about it." Absalom's response, both his silencing of Tamar and his making light of her circumstance, is odd given the narrator's depiction of the severity and humiliation of the crime.[38] This incongruity between the cruelty of the rape and Absalom's unusual response to his sister suggests that something more is going on beyond the surface meaning of Absalom's words.

---

[37] Ibid., 272.

[38] Ibid.

As the reader later recognizes, Absalom's advice masks an ulterior motive. He desires for his sister to be quiet and make light of what happened so that he can carry out his plan of revenge in secrecy (13:23–29). This understanding of Absalom's words makes the best sense of his response in v. 22, where he refuses to say anything good or bad about Amnon even though he hates his brother for raping Tamar. Absalom's silencing of Tamar mirrors his own refusal to say anything good or bad. The veil of secrecy that Absalom has created, combined with his deep hatred of Amnon, suggests to the reader that revenge is forthcoming from Tamar's blood brother, even if the plans for retaliation are not explicit.

Absalom's advice for Tamar is juxtaposed with his sister's devastation. The narrator describes Tamar as desolate (שֹׁמֵמָה) within the house of Absalom (v. 20). שֹׁמֵמָה, from the root שׁמם, within this context connotes being isolated due to affliction.[39] It refers to both the ravaged state of the thing/person that is "desolate" and the social separation that results. Hence, Tamar has been hushed and isolated because of the crime that was committed against her. Absalom silences Tamar, protecting her from public scorn while concealing his own hidden plot. In the process, however, he isolates her within his own house, leaving her desolate.

The structure of familial language in v. 20 reinforces Absalom's protection of the secret, i.e., Tamar's desolation. Five times within this verse, sibling relationships are mentioned (brother occurs four times and sister once). The word "sister" is placed in the middle, between two occurrences of the word "brother." Bar-Efrat has recognized a symmetrical pattern in this arrangement of familial terms:

her brother	your brother	my sister	your brother	her brother
(אָחִיהָ)	(אָחִיךְ)	(אֲחוֹתִי)	(אָחִיךְ)	(אָחִיה)
(Absalom)	(Amnon)	(Tamar)	(Amnon)	(Absalom)[40]

Fokkelman, following this schema, rightly observes the concentric pattern of "reference to Absalom/Amnon/Tamar/Amnon/Absalom" and the "possessive

---

[39] שׁמם often occurs with reference to land, suggesting a desolate or uninhabited place. It also, however, speaks of the resulting isolation of afflicted people or personified things (Isa 54:1; Lam 1:16, 3:11).

[40] Bar-Efrat, *Narrative Art*, 272–73.

suffixes, indicating the 3rd, 2nd, 1st, 2nd and 3rd person respectively."[41] The narrator makes both comments about Absalom at the beginning and end of the verse, providing the frame for the symmetry. Absalom's speech uses the familial terms (אָחִיךְ, אֲחוֹתִי, and אָחִיךְ) to describe Amnon and Tamar. Hence, the narrator shapes the story in a way that structurally reinforces Absalom's attempt to keep the situation under control. Absalom's speech focuses on Tamar as the center of his attention. His words surround her, however, within the context of her half-brother's crime. Moreover, the narrator circumscribes the whole of this event within the speech and interpretation of Absalom—an interpretation marked by silencing and trivializing as suggested above.

Therefore, though Absalom appears to have this situation under control socially and structurally, his actions result in his sister being silenced and isolated. She is doubly enclosed by the deeds of Amnon and the words of her older brother. The narrator's comment is appropriate: Tamar is left desolate (שֹׁמֵמָה, v. 20) within the house of Absalom. Hence, Absalom's response to Tamar's grief, both in the words that he uses and in the structure of the narrative itself, suggest that the brother intends to keep his sister's violation quiet. As suggested above, this silence, when viewed within the larger context of Absalom's vengeful plot against Amnon, serves to conceal the younger brother's plans. In this way, Absalom's initial post-rape actions provide a veil of secrecy over the rape, which looks forward to his eventual violent and calculated response.

At the end of the scene, the narrator's description of two post-rape responses—David and Absalom's—also anticipates the movement in this story toward further violence and eventual social fragmentation. In vv. 21–22, Absalom's reaction to Amnon's deed is compared and contrasted with David's response. Like his father, Absalom initially does not do or say anything to Amnon, speaking neither good nor bad to him. Unlike David, however, hatred drives Absalom's response since Amnon "raped Tamar, his sister" (עִנָּה אֵת תָּמָר אֲחֹתוֹ). David is greatly angered (וַיִּחַר לוֹ מְאֹד), but hate does not motivate his reaction. While both responses are negative, Absalom's is the more extreme. Hence, the narrator has contrasted the reactions of father and son. Furthermore, as the story will show, David's anger does not result in any form of punishment for Amnon. Thus, his outrage does not correspond to

---

[41] Fokkelman, *King David*, 112.

subsequent action. In light of this narrative detail, it is not surprising that the LXX adds, "but he would not punish [literally, 'chasten the spirit of'] his son Amnon, because he loved him since he was his firstborn."[42] The Hebrew describes David's emotion of anger but fails to explain why he does nothing to Amnon, his son. Hence, when one tries to make sense of MT, one is left with the discontinuity between David's angry response and his lack of resolve to do anything to address Amnon's rape of his daughter.[43]

The narrative's movement toward revenge can also be seen when one observes the dynamics of love and hate that have been prominent in this story. Absalom's hatred of Amnon moves the emotional trajectory of this story toward the violent retribution at the end of the chapter. At the beginning of 2 Sam 13, Amnon *loves* (וַיֶּאֱהָבֶהָ) his sister Tamar (v. 1). His *love* turns into *hate* after the rape in v. 15. At the end of the story, Absalom *hates* (שָׂנֵא) Amnon for raping his sister (v. 22). The dynamics move from *love* (v. 1 ff.) → *love/hate* (v. 15) → *hate* (v. 22). Amnon's initial love for Tamar is conflicted by the fact that the object of his love is the sister of his half-brother, Absalom. The rape is the pivotal and central event in the story, after which Amnon's love for Tamar turns into hate. His hatred, which leads to her rejection and expulsion (vv. 15–18), leaves Tamar desolate. The devastated sister returns to her brother Absalom, who, after learning of his brother's deeds, hates Amnon (v. 22). Absalom's silence, combined with his hatred for Amnon, creates a pregnant moment in the text, where the reader anticipates an inevitable response from the offended brother. David's failure to act against his firstborn suggests that Absalom's hatred will carry the day.

Absalom's Violent Response: Revenge against Amnon

Before turning to the issue of social fragmentation, a movement that has been alluded to already in the preceding analysis, I will examine elements within

---

[42] This reading assumes ולא יצב את רוח אמנון בנו כי אהבו כי בכורו הוא, following Kittel's (*BHK*) reconstruction of the Hebrew assumed by the LXX and supported by 4QSam[a] (וכי אהנבו כי בכורן הוא). See the suggestion in *BHS*. For full discussion of this textual problem see McCarter, *2 Samuel*, 319–20; and Conroy, *Absalom Absalom!* 153–53.

[43] Bar-Efrat states, "Tamar sits, a desolate woman, in her brother Absalom's house, David is very angry but takes no action, and neither does Absalom. This serenity exists only on the surface, however. Underneath, in Absalom's mind, there is unrest and agitation, as the narrator insinuates, and these will burst out and be expressed in action at a later stage" (*Narrative Art*, 274).

Absalom's revenge on Amnon. It is Absalom's retaliation on his half-brother that moves this story's rape into further male violence. As stated above, Absalom's silent hatred of Amnon is a pregnant expression that suggests that he plans to avenge his sister's violation (v. 22). After two years of waiting, Absalom's retaliation begins to take shape in 13:23 ff. He invites all the king's sons for a sheep-shearing feast at Baal-hazor. Absalom implores his father to come, but David refuses. After a long series of exchanges, David's reluctance finally gives way to Absalom's persistence. David consents to let Amnon go, but David himself does not attend the festival. This verbal wrestling between David and Absalom, set within the courtesy of a son's invitation, points to a veiled struggle between father and son, especially after the narrator's deliberate contrast of their responses to the rape of Tamar (vv. 21–22). David appears suspicious, but Absalom is able to overcome his father's doubts through persistence. The father yields twice to his son, suggesting to the reader that David has lost his ability to respond decisively to even small challenges within his household (v. 21). His earlier inaction with regard to Amnon makes this indecisive behavior more suspect.

David's fears are realized in v. 28 when Absalom immediately reveals his scheme to his servants. He will get his brother Amnon drunk and then slay him. Absalom's resolve and premeditation confirm for the reader that his earlier silence was a cover for his intention to seek revenge. The deed is carried out swiftly in v. 29. Amnon is killed and David's sons flee from the scene out of fear for their lives. The silent responses of David and Absalom in vv. 21–22 delayed the reader's expectation for a response to the crime committed against Tamar. Since David, the appropriate authority and offended party, did not address the rape of his daughter, Absalom responded to Amnon's violation of Tamar with the murdering of his half-brother.

However, Absalom's motivation for this violent retaliation is complicated by the politics within his family. Amnon, being David's firstborn (2 Sam 3:2), would be the most likely successor to David's throne. Eliminating Amnon would put Absalom in a better position to possess the kingdom. Thus, when Absalom asks for all of David's sons to gather in one place for the sheep-shearing feast, including Amnon the firstborn and the king himself, the reader suspects that Absalom might be planning more than vengeance for his sister. In fact, after the king's sons were invited, Absalom's first inquiry is for David himself to be present. Amnon's presence seems to be a secondary request. Hence, Absalom's plot appears to be about more than revenge. By drawing out the king and the king's sons away from the capital and to a location of his choosing, Absalom would have the upper hand should he attempt to revolt from his father's authority. Later, when Absalom's kills Amnon and his plan is revealed, the reader suspects that Absalom had initially intended to kill the king and usurp the throne.

Such an interpretation is consistent with the developments that follow in Chapter 15, when Absalom leads a *coup d'etat* against his father. In the present scenario, however, Absalom settles for one of his other premeditated objectives—to seek revenge on Amnon, whom he hates. Hence, Absalom's response, like other male responses in the rape narratives, ends with excessive violence—the premeditated murder of his half-brother and rival to the throne. As I have shown, however, his response is complicated within the themes of revenge and royal succession.

Social Fragmentation: Family Strife and Royal Succession

Throughout the preceding discussion, I identified trajectories of social fragmentation within the earlier stages of the narrative. Within the context of divine judgment, Nathan's oracle against the house of David predicts the eventual division and strife of the royal family (2 Sam 12:7–11). Thus, forces of social fragmentation are put in motion prior to the rape of Tamar through prophetic utterance. The rape acts as an important catalyst for the issues of family rivalry and succession that result. It is the first link in a whole chain of events that works toward the fulfillment of Yahweh's word against David. Within 2 Sam 13, the rape scene and the ensuing male responses make clear the family's growing divisions and conflict. Amnon's act of sexual violence upon Tamar sets half-brother against half-sister. Absalom's response of hate toward Amnon points to the eventual killing of the latter by the former. Absalom and David's varied responses to Amnon's crime also set in motion a developing tension between Absalom and David, leading to the son's rebellion against his father. This last tension, which was discussed briefly above, is worth exploring further since it points to the most obvious and profound illustration of social fragmentation within this narrative.

As suggested above, Absalom's verbal bout with his father in 13:24–27 is symptomatic of a developing conflict between father and son. Earlier in the story, the narrator foreshadows an impending clash between David and Absalom in vv. 21–22 through their contrasting responses to Amnon's rape of

Tamar. As the story progresses, the narrator develops a characterization of David in which the king appears to be losing control of his own house, opening the door for Absalom's revolt.

David's faltering authority can be seen throughout 2 Sam 13. First, David is an unwitting accomplice to the scheme of Jonadab and Amnon in v. 7. The king is portrayed as a pawn in his oldest son's plans to seduce Tamar. Second, David fails to respond to an injustice within his own house. When he hears about the rape, his response is appropriate—he is very angry (v. 21). However, he fails to do anything to punish Amnon for the rape of Tamar. Finally, when David fails to act on Tamar's behalf, Absalom takes it upon himself to avenge his sister. Hence, the son has usurped the father's role.

Absalom is also silent after the rape, refusing to say good or bad about Amnon (v. 22). It is clear, however, that he intends to respond to the crime, which he does by murdering Amnon at the end of Chapter 13. Absalom's plan of revenge, whatever the motivation, is in direct contrast with the inaction of David. When the father and king does not respond to such a crime, the blood brother takes justice into his own hands. Hence, the verbal sparring between David and Absalom in 13:24–27 is indicative of a growing conflict between father and son. In this way, the narrator, through the story of Amnon's rape of Tamar, has set the reader up for an inevitable power struggle between Absalom and David. Though Absalom's motivation for killing Amnon is framed in the language of revenge by Jonadab (v. 32), the narrator has made it clear that much more is at stake.[44]

Two discernable themes emerge from the preceding discussion that will continue to build in the chapters that follow: 1) Absalom's ambitions to become

---

[44] It is important to note that Jonadab, earlier described as Amnon's friend, has political motivation for depicting Absalom's act as one of revenge. The narrator has made it clear that David chose not to punish his son Amnon for the crime that he committed. By suggesting that Absalom had plotted his brother's murder from the time that Amnon raped Tamar, Jonadab sets the perspective of David over against Absalom's point of view. Hence, the counselor's words suggest that Absalom, by killing the king's firstborn son, has committed an act of rebellion against the king's authority. In addition, Jonadab counsels the king not to take this matter to heart (v. 33), language that reminds the reader of Absalom's advice to Tamar. Jonadab minimizes Amnon's death in order to assure the king that he has other options for an heir—Amnon alone is dead. Such words point to the king's control over the situation and suggest that Absalom acted alone in this matter.

king; and 2) David's faltering authority over his family and kingdom. Absalom, after fleeing the murder scene, spends three years in exile at Geshur (13:38). Through the mediation of Joab, which includes a long discussion between David and the woman from Tekoa, Absalom is eventually restored to the royal house (14:33). Upon his return, he once again begins to assert his authority, and eventually wins the heart of the people (15:6). His ambitions eventually lead to an outright rebellion against his father's kingship, causing David to flee from Jerusalem.

Throughout Chapters 14 and 15, the narrator characterizes Absalom as an ambitious young prince, who desires to rule in place of his father. At the same time, he is described as a man who is praised for his beauty (אִישׁ־יָפֶה) "from the sole of his foot to the crown of his head" (מִכַּף רַגְלוֹ וְעַד קָדְקֳדוֹ, v. 14:25). He also is popular among the people, promoting a standard of justice that is not present in his father's kingdom (15:1–6). The configuration of "beauty" (יָפֶה) and lack of justice from the king (cf. 15:4) point the reader back to Absalom's desolate sister, Tamar. She was "beautiful" (יָפָה, 13:1) and she received no justice from the king, her father.

This characterization, combined with Absalom's ambition, suggests to the reader that this son's desire to rule is connected in a complicated way to the events surrounding the rape of his sister. The narrator makes this connection more explicit to the reader when describing Absalom's children. Of his four children, his daughter is singled out for special attention. Her name is Tamar and she was "beautiful" (יְפַת מַרְאֶה). Hence, the narrator makes a clear connection between Absalom's daughter and his sister through their shared beauty and name. The placement of this narrative fact sets the reader up to hear Absalom's rebellion in Chapter 15 in light of the legacy of his sister Tamar. In the end, however, Absalom's ambition catches up to him. After a long struggle, his rebellion is eventually crushed, and he himself is killed violently by Joab, the commander of David's army (18:14–15), in spite of David's command to spare the life of his son (18:5).

In contrast to Absalom, David is depicted throughout this episode as a king who is indecisive and unable to deal with the strife that is dividing his family. He is portrayed as a man who has conflicting loyalties, a theme that began in 2 Sam 13:1–22 with his angry response to the rape of Tamar and his refusal to punish Amnon. Even after Absalom's premeditated murder of Amnon, David longs for Absalom while he is in exile (13:38). When Absalom is later killed during his revolt against the king, David weeps, wishing that he could have died in his son's place. His mourning puts to shame those who defended David and his kingship (19:6–7). Joab summarizes this contradiction well, telling David that he has humiliated those around him by "loving those who hate you and hating those who love you" (v. 7).

While Joab's words reflect a particular perspective given his role in killing Absalom, they nevertheless point to David's internal conflict and the growing divisions within David's kingdom. The king's internal conflicts have become inscribed writ large on the body politic. It is likely that David's love for Amnon prevented him from punishing his son for the rape of Tamar (cf. LXX). David's love for Absalom meant that he mourned not only for the death of his oldest son, Amnon, but also the exiled Absalom—his brother's murderer. After Absalom's death, David mourns for the very son who planned a conspiracy to dethrone him. David's loyalties are conflicted—a symbol of the division within his own house and kingdom.

David's family is fragmenting. His love protects his sons, even when the sons rape, plot murder, and seek to seize his throne. The women in David's house, however, are seized by others in his family, violated in public, and left desolate (cf. 13:20, 16:22). Ironically, David's love for those within his household has contributed to his family's division by the sword. In failing to address the disorder within his own house, David has become an ineffective king in the eyes of his officials, the people, and the reader. His love blinds him to the injustices committed by his sons, and his loyalty has protected those who have dishonored his family's reputation as Joab's words so poignantly state (19:7). The prophecy of Nathan has come to pass—the sword divides the house of David, and those within his own house have risen up against him (12:10–11).

Conclusion

The rape of Tamar, like the other two rape narratives, follows the progression of rape that provokes excessive male violence leading to social fragmentation. In this way, 2 Sam 13 displays characteristics that are common to this family of texts. However, 2 Sam 13 is set within a larger narrative context of royal succession and divine judgment, which provide this rape text with its particular dynamics and plot development. Nathan's oracle of judgment in 2 Sam 12 anticipates the violence and strife that characterizes David's family in 2 Sam 13 ff. The rape exacerbates existing tensions between two brothers, Amnon and Absalom, both potential successors to the throne of David. Thus, the rape intensifies issues of conflict that are already assumed within a context of royal succession. Moreover, David's post-rape silence and inaction create a rift between Absalom and his father, prompting the former to secretly plan revenge on his half-brother Amnon. Thus, the rape puts in motion forces of rebellion that lead to Absalom's eventual attempt to usurp the throne of his father. The social fragmentation of this text, represented by the relational discord within the family of David, fulfills the word of Yahweh against the king. Though David eventually gains control of his kingdom, David's family is marked with violence and the sword. Hence, forces of divine judgment and royal succession cause this story's rape to move toward the excessive male violence and social/familial discord that results.

CHAPTER FIVE

Conclusion: Configurations of Rape

Summary

The preceding discussion has examined three rape narratives—Gen 34, Judg 19, and 2 Sam 13—that display a similar configuration of an initial rape that leads to further retributive violence among males and results in some kind of social fragmentation. I have argued that these texts bear a family resemblance to one another in that they all contain these three elements and progression. Moreover, as stated in the first chapter, these texts share the common feature of responding to rape in an excessively violent way, even when a less violent option exists in the Hebrew Bible through the legal material. This last observation suggests that there are elements and dynamics that are intrinsic to each narrative that propel these texts toward their violent and socially fragmented ends. In Chapters Two through Four, I argued that each story, while displaying the characteristic progression of the rape texts' family resemblance, is marked by themes and forces that bring particular expression to the movement of the rape toward violence and social fragmentation. That is, each narrative contains within itself distinct traits that embody the family resemblance in ways that are unique to its own literary context.

In Gen 34, the sexual violence is set within the complex issues of negotiating the relationship between Jacob's family and the Hivites. Dynamics of how this Israelite family will deal with outsiders complicate and exacerbate the post-rape responses. Shechem's rape of Dinah, which is narrated briefly in 34:2, is the impetus for further interaction between the two groups.

There are two different responses from the males within Dinah's family— one from Dinah's father and one from her brothers. Jacob's reaction is one of silence. The reader later finds out that the father's response is based in his desire to live peaceably with the Shechemites (cf., 33:18–19, 34:30). Simeon and Levi, the two blood-brothers of Dinah, respond differently than their father Jacob. They along with their brothers perceive the event as a threat to group norms and boundaries. Hence, the brothers deceive the Shechemites, and Simeon and Levi slaughter the outsiders with the sword. The remaining brothers proceed to plunder the city (34:27–29). This excessively violent act of revenge creates strife between Jacob and his sons. The father is angered that the rash actions of his sons have given him a bad reputation among the people of the land (v. 30). The sons remain indignant with their father, asking if they should allow their sister to be treated like a prostitute (v. 31). For the brothers, Jacob's silence is unconscionable, while Jacob's judgment of Simeon and Levi's violent acts remain with the brothers to the end of the ancestral stories (Gen 49:5–7).

Hence, the brothers' retributive violence leads to two types of social fragmentation. One is internal to the family of Jacob and is represented by the enduring conflict between Jacob and his sons, particularly Simeon and Levi. The other is external and points to the Israelites' problematic relationship with the inhabitants of Canaan. Dinah, though her brothers remove her from the house of Shechem (34:26), is never heard from again in the story with the exception of a later genealogy (46:15). She remains desolate at the end of the story.

Thus, Gen 34 has elements that characterize it within the family resemblance of the rape texts in that it moves through the progression of rape → excessive male violence → social fragmentation. The story, however, is shaped by particular themes of how to negotiate and interact with this group of Canaanites. The rape, which quickly turns into issues of intermarriage between the two groups, forces the different perspectives of Jacob and his sons into conflict. The sexual violence, combined with the breaching of social norms, ignites the retaliatory violence of Jacob's sons.

Judges 19 describes the rape of a Levite's concubine within a larger framework of religious, social, and moral decline at the end of the book of Judges (17–21). The rape itself is set within the context of two hospitality scenes, with the rape scene described in language that evokes the legendary abomination and judgment of Sodom and Gomorrah. The rape provides a catalyst for the excessive violence and social disintegration that follow. The initial sexual violation ignites a civil war in Israel, which leads to the near extinction of the tribe of Benjamin. The repopulation of the decimated tribe leads to further killing and additional seizures of women, propelling this narrative further into an absurd display of violence.

The end result is clear for the reader. At the end of the period of the Judges, the rape of a woman has degenerated into the war of a nation against itself. The picture at the conclusion of this story is one of moral deterioration and increasing social chaos. The woman's divided body, which was defiled and broken, is an image of the larger social body of Israel. This social fragmentation characterizes the narrative movement at the end of the book of Judges when there was no king in Israel and "every man did what was right in his own eyes" (17:6, 21:25).

Hence, the rape of the Levite's concubine also follows the rape text progression of an initial rape that leads to further retributive violence among males and results in social fragmentation. However, the development and themes within Judg 17–21, framed with the narrator's evaluation of this period (17:6, 18:1, 19:1, and 21:25), move the rape of this woman toward the most extensive display of violence and social breakdown among the rape texts. Within the context of the moral and social decline at the end of the book of Judges, the rape functions as a spark that unleashes violent forces that move the story toward its increasingly chaotic conclusion.

Finally in 2 Sam 13:1–22, the rape of Tamar marks the beginning of succession struggles within David's family. Amnon, David's firstborn, rapes his half-sister Tamar. The complex familial relations within this text, which the narrator makes explicit in vv. 1–2, set off a chain reaction of male responses to the rape that exacerbate existing divisions within the royal house and create new tensions between David and Absalom.

Amnon's rape of Tamar, similar to the rape within Gen 34, elicits two responses—one from David and one from Absalom. The narrator of 2 Sam 13 marks the explicit contrast between David and Absalom in vv. 21–22. David, though initially angered by the news of Tamar's rape, refuses to do anything to Amnon, the king's firstborn son. Absalom, like his father, does not do anything to his brother initially. The narrator, however, includes the detail that Absalom hated Amnon because of the rape (v. 22). As I suggested earlier, Absalom's response anticipates his future plot of revenge that is carried out two years later in 13:23–29, when Absalom has Amnon killed.

The different responses to the rape set in motion the dynamics that fuel Absalom's eventual rebellion against his father's kingship in succeeding chapters. The resulting fragmentation of the royal family harks back to Nathan's oracle in 2 Sam 12, which announced that David's house would be marked and divided by violence. Hence, 2 Sam 13 follows the progression of rape to excessive male violence to social fragmentation. However, particular forces of family strife, within the context of royal succession and divine judgment, drive this story of rape toward its violent and socially fractured end.

The nature and extent of the three elements—rape, excessive male violence, and social fragmentation—differ among this family of texts. The rape in Gen 34 is narrated briefly as Shechem's violent seizure (לקח) and defilement (טמא) of Dinah. The sexual violation is one between a Hivite foreigner and a daughter of Israel, and moves quickly to issues of intermarriage between insiders and outsiders.[1] Thus, the rape acts as an impetus for the subsequent negotiations and hostilities between the two groups. In Judg 19, the gang rape of a Levite's concubine serves as a negative example of how hospitality goes terribly wrong in this period when "there was no king in Israel." Depravity has reached legendary status as Gibeah's acts exceed the deeds of Sodom and Gomorrah. Moreover, the rape serves as a catalyst for the chaotic and violent forces that mark the decline of this period when "every man did what was right in his own eyes." Amnon's rape of Tamar in 2 Sam 13 occurs between half-brother and half-sister. The sexual violence of the crime is the most explicitly narrated among the rape texts. Within the complex tensions of royal succession, the rape ignites hostilities between half-brothers (Amnon and Absalom) and conflicts between father and son (David and Absalom). The rape itself and the male responses that result are seen within the context of Yahweh's judgment on the house of David, where his house will be marked with violence.

The rape texts also have different reasons for moving from rape to excessive violence. In Gen 34, the motivation for Simeon and Levi's retaliation is directly related to their perception of how to interact with outsiders. The sons of Jacob collectively respond to Hamor and Shechem's intermarriage proposal with the rejoinder that they cannot allow their sister to marry an uncircumcised male (Gen 34:13–17). Their deception and violent slaughter of the Hivites point to the seriousness of the social breach in the minds of the brothers. Their

---

[1] Bechtel, "What If Dinah Is Not Raped?" 19–36; Keefe, "Rapes of Women," 79–97.

violence marks a clear division between insider and outsider, Israelite and Canaanite. Judg 19 frames the violent male responses to the rape within the larger social and moral decline of Israel during the period of the Judges. The initial rape of a Levite's concubine degenerates into a holy war of Israel with itself. Within this topsy-turvy world, a Levite's problematic justification for retaliation becomes the basis for the near extinction of the tribe of Benjamin at the hands of other Israelites. In 2 Sam 13, the move from rape to retributive violence is motivated by factors related to family strife and royal succession. Absalom's hatred for Amnon, following the rape of Tamar, fuels his desire for retribution. His motivation, however, is complicated by his own desires to seize the throne at a time when his father's power is apparently waning.

Finally, the social fragmentation that results in all three rape texts differs in nature and extent. Gen 34 ends with an enduring conflict between Jacob and his sons, particularly Simeon and Levi (cf. Gen 49:5–7). The initially peaceful relationship with the Hivites has been severed through the violent deeds of Jacob's sons, opening the possibility of future hostile acts from the peoples of Canaan. Thus, the social fragmentation in Gen 34 is both internal and external to the family. In the book of Judges, the excessively violent retaliation against Gibeah of Benjamin leads to escalating social and moral decline at the end of the story. In this period without a king, Israel commits acts of holy war against itself and proceeds to commit further deeds of excessive violence to replenish the decimated tribe of Benjamin. Within this context of inter-tribal warfare, the woman's defiled and severed body is a symbol of a broken and divided Israel at the end of the period of Judges. The social fragmentation within 2 Sam 13 is expressed through the family strife and divisions within David's household that result from the rape. Nathan's oracle in 2 Sam 12:10–12 moves toward fulfillment with Amnon's rape of Tamar and Absalom's premeditated retaliation against his half-brother. Violence and strife abound within the house of David in the events of 2 Sam 13, leading to the eventual revolt of Absalom against his father in succeeding chapters. The sword has divided David's family—brother rapes sister, brother murders brother, and son rebels against father.

Implications for Research

The present study has explored the thematic and developmental similarities between Gen 34, Judg 19, and 2 Sam 13. By analyzing these texts through narrative or literary criticism, this study has provided a thorough look at the different stories that deal with rape in the Hebrew Bible. In this way, my work contributes to the growing body of scholarship that addresses the issue of violence against women in the biblical texts. Such literature tends to emphasize the ways in which the Bible depicts violence against women,[2] creates or reinforces a culture of violence against women,[3] or, in some cases, frames the violence against women in terms of how it affects other men.[4] The present work emphasizes the first and last areas of emphasis. Through an examination of the rape texts, a family resemblance was uncovered that suggests a certain configuration of meaning on the topic of rape in narrative. The three rape stories in the Hebrew Bible move through similar progressions of rape to excessive male violence to some kind of social fragmentation. Hence, rape, at least as it is narrated within the biblical texts, is framed within a certain characteristic structure, even if each individual text bears out this family resemblance in ways that are particular to its themes and context.

Moreover, as the preceding analysis has shown, each of the texts moves through the rape progression because of forces that are tied predominantly to male issues and responses. Each of the rapes leads to further excessive violence among males. Harm done to the woman is a factor that motivates the retaliatory responses of the offended males (Gen 34:31, Judg 20:5–7, and 2 Sam 13:22).[5] However, the preceding analysis has shown that other issues—group norms regarding outsiders, chaotic lawlessness that results from the lack of a king, and issues of royal succession—move the rape forward toward further retributive violence among males and a resulting social fragmentation. In each of the three rape narratives, the woman is left desolate in the wake of the male violence. Hence, my conclusions are similar to those who have found that the biblical texts are concerned more with issues of men than of women, even when

---

[2] The literature is too vast to cite. For some representative studies, see Trible, *Texts of Terror*; Mieke Bal, ed., *Anti-Covenant: Counter-Reading Women's Lives in the Hebrew Bible* (JSOTSup 81; Bible and Literature Series 22; Sheffield; Almond, 1989); J. Cheryl Exum, *Fragmented Women*; Fewell and Gunn, *Gender, Power and Promise*; Scholz, *Rape Plots*.

[3] See Washington, "Violence and the Construction of Gender," 324–63; idem, "Lest He Die," 183–213; and Cheryl B. Anderson, *Women, Ideology, and Violence*.

[4] Pressler, *Family Laws*; and idem, "Sexual Violence," 102–12.

[5] As suggested in Chapter 3, Judg 20:5–7 is a disingenuous response. The Levite's speech is incongruous with the events narrated in Judg 19. Regardless, he uses the rape of his concubine to motivate the tribes' response against Gibeah.

addressing themes of sexual violence perpetrated against women. Carolyn Pressler, for example, has shown convincingly that Deuteronomic legal texts understand violence against women in terms of its effects upon men.[6] In this way, the legal literature seeks to reinforce and protect certain male privileges by making them law. The difference with biblical narrative, however, is that it has the ability to align the reader into a position of sympathy for the female victim, creating additional distance for the reader from the male perpetrator and the excessive male violence that follows.[7] For example, as discussed in 2 Sam 13, Tamar's extended pleas before and after the rape stand in stark contrast to Amnon's rash decisions to rape her and cast her away. The effect upon the reader is obvious. The reader stands in condemnation of Amnon, siding with the plight of the devastated Tamar. The narrator adds for emphasis the explicit detail that Tamar remained desolate within the house of Absalom (2 Sam 13:20). When Absalom's plot for revenge is complicated with his own desires to ascend to the throne, Tamar's desolation functions even more as a reminder of how this violent male response failed to address her situation. Hence, biblical narrative allows the reader to come to a set of judgments that are not available through an interpretation of the legal material.[8]

Finally, this study also provides a different way for narrative and literary-critical scholars to think about comparative analysis among biblical texts. When examining overlapping elements and themes in stories, scholars tend to use terms such as "type," "genre," or "motif."[9] While such designations are useful for suggesting similarities among texts, they tend to be overly deterministic and confining to the diversity of material found within the Hebrew Bible. The rape

---

[6] See Pressler, *Family Laws*, and idem, "Sexual Violence."

[7] It is interesting to note that in each of the three rape texts, the violence, beyond being excessive, is also framed within the context of judgment. Simeon and Levi's retaliation on Shechem receives enduring condemnation from Jacob (Gen 34:30, cf. Gen 49:5–7). The retaliation against Gibeah and Benjamin is an illustration of the social and political decline of this period that the narrator characterizes within the negative evaluation: "In those days, there was no king in Israel; every man did what was right in his own eyes" (Judg 17:6, 21:25). Absalom's vengeful plan against Amnon is further fulfillment of the strife and violence that falls upon David's house in accordance with Nathan's oracle of judgment in 2 Sam 12.

[8] Lapsley makes this point repeatedly in her analysis of the narrator's function in Judg 19. See Lapsley, *Whispering the Word*, esp. 47–49 and 64–67.

[9] Robert Alter's standard treatment provides a very useful understanding of biblical type scenes (*Art of Biblical Narrative*, 47–62). See also Fields, "Motif," 17–32.

texts present a challenge to literary criticism in that the narratives do not fit nicely into what scholars would recognize as formal genre categories. The themes, contexts, characters, and development are all shaped within particular structures that are unique to each individual story. Though the rape texts share the rape progression described above, they are very different stories in form and function. The complex insider/outsider story of crime and punishment in Gen 34 is not the same "type" as the tale of the topsy-turvy world at the end of Judges, nor is it of the same formal category as a story of sibling rivalry within the context of royal succession. By using the idea of a family resemblance, this study identified a similar progression of rape → excessive male violence → social fragmentation. All of the stories move from the initial rape in ways that are excessively violent, even when a less violent option is available within the Hebrew Bible through the legal material. However, as argued above, the reasons that these texts explode into retributive male violence are particular to the different themes and contexts of each individual text. Hence, the texts' similar subject matter of rape, the movement to excessively violent male responses, and the resulting social fragmentation, justify their family resemblance. Their individual expressions, however, mark them each as unique members of this family of texts.

BIBLIOGRAPHY

Abou-Zeid, Ahmed M. "Honour and Shame among the Bedouins in Egypt." Pages 243–60 in *Honour and Shame: The Values of Mediterranean Society*. Edited by Jean G. Peristiany. London: Weidenfeld and Nicolson, 1965.

Abu-Lughod, Lila. *Veiled Sentiments: Honor and Poetry in a Bedouin Society*. Berkeley: University of California, 1986.

Ackroyd, Peter R. *The Second Book of Samuel*. Cambridge Bible Commentary. London: Cambridge University Press, 1977.

Adams, James Luther, and Wilson Yates, eds. *The Grotesque in Art and Literature: Theological Reflections*. Grand Rapids: Eerdmans, 1997.

Aichele, George, and Gary A. Phillips. "Introduction: Exegesis, Eisegesis, Intergesis." *Semeia* 69/70 (1995): 1–18.

Alter, Robert. *The Art of Biblical Narrative*. New York: Basic, 1981.

Alter, Robert, and Frank Kermode. *The Literary Guide to the Bible*. Cambridge: Belknap, 1987.

Amit, Yairah. "Literature in the Service of Politics: Studies in Judges 19–21." Pages 28–40 in *Politics and Theopolitics in the Bible and Postbiblical Literature*. Edited by Henning Graf Reventlow, Yair Hoffman, and Benjamin Uffenheimer. Journal for the Study of the Old Testament: Supplement Series 171. Sheffield: JSOT Press, 1994.

———. "The Saul Polemic in the Persian Period." Pages 647–61 in *Judah and the Judeans in the Persian Period*. Edited by Oded Lipschits and Manfred Oeming. Winona Lake: Eisenbrauns, 2006.

Anderson, Arnold A. *2 Samuel*. Word Biblical Commentary 11. Dallas: Word, 1989.

Anderson, Cheryl B. *Women, Ideology, and Violence: Critical Theory and the Construction of Gender in the Book of the Covenant and the Deuteronomistic Law*. Journal for the Study of the Old Testament: Supplement Series 394. London: T & T Clark, 2004.

Azzoni, Annalisa. "The Private Life of Women in Persian Egypt." Ph.D. dissertation. Johns Hopkins University, 2000.

Bach, Alice. "Rereading the Body Politic: Women and Violence in Judges 21." *Biblical Interpretation* 6, no. 1 (1998): 1–19.

Bader, Mary Anna. *Sexual Violation in the Hebrew Bible: A Multi-Methodological Study of Genesis 34 and 2 Samuel 13*. Studies in Biblical Literature 87. New York: Peter Lang, 2006.

Bal, Mieke. "The Rape of Narrative and Narrative of Rape." Pages 1–32 in *Literature and the Body: Essays on Populations and Persons.* Edited by Elaine Scarry. Baltimore: Johns Hopkins University Press, 1984.

———. *Death and Dissymmetry: The Politics of Coherence in the Book of Judges.* Chicago: University of Chicago Press, 1988.

———. "Dealing/With/Women: Daughters in the Book of Judges." Pages 16–39 in *The Book and the Text: The Bible and Literary Theory.* Edited by Regina M. Schwartz. Oxford: Basil Blackwell, 1990.

———. "A Body of Writing: Judg. 19." Pages 208–30 in *A Feminist Companion to Judges.* Edited by Athalya Brenner. The Feminist Companion to the Bible 4. Sheffield: Sheffield Academic Press, 1993.

———. "Metaphors He Lives By." *Semeia* 61 (1993): 185–207.

———, ed. *Anti-Covenant: Counter-Reading Women's Lives in the Hebrew Bible.* Journal for the Study of the Old Testament: Supplement Series 81. Bible and Literature Series 22. Sheffield: Almond, 1989.

Bar-Efrat, Shimeon. *Narrative Art in the Bible.* Journal for the Study of the Old Testament: Supplement Series 70. Sheffield: Almond Press, 1989.

Beal, Timothy K. "Ideology and Intertextuality: Surplus of Meaning and Controlling the Means of Production." Pages 27–39 in *Reading Between Texts: Intertextuality and the Hebrew Bible.* Edited by Danna Nolan Fewell. Louisville: Westminster/John Knox, 1992.

Bechtel (Huber), Lyn M. "The Biblical Experience of Shame/Shaming: The Social Experience of Shame/Shaming in Biblical Israel in Relation to Its Use as Religious Metaphor." Ph.D. dissertation. Drew University, 1983.

———. "Shame as a Sanction of Social Control in Biblical Israel: Judicial, Political, and Social Shaming." *Journal for the Study of the Old Testament* 49 (1991): 47–76.

———. "The Perception of Shame within the Divine-Human Relationship in Biblical Israel." Pages 79–92 in *Uncovering Ancient Stones: Essays in Memory of H. Neil Richardson.* Edited by Lewis M. Hopfe. Winona Lake: Eisenbrauns, 1993.

———. "What If Dinah Is Not Raped?" *Journal for the Study of the Old Testament* 62 (1994): 19–36.

Bechtler, Steven Richard. *Following in His Steps: Suffering, Community, and Christology in 1 Peter.* Society of Biblical Literature Dissertation Series 162. Atlanta: Scholars Press, 1998.

Bergant, Dianne. "'My Beloved Is Mine and I Am His' (Song 2:16): The Song of Songs and Honor and Shame." *Semeia* 68 (1994): 23–40.

Birch, Bruce C. "Number." Pages 556–61 in vol. 3 of *International Standard Bible Encyclopedia.* Edited by Geoffrey W. Bromiley. 4 vols. Grand Rapids: Eerdmans, 1986.

Bird, Phyllis A. *Missing Persons and Mistaken Identities: Women and Gender in Ancient Israel.* Minneapolis: Fortress, 1997.

Block, Daniel I. "Echo Narrative Technique in Hebrew Literature: A Study in Judges 19." *Westminster Theological Journal* 52 (1990): 325–41.

Bohmbach, Karla G. "Conventions/Contraventions: The Meaning of Public and Private for the Judges 19 Concubine." *Journal for the Study of the Old Testament* 83 (1999): 83–98.

Boling, Robert G. *Judges: Introduction, Translation, and Commentary.* Anchor Bible 6A. New York: Doubleday, 1975.

Botterweck, Gerhard Johannes, and Helmer Ringgren. *Theological Dictionary of the Old Testament.* Translated by John T. Willis, Geoffrey William Bromiley, and David E. Green. 14 vols. Grand Rapids: Eerdmans, 1974–1998.

———. *Theologisches Wörterbuch zum Alten Testament.* 10 vols. Stuttgart: W. Kohlhammer, 1970–1998.

Bourque, Linda Brookover. *Defining Rape.* Durham: Duke University Press, 1989.

Brandes, Stanley. "Reflections of Honor and Shame in the Mediterranean." Pages 121–134 in *Honour and Shame and the Unity of the Mediterranean.* Edited by David D. Gilmore. American Anthropological Association Special Publication 22. Washington, D.C.: American Anthropological Association, 1987.

Brenner, Athalya, ed. *A Feminist Companion to Judges.* The Feminist Companion to the Bible 4. Sheffield: Sheffield Academic Press, 1993.

———, ed. *A Feminist Companion to Exodus to Deuteronomy.* The Feminist Companion to the Bible 6. Sheffield: Sheffield Academic Press, 1994.

———, ed. *A Feminist Companion to Genesis.* The Feminist Companion to the Bible 2. Sheffield: Sheffield Academic Press, 1997.

Brettler, Marc Zvi. "The Book of Judges: Literature as Politics." *Journal of Biblical Literature* 108, no. 3 (1989): 395–418.

———. *The Book of Judges.* Old Testament Readings. New York: Routledge, 2002.

Brownmiller, Susan. *Against Our Will: Men, Women, and Rape.* New York: Bantam, 1975.

Brueggemann, Walter. *Genesis.* Interpretation: A Commentary for Teaching and Preaching. Atlanta: John Knox, 1982.

———. *David's Truth in Israel's Imagination and Memory.* 2nd ed. Minneapolis: Fortress, 2002.

Buchwald, Emilie, Pamela R. Fletcher, and Martha Roth, eds. *Transforming a Rape Culture.* Minneapolis: Milkweed, 1993.

Burney, Charles F. *The Book of Judges: With Introduction and Notes; and Notes on the Hebrew Text of the Books of Kings: With an Introduction and Appendix.* New York: KTAV, 1970.

Camp, Claudia V. *Wise, Strange and Holy: The Strange Woman and the Making of the Bible.* Journal for the Study of the Old Testament Supplement Series 320. Gender, Culture, Theory 9. Sheffield: Sheffield Academic Press, 2000.

Camp, Claudia V., and Carole R. Fontaine, eds. "Women, War, and Metaphor: Language and Society in the Study of the Hebrew Bible." *Semeia* 61 (1993): 1–237.

Carden, Michael. "Homophobia and Rape in Sodom and Gibeah: A Response to Ken Stone." *Journal for the Study of the Old Testament* 82 (1999): 83–96.

Carlson, Rolf A. *David, the Chosen King: A Traditio-Historical Approach to the Second Book of Samuel.* Stockholm: Almqvist & Wiksell, 1964.

Caspi, Mishael Maswari. "The Story of the Rape of Dinah: The Narrator and the Reader." *Hebrew Studies* 26:1 (1985): 25–45.

Chance, John K. "The Anthropology of Honor and Shame: Culture, Values, and Practice." *Semeia* 68 (1994): 139–51.

Childs, Brevard S. *Introduction to the Old Testament as Scripture.* Philadelphia: Fortress, 1979.

Conroy, Charles. *Absalom Absalom! Narrative and Language in 2 Sam 13–20.* Analecta biblica 81. Rome: Biblical Institute, 1978.

Coombe, Rosemary J. "Barren Ground: Re-Conceiving Honour and Shame in the Field of Mediterranean Ethnography." *Anthropologica* 32 (1990): 221–38.

Crüsemann, Frank. *Der Widerstand gegen das Königtum.* Neukirchen-Vluyn: Neukirchener Verlag, 1978.

Day, Peggy L., ed. *Gender and Difference in Ancient Israel.* Minneapolis: Fortress, 1989.

Deacy, Susan, and Karen F. Pierce, eds. *Rape in Antiquity.* London: Duckworth, 1997.

Derrida, Jacques. "The Law of Genre." *Glyph* 7 (1980): 202–29.

DeSilva, David Arthur. *Despising Shame: Honor Discourse and Community Maintenance in the Epistle to the Hebrews.* Society of Biblical Literature Dissertation Series 152. Atlanta: Scholars Press, 1995.

———. *Honor, Patronage, Kinship, and Purity: Unlocking New Testament Culture.* Downers Grove: Intervarsity Press, 2000.

Dever, William G. *Who Were the Early Israelites and Where Did They Come From?* Grand Rapids: Eerdmans, 2003.

Diebner, Jörg Bernd. "Gen 34 und Dinas Rolle bei der Definition 'Israels.'" *Dielheimer Blätter zum Alten Testament und seiner Rezeption in der Alten Kirche* 19 (1984): 59–75.

Dijk-Hemmes, Fokkelien van. "Tamar and the Limits of Patriarchy: Between Rape and Seduction (2 Samuel and Genesis 38)." Pages 135–56 in *Anti-Covenant: Counter-Reading Women's Lives in the Hebrew Bible.* Edited by Mieke Bal. Journal for the Study of the Old Testament: Supplement Series 81. Sheffield: Sheffield Academic Press, 1989.

Dobbs-Allsopp, F. W. "Rethinking Historical Criticism." *Biblical Interpretation* 7 (1999): 235–71.

———. *Weep, O Daughter of Zion: A Study of the City-Lament Genre in the Hebrew Bible.* Biblica et orientalia 44. Rome: Editrice Pontificio Istituto Biblico, 1993.

Dumbrell, William J. "'In Those Days There Was No King in Israel; Everyman Did What Was Right in His Own Eyes': The Purpose of the Book of Judges Reconsidered." *Journal for the Study of the Old Testament* 25 (1983): 23–33.

Elliot, John H. "Disgraced Yet Graced: The Gospel According to 1 Peter in the Key of Honor and Shame." *Biblical Theology Bulletin* 25 (1995): 166–78.

Exum, J. Cheryl. *Fragmented Women: Feminist (Sub)versions of Biblical Narratives.* Valley Forge: Trinity, 1993.

Fewell, Danna Nolan, ed. *Reading Between Texts: Intertextuality and the Hebrew Bible.* Louisville: Westminster/John Knox, 1992.

Fewell, Danna Nolan, and David M. Gunn. "Tipping the Balance: Sternberg's Reader and the Rape of Dinah." *Journal of Biblical Literature* 110 (1991): 193–211.

———. *Gender Power and Promise: The Subject of the Bible's First Story.* Nashville: Abingdon, 1993.

Fields, Weston W. "The Motif 'Night as Danger' Associated With Three Biblical Destruction Narratives." Pages 17–32 in *"Sha'arei Talmon": Studies in the Bible, Qumran, and the Ancient Near East Presented to Shemaryahu Talmon.* Edited by Michael Fishbane and Emanuel Tov. Winona Lake: Eisenbrauns, 1992.

———. *Sodom and Gomorrah: History and Motif in Biblical Narrative.* Journal for the Study of the Old Testament: Supplement Series 231. Sheffield: Sheffield Academic Press, 1997.

Fish, Stanley. *Is There a Text in This Class? The Authority of Interpretative Communities.* Cambridge: Harvard University Press, 1980.

Fishelov, David. *Metaphors of Genre: The Role of Analogies in Genre Theory.* University Park: Pennsylvania State University Press, 1993.

Flanagan, James W. "Court History or Succession Document? A Study of 2 Sam 9–20 and 1 Kings 1–2." *Journal of Biblical Literature* 91 (1972): 172–81.

Flores, Diane. "Topsy-Turvy World." Pages 233–55 in *Egypt, Israel, and the Ancient Mediterranean World: Studies in Honor of Donald B. Redford.* Edited by Gary N. Knoppers and Antoine Hirsch. Leiden: Brill, 2004.

Fokkelman, Jan P. *King David (II Sam. 9–20 and I Kings 1–2).* Vol 1. of *Narrative Art and Poetry in the Books of Samuel: A Full Interpretation Based on Stylistic and Structural Analyses.* Assen: Van Gorcum, 1981.

Forshey, Harold O. "Court Narrative (2 Samuel 9–1 Kings 2)." Pages 1172–79 in vol. 1 of *The Anchor Bible Dictionary.* Edited by David Noel Freedman. 6 vols. New York: Doubleday, 1992.

Fowler, Alastair. *Kinds of Literature: An Introduction to the Theory of Genres and Modes.* Cambridge: Harvard University Press, 1982.

Freedman, David Noel. "Who Is Like Thee Among the Gods?' The Religion of Early Israel." Pages 315–35 in *Ancient Israelite Religion: Essays in Honor of Frank Moore Cross.* Edited by Patrick D. Miller, Paul D. Hanson, and S. Dean McBride. Philadelphia: Fortress, 1987.

———. "Dinah and Shechem, Tamar and Amnon." *Austin Seminary Bulletin: Faculty Edition* 105 (1990): 51–63.

Freedman, David Noel, and Frank Moore Cross. *Studies in Ancient Yahwistic Poetry.* 2nd edition. Grand Rapids: Eerdmans, 1997.

Fretheim, Terence E. "The Book of Genesis: Introduction, Commentary, and Reflections." Pages 319–674 in vol. 1 of *The New Interpreter's Bible.* Edited by Leander E. Keck. 12 vols. Nashville: Abingdon, 1994.

Friedman, Richard Elliot. *The Hidden Book in the Bible.* San Francisco: Harper SanFrancisco, 1998.

Frymer-Kensky, Tikva. "Law and Philosophy: The Case of Sex in the Bible." *Semeia* 45 (1989): 89–102.

———. *In the Wake of the Goddesses: Women, Culture, and the Biblical Transformation of Pagan Myth.* New York: Free Press, 1992.

———. "Sex and Sexuality." Page 1145 in vol. 5 of *The Anchor Bible Dictionary.* Edited by David Noel Freedman. 6 vols. New York: Doubleday, 1992.

———. "Virginity in the Bible." Pages 79–96 in *Gender and Law in the Hebrew Bible and the Ancient Near East.* Edited by Victor H. Matthews, Bernard M. Levinson, and Tikva Frymer-Kensky. Journal for the Study of the Old Testament: Supplement Series 262. Sheffield: Sheffield Academic Press, 1998.

———. *Reading the Women of the Bible.* New York: Schocken, 2002.

Fuchs, Esther. *Sexual Politics in the Biblical Narrative: Reading the Hebrew Bible as a Woman.* Journal for the Study of the Old Testament Supplement Series 310. Sheffield: Sheffield Academic Press, 2000.

Geller, Stephen A. "The Sack of Shechem: The Use of Typology in Biblical Covenant." *Prooftexts* 10 (1990): 1–15.

Gilmore, David D., ed. *Honour and Shame and the Unity of the Mediterranean*, American Anthropological Association Special Publication 22. Washington, D.C.: American Anthropological Association, 1987.

Globe, Alexander. "'Enemies Round About': Disintegrative Structure in the Book of Judges." Pages 233–51 in *Mappings of the Biblical Terrain: The Bible as Text*. Edited by Vincent L. Tollers and John Maier. Lewisburg: Bucknell University Press, 1990.

Gooding, David W. "The Composition of the Book of Judges." *Eretz-Israel* 16 (1982): *70–*79.

Graetz, Naomi. "Dinah the Daughter." Pages 306–17 in *A Feminist Companion to Genesis*. Edited by Athalya Brenner. The Feminist Companion to the Bible 2. Sheffield: Sheffield Academic Press, 1993.

Gravdal, Kathryn. *Ravishing Maidens: Writing Rape in Medieval French Literature and Law*. Philadelphia: University of Pennsylvania Press, 1991.

Gray, Mark. "Amnon: A Chip Off the Old Block? Rhetorical Strategy in 2 Samuel 13:7–15 the Rape of Tamar and the Humiliation of the Poor." *Journal for the Study of the Old Testament* 77 (1998): 39–54.

Gros Louis, Kenneth R. R. "Some Methodological Considerations." Pages 13–24 in *Literary Interpretations of Biblical Narrative II*. Edited by Kenneth R. R. Gros Louis and James S. Ackerman. Nashville: Abingdon, 1982.

Gros Louis, Kenneth R. R., and James S. Ackerman, eds. *Literary Interpretations of Biblical Narrative II*. Nashville: Abingdon, 1982.

Gunn, David M. *The Story of King David: Genre and Interpretation*. Journal for the Study of the Old Testament: Supplement Series 6. Sheffield: JSOT Press, 1978.

———. "What Does the Bible Say? A Question of Text and Canon." Pages 242–61 in *Reading Bibles, Writing Bodies: Identity and the Book*. Edited by Timothy K. Beal and David M. Gunn. New York: Routledge, 1997.

Gunn, David M., and Danna Nolan Fewell. *Narrative in the Hebrew Bible*. New York: Oxford University Press, 1993.

Hertzberg, Hans Wilhelm. *I & II Samuel: A Commentary*. Translated by J. S. Bowden. Old Testament Library. London: SCM, 1964.

Herzfeld, Michael. "Honour and Shame: Problems in the Comparative Analysis of Moral Systems." *Man* 15, no. 2 (1980): 339–51.

Higgins, Lynn A., and Brenda R. Silver, eds. *Rape and Representations*. New York: Columbia University Press, 1991.

House, Paul R., ed. *Beyond Form Criticism: Essays in Old Testament Literary Criticism*. Sources for Biblical and Theological Study 2. Winona Lake: Eisenbrauns, 1992.

Hudson, Don Michael. "Living in a Land of Epithets: Anonymity in Judges 19–21." *Journal for the Study of the Old Testament* 62 (1994): 49–66.

Hyman, Ronald T. "Final Judgment: The Ambiguous Moral Question That Culminates Genesis 34." *Jewish Bible Quarterly* 28, no. 2 (2000) 93–101.

Kamuf, Peggy. "Author of a Crime." Pages 187–207 in *A Feminist Companion to Judges*. Edited by Athalya Brenner. The Feminist Companion to the Bible 4. Sheffield: Sheffield Academic Press, 1993.

Kayser, Wolfgang. *The Grotesque in Art and Literature.* Translated by Ulrich Weisstein. New York: Columbia University Press, 1981.

Keefe, Alice A. "Rapes of Women/Wars of Men." *Semeia* 61 (1993): 79–97.

Kelso, Julie. "Reading the Silence of Women in Genesis 34." Pages 85–109 in *Redirected Travel: Alternative Journeys and Places in Biblical Studies.* Edited by Roland Boer and Edgar W. Conrad. London and New York: T & T Clark, 2003.

Kevers, Paul. "Étude littéraire de Genèse 34," *Revue biblique* 87 (1980): 38–86.

Klein, Lillian R. *The Triumph of Irony in the Book of Judges.* Journal for the Study of the Old Testament: Supplement Series 68. Sheffield: Almond Press, 1989.

———. "Honor and Shame in Esther." Pages 149–75 in *A Feminist Companion to Esther, Judith, Susanna.* Edited by Athalya Brenner. Feminist Companion to the Bible 7. Sheffield: Sheffield Academic Press, 1995.

Kressel, Gideon M. "Shame and Gender." *Anthropological Quarterly* 65, no. 1 (1992): 34–46.

———. "An Anthropologist's Response to the Use of Social Scientific Models in Biblical Studies." *Semeia* 68 (1994): 153–61.

Landy, Francis. "On Metaphor, Play and Nonsense." *Semeia* 61 (1993): 219–237.

Laniak, Timothy S. *Shame and Honor in the Book of Esther.* Society of Biblical Literature Dissertation Series 165. Atlanta: Scholars Press, 1998.

Lanoir, Corinne. "Le Livre des Juges, L'histoire et Les Femmes." *Foi et Vie* 96, no. 4 (1997): 55–71.

Lapsley, Jacqueline E. *Can These Bones Live? The Problem of the Moral Self in the Book of Ezekiel.* Beihefte zur Zeitschrift für die alttestamentliche Wissenschaft 301. Berlin: deGruyter, 2000.

———. "Shame and Self-Knowledge: The Positive Role of Shame in Ezekiel's View of the Moral Self." Pages 143–73 in *The Book of Ezekiel: Theological and Anthropological Perspectives.* Edited by Margaret S. Odell and John T. Strong. Society of Biblical Literature Symposium Series 9. Atlanta: Society of Biblical Literature, 2000.

———. *Whispering the Word: Hearing Women's Stories in the Old Testament.* Louisville: Westminster John Knox, 2005.

Lasine, Stuart. "Guest and Host in Judges 19: Lot's Hospitality in an Inverted World." *Journal for the Study of the Old Testament* 29 (1984): 37–59.

Leeuwen, Raymond C. van. "Proverbs 30:21–23 and the Biblical World Upside Down." *Journal of Biblical Literature* 105 (1986): 599–610.

Leitch, Vincent B. *Cultural Criticism, Literary Theory, Poststructuralism.* New York: Columbia University Press, 1992.

Lever, Alison. "Honour as a Red Herring." *Critique of Anthropology* 6, no. 3 (1988): 83–106.

Lichtheim, Miriam. *Ancient Egyptian Literature: A Book of Readings.* 3 vols. Berkeley: University of California Press, 1971–80.

Malina, Bruce J. *The New Testament World: Insights from Cultural Anthropology.* Rev. ed. Louisville: Westminster/John Knox, 1993.

Matthews, Victor H. "Hospitality and Hostility in Genesis 19 and Judges 19." *Biblical Theology Bulletin* 22, no. 1 (1992): 3–11.

Matthews, Victor H., and Don C. Benjamin. "Social Sciences and Biblical Studies." *Semeia* 68 (1994): 7–21.

———. "Amnon and Tamar: A Matter of Honor (2 Samuel 13:1–38)." Pages 339–66 in *Crossing Boundaries and Linking Horizons: Studies in Honor of Michael C. Astour on His 80th Birthday*. Edited by Gordon D. Young, Mark W. Chavalas, and Richard E. Averbeck. Bethseda: CDL, 1997.

———, eds. "Honor and Shame in the World of the Bible." *Semeia* 68 (1994): 1–161.

Matthews, Victor H., Bernard M. Levinson, and Tikva Frymer-Kensky, eds. *Gender and Law in the Hebrew Bible and the Ancient Near East*. Journal for the Study of the Old Testament: Supplement Series 262. Sheffield: Sheffield Academic Press, 1998.

May, David M. "Mark 3:20–35 From the Perspective of Shame/Honor." *Biblical Theology Bulletin* 17 (1987): 83–87.

Mayes, Andrew D. H. "Deuteronomistic Royal Theology in Judges 17–21." *Biblical Interpretation* 9, no. 3 (2001): 241–58.

McCarter, P. Kyle, Jr. "'Plots, True or False.' The Succession Narrative as Court Apologetic." *Interpretation* 35 (1981): 355–67.

———. *2 Samuel: A New Translation with Introduction, Notes, and Commentary*. Anchor Bible 9. New York: Doubleday, 1984.

Mendenhall, George E. *The Tenth Generation: The Origins of the Biblical Tradition*. Baltimore: Johns Hopkins University Press, 1973.

Meyers, Carol. *Discovering Eve: Ancient Israelite Women in Context*. New York: Oxford University Press, 1988.

Moore, George Foot. *Judges: Critical and Exegetical Commentary*. International Critical Commentary. New York: Charles Scribner's Sons, 1895.

Neyrey, Jerome H. *The Social World of Luke-Acts: Models for Interpretation*. Peabody: Hendrickson, 1991.

Niditch, Susan. "The 'Sodomite' Theme in Judges 19–20: Family, Community, and Social Disintegration." *Catholic Biblical Quarterly* 44 (1982): 365–78.

Noble, Paul R. "A 'Balanced' Reading of the Rape of Dinah: Some Exegetical and Methodological Observations." *Biblical Interpretation* 4, no. 2 (1996): 173–204.

Noth, Martin. "The Background of Judges 17–18." Pages 68–85 in *Israel's Prophetic Heritage*. Edited by Bernhard W. Anderson and Walter Harrelson. New York: Harper & Row, 1962.

O'Connell, Robert H. *The Rhetoric of the Book of Judges*. Vetus Testamentum Supplements 63. Leiden: Brill, 1996.

Odell, Margaret S. "An Exploratory Study of Shame and Dependence in the Bible and Selected Near Eastern Parallels." Pages 217–33 in *The Biblical Canon in Comparative Perspective: Scripture in Context IV*. Edited by K. Lawson Younger, Jr., William W. Hallo and Bernard F. Batto. Ancient Near Eastern Texts and Studies 11. Lewiston: Edwin Mellon, 1991.

Olson, Dennis T. "The Book of Judges: Introduction, Commentary, and Reflections." Pages 722–888 in vol. 2 of *The New Interpreter's Bible*. Edited by Leander E. Keck. 12 vols. Nashville: Abingdon, 1998.

Penchansky, David. "Staying the Night: Intertextuality in Genesis and Judges." Pages 77–88 in *Reading Between Texts: Intertextuality and the Hebrew Bible*. Edited by Danna Nolan Fewell. Louisville: Westminster/John Knox Press, 1992.

Peristiany, Jean G., ed. *Honour and Shame: The Values of Mediterranean Society*. London: Weidenfeld and Nicolson, 1965

Peristiany, Jean G., and Julian Pitt-Rivers, eds. *Honor and Grace in Anthropology.* Cambridge: Cambridge University Press, 1992.

Phillips, Anthony. "*NEBALAH.*" *Vetus Testamentum* 25 (1975): 237–41.

Pitt-Rivers, Julian. *The Fate of Shechem or the Politics of Sex: Essays in the Anthropology of the Mediterranean.* Cambridge: Cambridge University Press, 1977.

Polzin, Robert. *David and the Deuteronomist: 2 Samuel.* Vol. 3 of *A Literary Study of the Deuteronomic History.* Indiana Studies in Biblical Literature. Edited by Herbert Parks and Robert Polzin. Bloomington: Indiana University Press, 1993.

———. *Moses and the Deuteronomist: Deuteronomy, Joshua, Judges.* Vol. 1 of *A Literary Study of the Deuteronomic History.* Indiana Studies in Biblical Literature. Edited by Herbert Parks and Robert Polzin. Bloomington: Indiana University Press, 1993.

Pope, Marvin H. "Number, Numbering, Numbers." Pages 561–67 in vol. 3 of *The Interpreter's Dictionary of the Bible.* Edited by George A. Buttrick. 12 vols. Nashville: Abingdon, 1962.

Pressler, Carolyn. *The View of Women Found in the Deuteronomic Family Laws.* Beihefte zur Zeitschrift für die alttestamentliche Wissenschaft 216. Berlin: de Gruyter, 1993.

———. "Sexual Violence and Deuteronomic Law." Pages 102–12 in *A Feminist Companion to Exodus to Deuteronomy.* Edited by Athalya Brenner. The Feminist Companion to the Bible 6. Sheffield: Sheffield Academic Press, 1994.

Propp, William H. "Kinship in 2 Samuel 13." *Catholic Biblical Quarterly* 55 (1993): 39–53.

Rad, Gerhard von. *The Problem of the Hexateuch and Other Essays.* Translated by E. W. Trueman Dicken. Edinburgh: Oliver and Boyd, 1966.

Rashkow, Ilona N. "The Rape(s) of Dinah (Gen. 34): False Religion and Excess in Revenge." Pages 53–80 in *The Destructive Power of Religion: Violence in Judaism, Christianity, and Islam.* Vol. 3: Models and Cases of Violence in Religion. Recent Titles in Contemporary Psychology. Edited by J. Harold Ellens; Westport: Praeger, 2004.

Reis, Pamela Tamarkin. "Cupidity and Stupidity: Woman's Agency and the 'Rape' of Tamar." *Journal of the Ancient Near Eastern Society* 25 (1997): 43–60.

Ridout, George P. "Prose Compositional Techniques in the Succession Narrative (2 Samuel 7, 9–20; 1 Kings 1–2)." Ph.D. dissertation. Graduate Theological Union, 1971.

———. "The Rape of Tamar: A Rhetorical Analysis of 2 Sam 13:1–22." Pages 75–84 in *Rhetorical Criticism: Essays in Honor of James Muilenburg.* Edited by Jared J. Jackson and Martin Kessler. Pittsburgh Theological Monograph Series 1. Pittsburgh: Pickwick, 1974.

Rofé, Alexander. "Defilement of Virgins in Biblical Law and the Case of Dinah (Genesis 34)." *Biblical* 86:3 (2005): 369–75.

Rost, Leonhard. *The Succession to the Throne of David.* Translated by Michael D. Rutter and David M. Gunn. Introduction by Edward Ball. Historical Texts and Interpreters in Biblical Scholarship 1. Edited by John W. Rogerson. Sheffield: Almond, 1982. Translation of *Die Überlieferung von der Thronnachfolge Davids.* Beiträge zur Wissenschaft vom Alten und Neuen Testament 3/6. Edited by Rudolf Kittel. Stuttgart: Verlag von W. Kohlhammer, 1926. Reprinted in pages 119–253 of *Das kleine Credo und andere Studien zum Alten Testament.* Heidelberg: Quelle und Meyer, 1965.

Roth, Wolfgang M. W. "*NBL.*" *Vetus Testamentum* 10 (1960): 394–409.

Rozeé, Patricia D. "Forbidden or Forgiven? Rape in Cross-Cultural Perspective." *Psychology of Women Quarterly* 17 (1993): 499–514.

Russell, Letty M., ed. *Feminist Interpretation of the Bible*. Philadelphia: Fortress, 1985.

Russo, Mary. *The Female Grotesque: Risk Excess and Modernity*. London: Routledge, 1994.

Sakenfeld, Katharine Doob. "Feminist Uses of Biblical Materials." Pages 55–64 in *Feminist Interpretation of the Bible*. Edited by Letty M. Russell. Philadelphia: Fortress, 1985.

Sanday, Peggy Reeves. "The Socio-Cultural Context of Rape: A Cross-Cultural Study." *Journal of Social Issues* 37, no. 4 (1981): 5–27.

Scholz, Susanne. "Was It Really Rape in Genesis 34? Biblical Scholarship as a Reflection of Cultural Assumptions." Pages 182–98 in *Escaping Eden: New Feminist Perspectives on the Bible*. Edited by Harold C. Washington, Susan Lochrie Graham, and Pamela Thimmes. Sheffield: Sheffield Academic Press, 1998.

———. *Rape Plots: A Feminist Cultural Study of Genesis 34*. Studies in Biblical Literature 13. New York: Peter Lang, 2000.

Schroeder, Joy A. *Dinah's Lament: The Biblical Legacy of Sexual Violence in Christian Interpretation*. Minneapolis: Fortress, 2007.

Searles, Patricia, and Ronald J. Berger, eds. *Rape and Society: Readings on the Problem of Sexual Assault*. Boulder: Westview, 1995.

Seow, Choon-Leong. *Ecclesiastes: A New Translation With Introduction and Commentary*. Anchor Bible 18C. New York: Doubleday, 1997.

Shanks, Hershel, P. Kyle McCarter, Ronald S. Hendel, and Richard D. Nelson. "Has Richard Friedman Really Discovered a Long-Hidden Book in the Bible?" *Biblical Research* 15 (April 1999): 30–39, 44–46.

Simkins, Ronald A. "'Return to Yahweh': Honor and Shame in Joel." *Semeia* 68 (1994): 41–54.

Soggin, J. Alberto. *Judges: A Commentary*. Translated by John Bowden. Old Testament Library. Philadelphia: Westminster Press, 1981.

Speiser, Ephraim A. *Genesis*. Anchor Bible 1. New York: Doubleday, 1964.

Stansell, Gary. "Honor and Shame in the David Narratives." *Semeia* 68 (1994): 55–79.

Sternberg, Meir. *The Poetics of Biblical Narrative: Ideological Literature and the Drama of Reading*. Bloomington: Indiana University Press, 1987.

———. "Biblical Poetics and Sexual Politics: From Reading to Counterreading." *Journal of Biblical Literature* 111, no. 3 (1992) 463–88.

Stone, Ken. "Gender and Homosexuality in Judges 19: Subject-Honor, Object-Shame?" *Journal for the Study of the Old Testament* 67 (1995): 87–107.

———. *Sex, Honor, and Power in the Deuteronomistic History*. Journal for the Study of the Old Testament: Supplement Series 234. Sheffield: Sheffield Academic Press, 1996.

Sweeney, Marvin A. "David Polemics in the Book of Judges." *Vetus Testamentum* 47 (1997): 517–29.

Tanner, Laura E. *Intimate Violence: Reading Rape and Torture in Twentieth-Century Fiction*. Bloomington: Indiana University Press, 1994.

Tomaselli, Sylvana, and Roy Porter, eds. *Rape*. Oxford: Basil Blackwell, 1986.

Trible, Phyllis. *Texts of Terror: Literary-Feminist Readings of Biblical Narrative*. Philadelphia: Fortress, 1984.

————. *Rhetorical Criticism: Context, Method, and the Book of Jonah.* Minneapolis: Fortress, 1994.

Walls, Neil H. *The Goddess Anat in Ugaritic Myth.* Society of Biblical Literature Dissertation Series 135. Atlanta: Scholars Press, 1992.

Washington, Harold C. "Violence and the Construction of Gender in the Hebrew Bible: A New Historicist Approach." *Biblical Interpretation* 5 (1997): 324–63.

————. "Lest He Die in Battle and Another Man Take Her: Violence and the Construction of Gender in the Laws of Deuteronomy 20–22." Pages 185–213 in *Gender and Law in the Hebrew Bible and the Ancient Near East.* Edited by Victor H. Matthews, Bernard M. Levinson, and Tikva Frymer-Kensky. Journal for the Study of the Old Testament: Supplement Series 262. Sheffield: Sheffield Academic Press, 1998.

Webb, Barry G. *The Book of Judges: An Integrated Reading.* Journal for the Study of the Old Testament: Supplement Series 46. Sheffield: JSOT Press, 1987.

Weinfeld, Moshe. *Deuteronomy and the Deuteronomic School.* Oxford: Clarendon, 1972.

Wenham, Gordon J. "*beṯûlāh*: A Girl of Marriageable Age." *Vetus Testamentum* 22 (1972): 326–48.

————. *Genesis 16–50.* Vol. 2. Word Biblical Commentary. Waco: Word, 1994.

Westbrook, Raymond. "Punishments and Crimes." Pages 546–56 in vol. 5 of *The Anchor Bible Dictionary.* Edited by David Noel Freedman. 6 vols. New York: Doubleday, 1992.

Westermann, Claus. *Genesis 12–36.* Translated by John J. Scullion. Continental. Minneapolis: Fortress, 1995.

Whybray, Roger N. *The Succession Narrative: A Study of II Sam 9–20 and I Kings 1 and 2.* Studies in Biblical Theology. Second Series 9. Naperville, Allenson, 1968.

Wikan, Unni. "Shame and Honour: A Contestable Pair." *Man* 19, no. 4 (1984): 635–52.

Wittgenstein, Ludwig. *Philosophical Investigations.* Translated by G. E. M. Anscombe. Oxford: Basil Blackwell, 1958.

Woulde, Ellen van. "Does *ʿINNÂ* Denote Rape? A Semantic Analysis of a Controversial Word." *Vetus Testamentum* 52, no. 4 (2002): 528–44.

Wyatt, Nicolas. "The Story of Dinah and Shechem." *Ugarit-Forschungen* 22 (1990): 433–58.

Yates, Wilson. "An Introduction to the Grotesque: Theoretical and Theological Considerations." Pages 1–68 in *The Grotesque in Art and Literature: Theological Reflections.* Edited by James Luther Adams and Wilson Yates. Grand Rapids: Eerdmans, 1997

Yee, Gale A. "Ideological Criticism: Judges 17–21 and the Dismembered Body." Pages 146–70 in *Judges and Method: New Approaches in Biblical Studies.* Edited by Gale A. Yee. Minneapolis: Fortress Press, 1995.

————. *Poor Banished Children of Eve: Woman as Evil in the Hebrew Bible.* Minneapolis: Fortress, 2003.

————, ed. *Judges and Method: New Approaches in Biblical Studies.* Minneapolis: Fortress, 1995.

Zeitlin, Froma. "Configurations of Rape in Greek Myth." Pages 122–51 in *Rape.* Edited by Sylvana Tomaselli and Roy Porter. Oxford: Basil Blackwell, 1986.

INDEX OF BIBLICAL REFERENCES

INDEX OF AUTHORS AND SUBJECTS

and sons, 27, 55–57, 61–65, 63–64n, 134, 137, 139n (*see also* Simeon and Levi)

Jebus, 74, 80–81, 81n (*see also* Jerusalem)
city of the Jebusites, 80, 81, 83

Jephthah's daughter, 11, 96–97n

Jerusalem, 61n, 80, 130 (*see also* Jebus)

Joab, 130, 131

Jonadab, 110–13, 112n, 129, 129n

–K–

Kamuf, Peggy, 93n

Kayser, Wolfgang, 93n

Keefe, Alice A., 4n, 8, 8n, 12–13, 13n, 19, 19n, 99, 99n, 136n

Kelso, Julie, 31n

Kevers, Paul, 59n

Klein, Lillian R., 16n, 69n, 71n,

Kressel, Gideon M., 15n

–L–

Landy, Francis, 4n

Laniak, Timothy S., 16n

Lapsley, Jacqueline E., 16n, 67n, 139n

Lasine, Stuart, 68n, 74n, 80n, 86n, 87n, 91, 91n, 92n, 94, 94n, 99n

Leah, 31–32, 34, 59

Leeuwen, Raymond C. van, 68n

Leitch, Vincent B., 5n

Lever, Alison, 15n

Levite priest, 7, 39, 72n, 84–85n, 89, 92–93n
and the Ephraimite, 82–84
and excessive violence, 92–93, 92–93n
and father-in-law, 74–79, 74n, 77n
negative characterization of, 74, 78–79, 90–96
and parallels between Judg 17–18 and 19–21, 71
response to rape, 90–95

Lichtheim, Miriam, 68n

Lot, 82n, 85, 87–88, 87n

–M–

Malina, Bruce J., 16n

Marbök, Johannes, 8n

Matthews, Victor H., 3n, 14n, 15n, 22n, 67n, 74n, 82n, 87n, 104n, 108n, 109n, 116, 116n, 117n

May, David M., 16n

Mayes, Andrew D. H., 69n

McCarter, P. Kyle, 21n, 102n, 108n, 109n, 112n, 116n, 118n, 119n, 120n, 121n, 126n

Mendenhall, George E., 121n

Meyers, Carol, 11n

Mizpah, 96, 96–97n

mob, at Gibeah (*see* Gibeah, men of)

Moore, George Foot, 74n

–N–

Nathan's oracle, 43n, 101, 103–4, 107, 110, 128, 131, 136, 137, 139n

Nelson, Richard D., 21n

Neyrey, Jerome H., 16n

Niditch, Susan, 86n, 87n

Niehr, H., 34n

night, as motif, 74, 77–78, 78n, 80, 85

Noble, Paul, 27–28, 28n, 47, 47n

Noth, Martin, 69n

numbers, significance of, 77n

–O–

O'Connell, Robert H., 69n

Odell, Margaret S., 16n,

Oholah, 38n

Oholibah, 61n

Olson, Dennis T., 69n, 71, 71n, 72n, 75–76, 75n, 76n, 79n, 93n, 94n, 97n

–P–

Penchansky, David, 87n

people of the land (*see* Canaanites; Hivites; and Shechem, people of)

Studies in Biblical Literature

This series invites manuscripts from scholars in any area of biblical literature. Both established and innovative methodologies, covering general and particular areas in biblical study, are welcome. The series seeks to make available studies that will make a significant contribution to the ongoing biblical discourse. Scholars who have interests in gender and sociocultural hermeneutics are particularly encouraged to consider this series.

For further information about the series and for the submission of manuscripts, contact:

Peter Lang Publishing
Acquisitions Department
P.O. Box 1246
Bel Air, Maryland 21014-1246

To order other books in this series, please contact our Customer Service Department:

(800) 770-LANG (within the U.S.)
(212) 647-7706 (outside the U.S.)
(212) 647-7707 FAX

or browse online by series at:

WWW.PETERLANG.COM